THE LANCASTER

Gordon A. A. Wilson

Photographs by Martin Keen

AMBERLEY

GORDON A. A. WILSON is a retired military and commercial pilot and is the author of Amberley's best-selling *Lancaster Manual 1943*. He flew with the Canadian Armed Forces 414 Electronic Warfare Squadron, flying target aircraft on secret missions to test the defences of North America, and as a maintenance test pilot. He subsequently flew for thirty years for a major airline and since retiring has worked as a ground school instructor for Air Canada and as an aviation consultant writing standard operating procedures manuals. He lives in British Columbia, Canada.

MARTIN KEEN is a professional photographer and runs Silksheen Photography. He is the official photographer for Lincolnshire Aviation Heritage Centre and is also a member of the small team that maintains and operates Lancaster NX611. He lives in the heart of Lincolnshire, just a short distance from the former RAF East Kirkby.

To all those young men of Bomber Command who sacrificed their youth
and to those that gave the ultimate sacrifice that I and my wife Emily could grow up in freedom in 1940s Europe.

This edition published 2017

Amberley Publishing
The Hill, Stroud
Gloucestershire, GL5 4EP

www.amberley-books.com

Copyright © Gordon A. A. Wilson and Martin Keen, 2015, 2017

The right of Gordon A. A. Wilson and Martin Keen to be identified as the Author of this work has been asserted in accordance with the Copyrights, Designs and Patents Act 1988.

ISBN 978 1 4456 7108 6 (paperback)
ISBN 978 1 4456 3427 2 (ebook)

British Library Cataloguing in Publication Data.
A catalogue record for this book is available from the British Library.

Typesetting by Amberley Publishing.
Printed in the UK.

CONTENTS

ACKNOWLEDGEMENTS

My wife Emily for her total support, which allowed me to complete this book; your love and encouragement for fifty-one years has truly been a blessing. You are not a bad proofreader either! My daughter Jennifer, a librarian, and her husband Cameron for their encouragement and for explaining to Emmett and Kalan why 'grandpa cannot come out to play right now'. Thank you Jennifer for building my website (www. aviationauthor.com). My son Mark, an airline pilot, who is 'carrying on the family flying career where I left off' and can appreciate what the young Lancaster pilots faced seventy years ago.

Jonathan Reeve, who conceived the project and encouraged (cajoled) me to write this second book on the Lancaster; thank you, it has been quite the journey.

Martin Keen, Silksheen Photography (www.silksheenphotography. co.uk), for his professional approach to providing, finding and arranging the images that make this book so appealing. Thank you, my friend. It has been great working with you.

Peter Mansbridge OC, who kindly wrote the preface about his family connection with the Lancaster. Bill Blackman, Bill Pearson, John Plenderleith and Art Sewel, thank you for talking with me about your wartime experiences – not all pleasant memories.

Bomber Command Museum of Canada archivist and librarian Dave Birrell. A personal thank you Dave for all you have done to assist and support me in researching both Lancaster books.

Bomber Command Museum of Canada, Greg Morrison, John Phillips; Doug Bowman (www.ArcherPhotoworks.ca); Lincolnshire Aviation Heritage Centre, Andrew Panton; Dave Stubley (www.lincsaviation. co.uk/museum/the-aircraft-recovery-group.htm); Gary Bainbridge (http://summerof44.org.uk); Canadian Warplane Heritage Museum, Captain Don Schofield, Al Mickeloff, Pauline Johnstone; Canadian Museum of Flight, Terry Brunner and archives staff; Western Canada Aviation Museum, Pam McKenzie and archives staff; Canadian Aviation Historical Society, Jerry Vernon; Ann Allen (née Shelson) for sharing her father's story and memorabilia; Alex Bennett and Annie Campbell, Amberley Publishing, professional, knowledgeable and efficient editors who made the whole process a pleasurable experience; ILL program, Surrey Public Library (BC); Access Copyright; Canada Council for the Arts; Gary Vincent, Geoff Pickard, Bill Pearson, Malcolm Dewar for use of their Lancaster libraries; interviewees and those of you who sent/gave me relevant information for my research; our family friends, who all have shown support and interest. Thank you.

For those of you who I have not mentioned due to my own oversight, my apologies; rest assured that your contributions were greatly appreciated and will add to the success of this book.

PREFACE

My mother used to tell us about how she would lie awake in the middle of the night during the war listening for something very distinctive: the pounding drone of those spectacular Rolls-Royce Merlin engines powering the mighty Lancasters home after night missions in the skies over Nazi-occupied Europe. Mother was in her late teens at the time, and like so many other Lincoln girls her age she'd become friends with many of the young English and Canadian aircrew who called her city home during the war.

In my mother's case, the young Brenda Jones was very friendly with a particular young wing commander, Stanley Mansbridge, a soon-to-be-decorated navigator and bomb aimer with 5 Group, No. 49 Squadron. They would get married in 1943. They're both gone now, but both lived full and exciting lives which have left their children, grandchildren and great-grandchildren with wonderful memories. Many are from the war years, and more than a few are about the Lancaster.

My father flew in twenty different aircraft between 1939 and 1945, but the one he always remembered best was the 'Lanc'. Of his fifty-one missions through two tours, most were on the four-engined pride of Bomber Command, and many of the targets carried names famous in the annals of that conflict: Hamburg, Spezia, Cologne, Friedrichshaven, Peenemunde.

It was for that Peenemunde raid, in August of 1943, knocking out – at least for a while – the Nazi rocket installation, that he was awarded the Distinguished Flying Cross, pinned on him by the king himself at Buckingham Palace. A very special moment, to be sure.

It was seventy-one years later, in May of 2014, nine years after my father's passing, that I took that same DFC on its first flight on a Lancaster. I thought it was a different way of remembering my dad, and honouring the great aircraft at the same time.

While there were well over 7,000 Lancasters built, there are only two left flying in the world – one in Britain and one in Canada. The good folks at the Canadian Warplane Heritage Museum in Mount Hope, Ontario, were kind enough to take me for a ride on the Canadian 'Lanc' as part of a CBC (Canadian Broadcasting Corporation) documentary we were putting together for *The National*. It was an incredibly emotional moment for me, and I think for the crew flying VRA as well, because, standing behind the pilots as we flew over south-western Ontario, I pulled the original cushioned medal box out of my flight jacket's inside pocket, opened it up, and we all stared at the silver DFC.

It obviously made me feel close to my father in that moment, but it was more than that. I think all of our thoughts were also about the other men and women who had contributed in that era and that plane. Those who had built the Lancasters, trained on them at bases across Britain and all over Canada, and all those brave young men who had risked their lives – and in far too many cases given them – in a cause they felt was so just and so important.

The Lancaster was and is an amazing feat of engineering. Standing or sitting in it these days is a pleasure and it's genuinely awe-inspiring. Trying to imagine what it must have been like in the war years is almost terrifying – the deafening roar of the engines, the beer-can-thin fuselage, the incredibly tight space. How those brave crews were able to go up in the air, in those conditions, mission after mission, knowing the odds were increasingly against them is something those of us today can simply not comprehend.

Gordon Wilson has again captured the story of the mighty Lancaster in this, his latest book. I think when you read it and glance through the pictures, you too will understand why those who flew the 'Lanc' loved it so much – and why those of us who are here today owe it and them so much too.

Peter Mansbridge

Mr Peter Mansbridge OC (Officer of the Order of Canada) is the chief correspondent of CBC (Canadian Broadcasting Corporation) News. He anchors CBC's flagship nightly news program, *The National*, and all CBC News specials. He is also host of CBC News Network's *Mansbridge: One on One*. Mansbridge began his career in 1968 in Churchill, Manitoba, where he helped develop CBC Radio's news service to northern Canada. In 1971 he moved to Winnipeg as a reporter for CBC Radio and in 1972 joined CBC Television. He became *The National*'s reporter in Saskatchewan in 1975 and in 1976 was named one of the program's parliamentary correspondents in Ottawa. He became chief correspondent and anchor of *The National* in 1988.

In more than forty years with CBC News, Mansbridge has provided comprehensive coverage of the most significant stories in Canada and around the world. He has interviewed countless international leaders and he remains the only Canadian journalist to have interviewed both US President Barack Obama and British Prime Minister David Cameron.

During a decorated career, Mansbridge has received twelve Gemini Awards for excellence in broadcast journalism. He has received nine honorary degrees from universities across the country and has also been recognised by leading universities in the United States and the United Kingdom. In 2008 Mansbridge was made an officer of the Order of Canada by Governor General Michaëlle Jean. In 2009 he was named Chancellor of Mount Allison University in New Brunswick.

Peter Mansbridge was born in London, England, in 1948 and now resides in Stratford, Ontario.

Left: Author Gordon Wilson pictured here in the Avro (Canada) CF-100 Canuck, a type he flew in active service. (Gordon Wilson)

Right: Peter and Stanley Mansbridge. (Peter Mansbridge)

Left: Wing Commander Stanley Mansbridge DFC. (Peter Mansbridge)

Right: The Distinguished Flying Cross awarded to Wing Commander Stanley Mansbridge. (Peter Mansbridge)

1

THE AVRO LANCASTER

There is a statue near Durham Tees Valley Airport, previously known as Teesside International Airport, that looks oddly out of place to all but those fortunate enough to know the history behind this solitary figure dressed in Second World War flying clothing. The statue is of a male airman standing to attention and saluting, and is situated in front of the St George Hotel, which was formerly used as the wartime officers' mess of Royal Air Force (RAF) Middleton St George. The RAF, the world war and the young airman are all gone from there now, and all that remains of that era are some old buildings, memorabilia, the memories of the local elderly population, clouded by age, and the imposing statue.

The statue is suitably placed in a Royal Canadian Air Force (RCAF) Memorial Garden, outside the front entrance to the St George Hotel. It is of Pilot Officer Andrew C. Mynarski, RCAF, who was awarded the Victoria Cross (VC), the British Commonwealth's highest award for bravery in the face of the enemy. Unfortunately the VC was awarded to Mynarski posthumously.

Mynarski was stationed at Middleton St George with No. 419 'Moose' Squadron RCAF in June 1944, flying as a mid-upper air gunner. Born and raised in Winnipeg, Manitoba, Canada, he was twenty-seven years old when he took off at 21.44 on a bombing mission to the rail marshalling yards in Cambrai, France. It was 12 June 1944. The actual bombing, however, their thirteenth mission as a crew, would take place early the next morning, on Friday 13 June – definitely a concern for a typically superstitious bomber crew.

Shortly after crossing the French coastline their aircraft, KB726 VR-A, was attacked by a Junkers Ju 88 night fighter from below. Both port engines were damaged and burst into flame. Hydraulic lines leading to the rear gun turret were severed and also burst into flames. The order was given by the pilot to abandon the aircraft. Mynarski left his mid-upper gun turret and made his way to the rear escape door. Through the smoke and flames in the rear fuselage he could see his friend, rear gunner Pilot Officer G. P. (Pat) Brophy, desperately trying to get out of his jammed turret.

Mynarski made the instant decision to rescue his friend and not bail out the escape door to safety. Disregarding the fact that his clothes and parachute were on fire, he attempted in vain to free Brophy from the jammed turret. Brophy indicated to him that it was hopeless and he should save himself and bail out. Reluctantly, Mynarski left his comrade and backed up through the flames again to the escape door. Prior to jumping out of the aircraft, Mynarski paid a final tribute to his comrade – he stood up and, before jumping out the door, saluted his doomed friend; hence the posture of the statue at the St George Hotel.

Witnesses apparently saw him descend in flames. When found, he was so severely burnt that he died shortly thereafter. How do we know all these details of the story? When the aircraft crashed, Brophy was miraculously thrown clear to live and tell his remarkable story. Brophy recounted in later years, 'I'll always believe that a divine providence intervened to save me because of what I had seen, so that the world might know of a gallant man who laid down his life for his friend.'

Mynarski's aircraft was the Second World War Bomber Command's four-engine heavy bomber, the famous Avro Lancaster. The Lancaster story is perpetuated both by the 1955 film *The Dam Busters*, starring Michael Redgrave and Richard Todd, and the fact that there are two examples flying in the world today, one in Britain and one in Canada. Films, magazines, media interest, veteran remembrance and, of course, aviation enthusiast interest has built the Avro Lancaster into the legend it truly is.

The Avro Lancaster is a four-engine, all-metal, mid-wing cantilever monoplane with an oval-shaped fuselage. The wide tail section has twin elliptical fins and rudders. It was initially powered by four wing-mounted twelve-cylinder Merlin engines with three-bladed propellers (airscrews). The propellers were originally 'needle blade', switching later to Hamilton Standard 'paddle blade' type. It has two main landing gears (undercarriage) that retract hydraulically rearward into the inner-engine nacelles, and a non-retractable tailwheel. The cockpit has a distinct greenhouse look, with the forward gun turret and bomb aimer's bubble making up the nose of the aircraft.

Halfway back, on top of the fuselage, is the mid-upper gun turret. The rear gunner's turret is at the very rear of the fuselage aft of the tailplane. The thirty-three-foot bomb bay extends underneath the fuselage and is concealed behind two long bomb bay doors. Some aircraft have the H2S radar bubble hanging down from the fuselage aft of the doors. The distinguishing feature of the interior is the two waist-high spars that pass through the fuselage. The aircraft is entered by a door on the aft starboard of the fuselage.

The wartime Lancaster had a crew of seven. At the front of the fuselage the bomb aimer has two positions: lying on the floor looking through the bombsight, or standing up manning the two Browning .303 guns on the front gun turret. The bomb computer is on the port side and the bomb release selector is on the starboard side. The nose compartment also contains a small escape hatch that was totally inadequate for aircraft escape, which is reflected by the low escape rate compared to other aircraft.

Above and behind the nose compartment, on top of the bomb bay, sits the single pilot on a raised platform, port side, with the flight engineer (F/E) beside him on the starboard side. The F/E has the fuel gauges and selectors on a panel behind him! His seat is collapsible, folding back against the fuselage side, and is known as 'second dickey seat'. Next aft was a curtain separating the navigator's table on the port side from the cockpit. The navigator sits sideways facing the port side of the fuselage. The wireless operator is immediately aft of the chart table facing forward. His instruments form the left-hand edge of the navigator's table.

The two wing spars are next before the floor drops away at the end of the bomb bay – an obstacle course at the best of times, a trap at the worst. The mid-upper gunner is seated in a slung canvas support under his turret in the top of the fuselage. Behind the turret is the entrance door on the starboard side of the fuselage. Further aft are the Elsan toilet, basically a barrel with chemicals in it with a seat on top (only to be used in dire emergencies and, of course, level flight), and then the entrance door to the rear turret, reached after crawling across the tailplane spar – a lonely existence away from the rest of the crew

The famous Rhine Valley Dams mission is one of many that involved the Lancaster. There were more Victoria Crosses (ten in all) for bravery awarded to crew members of the Lancaster than any other aircraft. Unlike the fighter pilots, who performed their mission alone in their aircraft and gathered afterwards to tell each other of the events, the bomber crew lived the terror, excitement and satisfaction of a 'job well done' together. The crew bonding and team spirit of the seven-member crew during wartime was never forgotten and, at the many reunions over the years, those remaining always toasted those crew members that had passed away with the words, 'We will remember them.'

Queen's Jubilee

We are very fortunate that in 2015 we have the opportunity to still observe this great aircraft in flight. A few years ago, the sight of the Lancaster flying above The Mall in London towards Buckingham Palace to celebrate the queen's Diamond Jubilee was breathtaking. It was 4 June 2012 and the sight and sounds of the famous bomber, surrounded by an escort of vintage fighters, flying above a million loyal subjects and spectators, was one for the history books.

That particular Lancaster, belonging to the Battle of Britain Memorial Flight (BBMF), is the only Lancaster aircraft maintained by the RAF in flying condition. It is surprising that the Lancaster is around today at all, seventy-plus years later, which is a tribute to the designer and the ruggedness of the aircraft. That the aircraft has been preserved in flying condition is an acknowledgement of the tremendous affection that still exists for the Lancaster and the part it played in the bomber campaign of the Second World War.

BBMF PA474

The BBMF Lancaster, PA474, rolled off the production line at the Vickers-Armstrongs Broughton factory at Hawarden Field, Chester, on 31 May 1945. The war in Europe had ended on 8 May 1945 and so it was allocated to the 'Tiger Force' against Japan. The war in the Far East also ceased before the aircraft was deployed, and after a period of storage it ended up doing survey work with No. 82 Squadron in Africa. Returned to England in 1952, it eventually assumed flying laboratory duties, testing aerofoil sections, at the Royal College of Aeronautics at Cranfield.

In 1964 the aircraft was adopted by the Air Historical Branch with a view to preparing it for exhibit at the RAF Museum in Hendon. In 1965, fate intervened. Wing Commander D'Arcy of No. 44 Squadron assumed care of the Lancaster and began a restoration program. In 1967

permission was obtained to fly the aircraft regularly, and in 1973 it was transferred to the BBMF, where the restoration and preservation has continued. Since 2012 it has worn the markings of No. 617 'Dambuster' Squadron KC-A *Thumper Mark III*.

CWHM FM213

The Canadian flying example belongs to the Canadian Warplane Heritage Museum (CWHM) in Hamilton, Ontario. It rolled off the production line at Victory Aircraft limited, Malton, Ontario, and was delivered to England in the spring of 1945. It was subsequently returned to Canada in August and after modifications assumed duty with 107 Rescue Unit, Royal Canadian Air Force, until 1963. In 1964 it was declared surplus and was obtained by the Goderich branch of the Royal Canadian Legion. It was acquired by the museum in 1977 and, after an eleven-year restoration project, it took to the skies again in 1988. It has worn the markings of KB726 as a memorial to Pilot Officer Andrew Mynarski, who earned his Victoria Cross while flying in that particular aircraft.

These seventy-year-old aircraft, in 2015, are fine examples of the state of aviation development during the latter days of the Second World War. That they are still flying is a great tribute to the aviation community that has built up over the years since the Wright brothers decided to defy gravity with a powered machine. Human beings have always been fascinated by the three elements of life that surround us – the earth, the sea and the sky. The Lancaster was very much a part of the sky story, and it is very fitting that it takes its place among the great achievements of aviation history. The two surviving Lancasters flew together in Britain during the summer of 2014. It is a tribute to all those people who were involved in the design, manufacture and development of the Lancaster that these two aircraft graced the skies of Britain together over the very airfields that housed their wartime predecessors. See chapter 7 for a full account of the Lancaster experience in Britain.

The original Lancaster design evolved from another Avro aircraft, the Manchester, which had one very important fuselage design feature that contributed to the ultimate success of the Lancaster aircraft: the special bomb bay. The war was accelerating aircraft and power-plant development and designers were often thinking of the next aircraft before the original aircraft had reached its final production model. The need for faster and more manoeuvrable fighters and bombers that could carry heavier loads longer distances was paramount, as the enemy increased the performance of their own aircraft. Let us go back and examine the origins of the Lancaster, beginning in 1918.

At the end of the First World War – 'the war to end all wars' – progress in aircraft design emphasised speed, passenger comfort and long flights, and it was not until the volatile political situation in 1930s Germany became apparent that Britain realised the vulnerability of its air forces. The bomber force at the end of First World War comprised of the Royal Flying Corps (RFC) de Havilland DH.4 and DH.9 and the Royal Naval Air Service (RNAS) Handley Page O/100 and V/1500. All these aircraft were biplanes and, in the case of the de Havilland aircraft, single-engine. In the spring of 1918, the RFC and RNAS joined together to form the Royal Air Force (RAF).

Another biplane, the twin-engine Vickers F.B.27 Vimy, deserves mention. After the war it was famous for the first non-stop crossing of the Atlantic Ocean, from Newfoundland to Ireland. This was closely followed by another long-distance flight: Britain to India. The inter-war bombers were the Handley Page Hyderabad and Vickers Virginia, the last of the mainly wood biplanes. The departure of Sir Hugh Trenchard as Chief of the Air Staff in 1930 also changed the RAF focus away from the bomber force. The progress and initiatives of aircraft bomber design were slowed because of this. However, in spite of this change in direction, the inclusion of more metal components in construction signalled the transition to the all-metal aircraft.

The Air Ministry requirements for the bomber to carry up to twenty-four troops hindered the development of the pure bomber. The bomber had this restrictive dual role as a transport aircraft. The Fairey Hendon was the first monoplane bomber to fly, but saw very limited service, being a light bomber capable of lifting only 1,600 lbs of bombs. The search was now on to find a heavy bomber for the RAF, and the following prototypes appeared in response to Air Ministry specifications.

The Armstrong Whitworth A.W.23, the Bristol Type 130 and the Handley Page H.P.51 were the aircraft submitted that still incorporated the requirement to carry troops. A subsequent specification abolishing the transportation requirement resulted in a major advancement in heavy bomber design. The Handley Page H.P.51 Harrow, first flight 10 October 1936, and the Armstrong Whitworth A.W.38 Whitley, first flight 17 March 1936, were both ordered into production before their first flight due to the gathering strength, supposedly restricted to civilian transport aircraft, of the undisguised military ambitions of the Nazi Germany Luftwaffe.

Separate specifications had placed the emphasis on speed rather than weight-carrying ability. The results were the Vickers Type 271, later developed as the Wellington, and the Handley Page H.P.52 Hampden. The Wellington actually achieved heavy bomber status, with its 4,500 lbs of bombs carried for 2,000 miles. The Hampden, meanwhile, was definitely a medium bomber, carrying 2,000 lbs of bombs a distance just less than 1,900 miles.

By 1935 production was underway to replace most of the remaining biplane bombers with metal monoplane aircraft. The Hawker Hind biplane was an exception; it was manufactured to meet the need for a light bomber trainer. The Fairey Battle and Bristol Blenheim joined the bomber fleet as light, fast bombers. These decisions coincided with the formation of RAF Bomber Command at Uxbridge on the 14 July 1936. Finally, after eighteen years, the RAF had recognised the importance of organising the strike force as a separate entity to the defence force. History recorded that it was three short years until the bomber force would be called upon to perform its function of carrying destruction to the enemy and, just as importantly, returning aircraft and crew safely to home base.

The Air Ministry specifications had the foresight to measure the distance, albeit initially straight-line, between the bases in England and Berlin and include that in their requirements. Also included were the types and shapes of bombs available as they progressed. The old machined style changed to a cast style to improve the aerodynamics and make the behaviour of the bomb more predictable. Initially the utility bomb was 250 lbs, but that soon gave way to heavier bombs up to 2,000 lbs and eventually specialty bombs up to 22,000 lbs. It would take a special aircraft to carry these large bombs to the target: that aircraft would turn out to be the Avro Lancaster.

Bomber aircraft development continued, with two types being considered: the fast, light bomber or the heavy, load-carrying bomber, with its ominous troop-carrying role. The discussion on two versus four engines persisted, with the argument that the benefit of four engines was negated by such things as extra weight, drag, maintenance cost, fuel consumption and heavier wing construction. The engines themselves were divided into two main types, the air-cooled radial or inline liquid-cooled engine. Crew positions were now being specified with the addition of gunners, navigator, wireless operator, bomb aimer and pilot(s). There was no thought to lengthening the take-off area, so performance had to drastically improve to take the heavier bomb loads off the same airfield.

These were the challenges Roy Chadwick, Avro's chief designer, had to contend with. Chadwick worked for the A. V. Roe Company, known as Avro, which was founded in 1910. The company was named after the founder, Sir Edwin Alliott Verdon-Roe OBE, Hon FRAes, FIAS, a pioneer aircraft manufacturer and pilot. Although he was born in England, it is interesting to note that he went to Canada in 1891 to train as a surveyor. A downturn in the markets caused him to return to England and seek other opportunities. During his time with the Merchant Navy he became interested in the flight of the albatross, often observed during his voyages.

A short exposure to the world of aircraft design caused him to start building models, and a subsequent winning design in a 1907 *Daily Mail* competition resulted in his attempt to build a full-size aircraft based on his winning entry. Despite many setbacks, he became the first Englishman to fly a British-made aircraft, his own aircraft, the Roe 1 biplane, in July 1909. The next year he founded Avro at Brownsfield Mill, Manchester, with his brother Humphrey. A great personal tragedy was the loss of two sons, killed while serving with the RAF during the Second World War.

Avro produced the Roe biplane followed by the Avro 500. Avro then produced the first aircraft with an enclosed cockpit. The Avro 504 became famous for the Royal Naval Air Service raid on the Zeppelin sheds at Freidrichshafen during November 1914. However, its real claim to fame was the fact that more than 8,000 were built over twenty years as trainer aircraft for the RFC and the newly founded RAF. Roe sold the company to J. D. Siddeley, who in 1935 sold it again to become part of the Hawker Siddeley Aircraft Group.

The inter-war years saw the introduction of the Tutor and Anson. The war years saw the Manchester and the Lancaster, which created a number of follow-on types. The York, Lincoln, Lancastrian and Shackleton were all derivatives of the basic Lancaster design. Where did this basic design for the Avro Lancaster come from? Who was responsible for the outside-the-box thinking to produce such a successful aircraft? That person was Roy Chadwick CBE, FRAes. He was following in a line of family engineers, which accounted for his interest in aircraft models at age ten. The year was 1903, and the entire world was fascinated with flight; as it developed from balloons to gliders, thoughts turned to powered flight – the sky was now no limit.

In 1918, after studies at the Manchester School of Technology, Chadwick joined the fledgling Avro Company as a draughtsman and personal assistant to Alliott Verdun-Roe. Drafting the first enclosed-cockpit monoplane, the Type F, was followed by the 500 series of aircraft, leading to the successful 504. Chadwick then went on to design the 504K, which was sold worldwide. During the First World War there were rapidly changing requirements for offensive aircraft, and the bomber aircraft became an entity. Chadwick designed the Avro Pike, which was unique in that it had internal stowage for the bombs – shades of the massive internal stowage area of the Lancaster. The Pike also had a gun turret aft of the biplane wings. Continuing his bomber theme was the world's biggest single-engine bomber, the Avro Aldershot.

Seaplanes, Arctic exploration planes, lightweight, ambulance, racer, autogiro and long-distance (Avro Avian) aeroplanes all came off the drawing board. The successful Avro Tutor and Cadet, followed by the extremely successful Anson, were all leading to the forerunner of the Lancaster: the Manchester. Chadwick's forethought and brilliance had designed the large, enclosed bomb bay for the Manchester. This in turn led to the ultimate development of more horsepower, four engines and the wider wings of the Lancaster.

The Avro York was developed from the Lancaster as a long-range transport. The York carried Sir Winston Churchill, King George VI and Lord Louis Mountbatten on their personal flights. He next developed a larger long-range bomber called the Avro Lincoln. The Avro Lancastrian was a very long-range aircraft, with a range close to 4,350 miles. He also designed Britain's first pressurised airliner, the Avro Tudor. The Avro

Shackleton was a further development of the theme, as a maritime patrol aircraft. Could he make the next big leap to the jet age?

In 1947 Chadwick had already thought of a delta-wing jet aircraft with internal bomb bay – it subsequently became the Avro Vulcan, which, thanks to the enormous effort of aviation enthusiasts, has taken to the skies again in this century as an air-show-display aircraft. Unfortunately, Chadwick was killed in a flying accident in 1947 and never saw his Shackleton or Vulcan fly. Perhaps it was a fitting tribute to him, notwithstanding the aircraft, that the BBMF Avro Lancaster PA474 and the Avro Vulcan XH558 G-VLCN flew together at the RAF Waddington air show on 5 July 2008. The Lancaster story had all started with an Air Ministry specification, a drafting board and Chadwick's brilliant, creative mind.

Just prior to the Second World War, Air Ministry specifications were changing. Air craft were now dually required to be able to carry torpedoes for shipping attacks, as well as the standard bomb load. The torpedoes would necessitate a long compartment if they were to be carried internally. Chadwick had this in mind when he was designing the Type 679 Manchester in response to Air Ministry Specification P.13/36 for a twin-engine bomber. He positioned both wing spars midway in the fuselage centre section to allow an interrupted bomb compartment beneath. It was certainly an engineering challenge, but the design decision proved itself invaluable for the future development of the Manchester into the Lancaster. The Manchester Mk I first flew in August 1939 with two Rolls-Royce Vulture twenty-four-cylinder engines that eventually proved underpowered and unreliable. Less than two years later, the Mk III flew with four Rolls-Royce Merlin engines, which in effect was the birth of the Lancaster. Rolls-Royce already had an established history of manufacturing luxury cars to exacting standards.

Francis K. Mason, in his book *The Avro Lancaster*, says that 'the Avro design staff, led by Chadwick, had, as early as February 1939, been examining the possibility of introducing a four-engine project, the Type 683, based on the Manchester but with four Rolls-Royce engines'. The Manchester was tested by the seasoned crews of No. 207 Squadron, No. 5 Group, at Waddington. The cooling problem with the Vulture engine was causing an abnormally high and unacceptable failure rate. The directional problem in the event of an engine failure had been addressed by enlarging the fins and the addition of a central fin, which was later removed. Restrictions were imposed as to performance to lessen the number of problems with engine heat.

The Manchester was relegated to training heavy bomber crew conversion units in 1942 until the spares for the Vulture engines dwindled away and the aircraft was grounded. The Manchester production line was now being considered for the Handley Page Halifax, and that would have been totally unacceptable to Chadwick and the Avro Company. The commonality of the two Avro aircraft, the Manchester and Lancaster, was pointed out to the Air Ministry in the hope of getting the go-ahead for the Type 683 Lancaster. Avro got the approval for a prototype with the proviso that it had to show its superiority with regards to its peers.

A Manchester, BT308, was taken out of the production line and modified with the addition of Merlin X engines, the XX engine not being available at that time. On 9 January 1941 the Manchester III, named for security purposes but in effect the Lancaster, went airborne with the central fin in place. By February the Lancaster had been returned to Avro for installation of a wider tailplane, larger fins and rudder, and removal of the unnecessary central fin. Further testing at the Airplane & Armament Experimental Establishment (A&AEE) at Boscombe Down revealed that the aircraft was faster than originally designed. This was probably due in part to the engine cowlings. The heating and cooling system would require extensive modification due to the variance of temperatures at different crew positions.

Thirty-two years later and another Avro aircraft, the Avro CF-100 Canuck, exhibited similar tendencies. In my book *NORAD and the Soviet Nuclear Threat* I stated that the CF-100 'was notorious for the lack of, or too much heat, depending where you sat in the cockpit. The pilot froze and the Electronic Warfare Officer sweated.' The more things change the more they stay the same, in some instances!

The Rolls-Royce Merlin engine made the Lancaster and Handley Page Halifax bombers, and at the same time made the stable of fighter aircraft. The Supermarine Spitfire, the Hawker Hurricane and the twin-engine de Havilland Mosquito all benefited from the Merlin engine as it continued its development throughout the war. It was the heart of these aircraft which took to the skies day after day and night after night; courage, bravery and determination were the heart of the aircrew that flew them, sometimes against terrible odds of expected attrition.

The Merlin engine was a liquid-cooled V-12 piston aero-engine of twenty-seven-litre displacement. It was originally known as the PV-12, standing for private venture, twelve-cylinder, as Rolls-Royce received no funding from the government for engine development. The Merlin engine was developed from the Kestrel engine to increase the available horsepower, as both the size and expected performance of aircraft were increasing at an accelerating rate. The biplane era was coming to an end and the monoplane reigned supreme in the designer's mind.

The Rolls-Royce engine-naming convention dictated that the new engine would be named after a bird of prey. The Merlin, a northern hemisphere falcon, joined the list of engine names in the tradition of the Kestrel, Peregrine and Vulture. It was eventually superseded by the Griffon engine. The Merlin was built at the Rolls-Royce factories in Derby, Crewe and Glasgow, and by Ford of Britain at the Old Trafford factory near Manchester. Close to 150,000 engines were built by the time production ceased in 1950.

The development of the Merlin was not without its problems. Typical engine problems that were dealt with effectively by Rolls-Royce led to the overall success of the Merlin. The problems that were solved included coolant leaks, cracked cylinder heads, excessive bearing wear and accessory gear train failures.

The second prototype Lancaster, DG595, was brought up to an all-up weight of 60,000 lbs and dived at maximum speeds to test the aerodynamics of turrets operating from side to side. The third and final prototype, DT810, was flown on 26 November 1941 with Bristol Hercules VI engines. This Lancaster was known as the Mk II and was constructed as an example of an alternate engine installation in case of shortage of Merlin XX engines.

The Bristol Engine Company Hercules engine was a totally different type of engine to the Merlin. It was a fourteen-cylinder two-row supercharged and air-cooled radial engine with a 38.7-litre displacement. The major version was the Hercules V1 engine, developing 1,650 horsepower, similar to that of the Merlin XX engine. It was a radically different design in that it featured 'sleeves' within the cylinder wall rotating and moving up and down to control the movement of the inlet air mixture and exhaust gases at the appropriate time in the combustion cycle. Designed by Sir Roy Fedden, the 'sleeve' design allowed better volumetric efficiency and higher compression ratios, and thus improved its thermal efficiency. In other words, more power from the same octane level. Developed from the Perseus engine, the Hercules engine was first available in 1939.

Bomber Command aircraft powered by the Hercules engine were the Handley Page Halifax, Short Stirling, Vickers Wellington and Avro Lancaster. The Hercules engine also powered Bristol's own Beaufighter, which saw duty as a night fighter and fighter-bomber. In post-war civilian life it powered the Handley Page Hastings and the Bristol Freighter. Over 57,000 engines were built, with the engine's main concern being how to maintain sufficient sleeve and cylinder lubrication with the oil technology of the 1940s.

The Merlin engines were built under licence in the USA to ensure a steady supply, and, despite the U-boat activity in the North Atlantic, this proved successful. The Ford Motor Car Company showed interested in the project, but subsequently declined the contract, which was offered to the Packard Motor Car Company of Detroit, Michigan, based on Rolls-Royce's impression of its high-quality engineering.

The first Packard Merlin 28 (Mk XX) engine ran in August 1941 and was designated by the United States Army Air Force as the V-1650-1. Modifications included main crankshaft bearing metals and the Wright supercharger for a high-altitude Packard Merlin engine, destined for the North American P-51 Mustang, designated the V-1650-3. Just over 55,000 engines were completed by Packard. These engines are sought after today by the contestants in the 'Unlimited' class of the Reno Air Races.

The first production Lancaster, R7527, first flew on 31 October 1941, nine months after the prototype. It was modified and had the ventral turret removed as ineffective. Based on further evaluation, the number of fuel tanks was increased to six and the maximum all-up weight to 65,000 lbs for future production aircraft. The aircraft had a crew of seven – the pilot, navigator, flight engineer, wireless operator, mid-upper gunner, bomb aimer/nose gunner and tail gunner. The Lancaster was now ready for squadron service, and joined the Bomber Command inventory of heavy bombers.

There are three gunnery positions on the Lancaster: the front (nose) turret, operated by the bomb aimer, plus the mid-upper and rear (tail) turrets. They all have the Colt-Browning 0.303-inch machine guns. The nose and mid-upper have two guns. The rear has four guns. The gun had not changed much for many years before 1939. It was a belt-fed machine gun that had some modifications for use in the Lancaster: the muzzle was lengthened and chromed, with cooling fins added. There was always a debate as to whether the gun was heavy enough against the fighter's armoured plating, but the gun and its ammunition had the advantage of being light, meaning the bomber could carry more bomb load. BSA and Vickers built this British version of the gun, referred to as the Mk II. It weighed twenty-four pounds and had a range of 3,000 feet.

Production of the Avro Lancaster was by five companies, in addition to the A. V. Roe & Co. Ltd factories at Newton Heath in Manchester, Woodford in, Cheshire and Yeadon in West Yorkshire. The other manufacturers were Austin Motors Ltd of Longbridge, Birmingham; Metropolitan-Vickers of Mosley Road and Old Trafford, Manchester; Sir W. G. Armstrong Whitworth Aircraft Ltd of Whitley, Coventry and Bitteswell, Warwickshire; Vickers-Armstrongs of Castle Bromwich, Birmingham and Hawarden, Cheshire; and the only overseas manufacturer, Victory Aircraft of Malton, Ontario, which produced 430 aircraft of the 7,374 Lancaster total.

The Victory order was in two parts, 300 and 130, before production was halted. Allocated serial numbers were KB700 to KB999 and FM100 to FM229. Serial number KB855 and up had the Martin electric mid-upper turret with 0.50 guns positioned further forward on the fuselage. Over 100 Canadian-built Lancasters were lost, nearly 25 per cent, due to enemy action or training accidents. KB732, serving with No. 419 RCAF Squadron, was the high-time survivor among Canadian-built aircraft, with eighty-three missions.

A whole publicity campaign was built around the first Canadian built Lancaster, KB700. It was filmed by a documentary crew during construction, the ferry flight to England and its first mission to Berlin. Rushed to completion, S/L Reg Lane DSO took it on its first flight at Victory Aircraft, Malton, on 1 August 1943. Despite many snags, Lane decided to carry on as planned to Dorval Airport, Montreal, to maintain the publicity momentum. It was repaired for about a month before proceeding overseas to No. 405 RCAF Squadron in England. Not compatible with the No. 405 Squadron Rolls-Royce Merlin aircraft, it was transferred to No. 419 RCAF Squadron, which used Packard Merlin engines.

KB700 was named the *Ruhr Express* for propaganda reasons. Tragically, it crashed and burned at Middleton St George in January 1945. This destroyed the aircraft's planned victorious return to Canada and the propaganda campaign.

THE *RUHR EXPRESS*

George Sines 6 August, 1943
(an employee of Victory Aircraft Ltd)

May the Gods above you ever bless,
And keep you safe, the *Ruhr Express*,
May you do your job and do it well,
And blow the Axis clean to hell.

We saw you born you wondrous thing,
We watched you grow and then take wing,
May you fly long though war-torn days,
And give us cause to sing your praise.

The job is hard you have to do,
But, we have faith you'll see it through,
May we have ever cause to bless,
Our new ship born, the *Ruhr Express*

We have waited long to see the day,
When you would take wings and fly away,
At last you roar a thunderous tune,

And Hitler too will hear it soon.
So here's to you the *Ruhr Express*,
Speed on your way, may Heaven bless,
Your every effort this war to cease,
So once again we live in peace.

Here's to the men your gallant crew,
The RCAF who will see you through,
God Save The King, may Heaven bless,
Your crew and you, the *Ruhr Express*.

Some 160 Lancasters were flown back across the Atlantic Ocean to prepare for service in the Pacific against the Japanese forces. VJ Day was declared before they saw any action, and the aircraft were disposed to storage sites throughout Canada, with the western prairie sites preferred due to the drier climate. Many were scrapped and the local farmers benefited from the many usable parts. In the late 1940s the Cold War situation was increasing, which resulted in some of the Lancasters being modified to 10MR/MP status – maritime reconnaissance, maritime patrol. There were other variants such as the 10AR, arctic reconnaissance; 10N, navigation trainer; and 10SR, air-sea rescue. By April 1964, the RCAF had retired the Lancaster from active military duty.

However, the venerable Lancaster had a civilian career in the late 1940s with the Canadian government's Trans-Atlantic Air Service and Trans-Canada Airlines, which operated a transatlantic passenger service – now everyone, finances permitting, could cross the Atlantic quickly. Spartan Air Services used the Lancaster for survey work across the vast northern regions of Canada.

There is no doubt that the decision by Bomber Command to concentrate on the four-engine heavy bomber was the correct one. The fact that the heavy bomber carried three times the bomb load of the medium bomber alone is justification. This was still done by just one pilot. The Empire Training Scheme was training pilots at its maximum capacity and probably would not have been able to train sufficient pilots to drop the same weight of bombs using the required medium bombers.

The three main types of heavy bomber were the Halifax, the Stirling and the Lancaster. The Lancaster proved beyond a doubt that it was the superior bomber and could carry more bombs further, with an ease of handling important for inexperienced pilots. The tons dropped per aircraft loss are 107 tons for the Lancaster and 48 for the Halifax. It had a relatively better accident rate and the casualties were less. The ruggedness of the Lancaster allowed for aggressive evasive manoeuvres and often allowed the Lancaster to return home 'on a wing and prayer'. The double waist-high spars not only held the aircraft together in the air but contributed to surviving crash landings.

It is estimated that over 1 million men and women worked on producing the aircraft that was the backbone of Bomber Command's heavy bomber fleet. Lancaster – it is a name that evokes memories of single heroic deeds and mass formations of aircraft attacking the enemy, and at the same time reminds us all of the great – sadly, for many the ultimate – sacrifice made by all the personnel in Bomber Command.

The Avro Lancaster – truly a British
aviation icon. (Martin Keen)

Right: Lancaster B.I PA474 of the Battle of Britain Memorial Flight. (Martin Keen)

Left: The Bomber Command Museum of Canada's Lancaster B.X, FM159. (Doug Bowman)

PA474 is based at RAF Coningsby in Lincolnshire and is one of only two currently airworthy examples of the Lancaster. (Martin Keen)

Above and right: The superb Mynarski memorial at the former RAF Middleton St George. (Martin Keen)

Above and left: Lancaster PA474 of the BBMF, captured here passing over the Derwent Dam on 16 May 2008 for the sixty-fifth anniversary of the famous Dambusters Raid. (UK Open Government Licence)

Above: Lancaster B.X FM213 of the Canadian Warplane Heritage Museum. (Martin Keen)

Right: Lancaster PA474 of the BBMF performs a poppy drop over The Mall to commemorate the fiftieth anniversary of VE Day on 8 May 1995. (UK Open Government Licence)

Far left and top left: The Avro Manchester. This aircraft type proved to be a troublesome design for the Royal Air Force, Rolls-Royce and Avro to master, but did lead directly to the far superior Lancaster. (Via Martin Keen)

Middle left and bottom left: Lancaster production line. (Via Martin Keen)

An airworthy Merlin 24 ready for installation on
Lancaster NX611 at the LAHC. (Martin Keen)

Opposite: Merlin 24 engines running faultlessly on NX611. (Martin Keen)

Below: With the Lancaster becoming such a familiar and successful design during the war, Avro was eager to publicise the aircraft's success in the media of the time. (BAE Systems Heritage Museum)

Above and overleaf: The *Ruhr Express*, the first Lancaster B.X built by Victory Aircraft of Canada. (Canadian Forces Joint Imagery Centre)

2

THE LANCASTER SQUADRONS

Some of the Lancaster Squadrons were steeped in British aviation history, often with their roots going back to the air battles of the First World War. The majority were established as the RAF built up its force to meet with the demands of the Second World War. It all began with the decision to have a formal approach to military aviation in 1911 and the formation of an air battalion within the Royal Engineers. This organisation was headquartered at South Farnborough; the name Farnborough was later to become synonymous with the British aviation industry.

Farnborough Airport has a long history with aviation in Britain. His Majesty's Balloon Factory, the Army's balloon factory, was located there from 1904 to 1906 and was part of the Army School of Ballooning. In 1908, Samuel Cody made the first powered flight in Britain at Farnborough. By 1912 the Balloon Factory was renamed the Royal Aircraft Factory, which in turn became the Royal Aircraft Establishment in 1918. A long association with Farnborough was to follow.

The Royal Flying Corps (RFC) was founded on 13 May 1912. The RFC was tasked with fighter (scout), bomber and observation duties. The RFC squadrons played a vital role in battlefield management, being the eyes of the Army. The aircraft, organised in squadrons, were assigned communication, reconnaissance, observation (aerial photography) and artillery direction duties. On 1 April 1918 the present-day Royal Air Force was formed, incorporating some of the original squadrons.

The squadron was comprised of 'flights', referred to as A Flight, B Flight, etc. The different squadrons belonged to 'wings', which were incorporated in 'groups' within Bomber Command. As an example, the first RAF VCs awarded, both posthumously, were to P/O D. Garland and Sgt T. Gray of No. 12 Squadron, No. 76 Wing (Advanced Air Striking Force), No. 1 Group, Bomber Command, flying a Fairey Battle in a bombing mission to destroy a bridge across the Albert Canal.

The RAF Bomber Command groups during the Second World War were initially numbered 1, 3, 5 and 8, with No. 8 never becoming operational. Subsequently, in 1942 No. 8 became the Pathfinder Force (PFF) Group. No. 6 Group was formed later to include all of the RCAF squadrons. The number of aircraft, and hence the size of all the components in a group, varied as per operational necessity, attrition, serviceability and availability. The strength of the group varied on a daily basis, especially following a large bombing mission.

The RAF Bomber Command stations were located in the eastern half of England, close to Germany to cut flying time, but far enough away to be out of the area of greatest enemy fighter activity in the south, stretching from Middleton St George, Durham, in the north to Wratting Common, Cambridgeshire, in the south.

Each squadron had a badge or emblem signifying its history, present tasking or other significant association. The BBMF Lancaster is presently, in 2015, painted to represent aircraft DV385 KC-A *Thumper Mark III* of No. 617 (Dambuster) Squadron. The No. 617 Squadron badge is an image of a dam being breached with the French motto meaning, 'After me, the flood.' The badge has the standard RAF surround with the numbers 617 and the royal crown.

The Mynarski Lancaster of the CWHM is painted to represent aircraft KB726 of No. 419 (Moose) Squadron RCAF. The No. 419 Squadron badge is an image of a moose attacking with the Cree language motto 'Moosa aswayita'. It has the words 'Royal Canadian Air Force' and number '419' surrounding the moose image. At the head of the badge is the royal crown.

The first squadron in the RAF to take the Lancaster on strength was No. 44 Squadron. Its badge shows an elephant with the motto 'Fulmina regis iusta' ('the king's thunderbolts are righteous'). The king was Lo Bengula, chief of the Matabeles. The elephant was used to indicate heavy attacks. The squadron was formed in July 1917 and was known for pioneering the use of the Sopwith Camel for night operations. One of its first commanding officers was a young Major Harris. He, Sir Arthur T. Harris, Marshal of the Royal Air Force, subsequently unleashed the biggest assault on the German homeland a quarter of a century later, in an ironic twist of fate.

The squadron was disbanded in 1919 and did not see service again until it was reformed at Wyton, Huntingdon, as a bomber squadron in 1937. It moved to Waddington, Lincolnshire, and reequipped with Bristol Blenheims and then Handley Page Hampdens. Its name was changed to No. 44 (Rhodesia) Squadron in 1941 to acknowledge the contribution of Rhodesia to the war effort. In 1942 the squadron became the first to convert totally to the Lancaster.

Its first sorties were minelaying in the Heligoland Bight in March 1942, followed by a daring unescorted daylight raid on the MAN diesel factory at Augsburg. Squadron Leader John D. Nettleton won the Victoria Cross during this raid and managed to bring his crippled aircraft, with crew, home after successfully bombing the target. No. 44 Squadron continued its illustrious career with attacks on German industrial areas, ports and U-boat shelters, not to mention V-weapon facilities and Italian targets. Two moves to Dunholme Lodge and Spilsby, both in Lincolnshire, completed its wartime record. Re-equipped with Avro Lincolns after the war, No. 44 Squadron finally paid a long visit on detachment to Rhodesia; the wartime thank you was complete.

Squadrons and conversion units were quickly formed with the Lancaster. No. 207 Squadron at Bottesford, Leicestershire and 83 and 106 at Coningsby, Lincolnshire, were followed by No. 50 Squadron in May 1942 at Skellingthorpe, Lincolnshire. These initial squadrons were followed by fifty-six others up until April 1945. They included one Polish squadron and one New Zealand squadron, plus thirteen Canadian and three Australian squadrons.

The markings on the Lancaster can be somewhat confusing at times. Each aircraft has a designated production number. The squadron itself was given a code. The aircraft was assigned to a flight and carried its own personal code beside the roundel. For example, the Mynarski Lancaster of the CWHM carries the markings VR (Roundel) A. The VR signifies an aircraft belonging to No. 419 RCAF Moose Squadron, and the A refers to aircraft number KB726.

The roundel is a circular identification mark used by RAF aircraft to identify them to ground forces and other aircraft. It originated in the First World War and consists of two rings of colours, white and blue, surrounding a red centre. It was in fact a copy of the identification used by France, a tricolour cockade (a roundel of red and white with a blue centre), but with the colours reversed. The intention originally was to prevent the loss of aircraft due to friendly ground fire; the Army during those early years of aviation tended to fire at all 'flying machines'. The RCAF used the roundel with various forms of the maple leaf as the red centre.

To further confuse the present-day historian and aircraft aficionado, the aviation museums have repainted and re-lettered the aircraft. The BCMC, CWHM and East Kirkby museums have settled upon a colour scheme to represent a particular aircraft. The BBMF has changed the colour scheme and markings to represent many aircraft over the years. In addition, an aircraft's raids and any special accomplishments were often painted by the squadron on the fuselage below the cockpit. The more adventuresome aircraft and crew had 'nose art' representing its name and phrases painted on the front of the fuselage – a personal touch to an otherwise impersonal war machine.

The squadrons were scattered all over the eastern part of the country and their landing patterns were very close to each other, which, during times of high stress, got quite confusing under the cover of darkness and bad weather. To further complicate the situation, the squadrons were relocated and combined with other squadrons from time to time. The stations were often named for the nearest small village to the appropriated fields. Unusual names became household names, such as Little Snoring and Elsham Wolds.

The aircraft were delivered to the squadrons by the Air Transport Auxiliary from the various manufacturing factories. The pilots were a very flexible group as they flew all types of aircraft to all destinations, flying many different types in the same day, often without much of a checkout. They did carry a standard checklist that applied to all aircraft, called a 'Blue Book'. They were instructed 'to go from A to B and don't bend the aircraft'. One of the famous female pilots was Joan Hughes, a diminutive British girl who once impressed the Avro workers by looping a Lancaster over their factory.

At the beginning of hostilities Bomber Command had twenty-seven airfields, all with grass-surface runways! At its peak in 1944 it had sixty-seven operational and sixty-one training airfields, and all but two were hard-surface runways. The requirements for runways changed as the aircraft got bigger and heavier. Initially the main runway was 1,400 yards, with the two subsidiary runways at 1,100 yards. The main runway was increased to 1,600 yards and finally, by 1941, to 2,000 yards and the subsidiary to 1,400 yards. In today's money, an airfield would cost £48 million to construct.

Because of the constant night operations of Bomber Command, a standard lighting system was adopted for the airfields. The Mk II system was widely used and consisted of the landing strip lights plus all the auxiliary lights, such as outer circuit lights, taxiing track lights, dispersal floodlights and angle-of-approach indicators. The whole system was controlled by the Watch Office.

A bombing mission could not be declared a success until the aircraft and crew were safely parked at dispersal, preferably at their home station. Having evaded the fighters, the barrage of flak and the risk of mid-air collision, and having crossed the sea to England, the Lancaster pilot faced the challenge of landing his aircraft and crew in the sometimes miserable weather of his home island. He did not have the benefit of the modern Instrument Landing System (ILS), but he did have some assistance thanks to the pioneering work of the Telecommunications Research Establishment and the technicians who implemented their discoveries.

One of the leading scientists involved in the development of the blind landing system was Robert J. Dippy. Dippy had started his work in 1937, but it was deemed 'not a priority' for daylight operations. By 1942 the situation had changed, as massive losses had driven the RAF to adopt night bombing missions. This necessitated the invention of navigation systems to get the bomber to its target, such as Gee, and navigation systems to get the bomber back to home base and land in inclement weather. These systems required technicians to install and maintain them both in the aircraft and on the airfield.

One of those technicians was Malcolm Dewar, now Dr, who, because of his amateur radio hobby in his youth, was posted to the Telecommunications Section of the RAF during the 1940s. He was later assigned to the famous Telecommunications Research Establishment (TRE) in Malvern, Worcestershire, to learn the top-secret intricacies of the 'landing beam' navigational aid. TRE had taken over Malvern College, an independent boys' boarding school, and Dewar was billeted in a local hotel during his training. Returning to his squadron, No. 12, based at Wickenby, Lincolnshire, he set up the runway landing system there. He was also responsible for the radio telephone in the control tower. During heavy work periods, if he was available, he would assist with the transmitters and receivers in the squadron's Lancasters.

When asked about setting up the landing system, Dewar said that 'it consisted of driving a vehicle up on a ramp to project the beam down the length of the runway and beyond. Calibration to ensure perfect alignment of the beam was carried out mechanically. The entire transmitting apparatus was mounted in the back of the vehicle with the antennae unfolded in two arms. The basic principal was that there were two sectors, left or right of the beam, relayed to the pilot and it was necessary to follow the instrument indications to line up with the runway.'

One night Dewar was listening to the Watch Office talking to an aircraft, Easy 2, that had aborted its mission as the bomb bay doors would not open. It was instructed to hold at 3,000 feet while clearance was received for the aircraft to proceed to a specially designated crash airfield. These special stations had better facilities for taking care of disabled aircraft, especially if a fiery crash was involved. Dewar recounted, 'Just then I heard the aircraft pass low overhead and was about to call the Watch Office to tell them of its position when the aircraft crashed close by into the bomb storage site. There were no survivors and I was lucky that the aircraft missed me and that the bomb site did not explode.'

East Kirkby, Lincolnshire, is such an example of a standard airfield. Formerly the home of Nos 57 and 630 Lancaster squadrons, it is now the home of the Lincolnshire Aviation Heritage Centre (LAHC). A full description of this facility is covered in chapter 6. The 'new' Bomber Command stations required during hostilities were acquired – a nice, soft phrase – from local farmers for the use of the government. The acquired locations had to be suitable for an airfield. One consideration was the topography, which needed to allow the bombers to get airborne with their heavy loads and to land with as few local obstacles as possible.

The land for East Kirkby was mostly from the Hagnaby Grange Farm, situated fourteen miles north of Boston, Lincolnshire, in the parishes of East Kirkby and Hagnaby. It was built in 1942–3 by the principal contractor, John Laing & Son Ltd.

The airfield consisted of a designated primary runway, 02/20, into the prevailing wind, with a length of 2,000 yards, and two other subsidiary runways, forming a core triangle. The other two runways were 08/26 and 13/31, both 1,400 yards in length. Runways were given their number by their magnetic bearing, adjusted to the nearest ten degrees. The main runway at East Kirkby was nearly north/south as its number was 02, 020 degrees magnetic and 20, 200 degrees magnetic, with north being 360 and south 180.

The whole inner field was surrounded by a perimeter track which joined the ends of all runways and allowed aircraft to taxi to and from the twenty-seven pan-type and eight loop-type hardstands from any runway. It was on these hardstands that all daily maintenance, minor repair work and bomb loading would take place. This could be quite pleasant in the summer months, but in the dark, cold and wet of a Lincolnshire winter it could be very challenging to keep the serviceability and morale up.

The airfield was built to Class A standard, with two T2 hangars and one B1. To the north-west was the village of East Kirkby. Beyond that was the dispersed camp consisting of accommodation and facilities, including sick quarters, for approximately 2,000 men and 500 women. The bomb store, or ammunition dump, was located to the north-east of the runways. In August 1943 East Kirkby accepted its first resident squadron, No. 57 Squadron, flying Lancasters. Shortly after, in November, B Flight was separated from No. 57 Squadron and became No. 630 Squadron. Unusually, it continued to reside and operate from East Kirkby until the end of hostilities. Both No. 57 and No. 630 Squadron were part of No. 5 Group.

Fighting a war was always thirsty work, and the East Kirkby station was no exception. The local pub, the Red Lion, was kept busy with the hard-working occupants of the airfield. The one-room pub was normally full, and the patrons flowed down the passageway to the street. In addition to the pub, the landlord operated a butcher shop in the same building, which supplied sausages to the troops. Britain was full of local pubs that catered to the operational life on an active RAF station. For those working long hours on the ground and for those risking their lives in the air, the local pub and the RAF mess played an important part in the social scene of the times.

Those on the ground were not free from danger either. In the early morning hours of 4 March 1945, a Luftwaffe Ju 88 strafed the airfield, causing one death and several wounded. Not long after, on 17 April 1945, in the closing weeks of the war, a bombed-up No. 57 Squadron Lancaster, PB630, caught on fire and caused extensive casualties and damage. Six Lancasters were totally destroyed and fourteen were damaged by the inferno caused by exploding bombs. The station took a week to recover to full operational status.

In the early years of the war each station had one 'satellite' – an alternate landing ground. Due to the build-up of resources, this one satellite became two, one of which was brought up to station status. A group consisted of fifteen stations: five were parent stations and ten were expected to facilitate sixteen bomber aircraft. Twelve were designated operational, and three were heavy conversion units (HCUs). By 1943 it was realised that

the organisation of stations had become inefficient and an intermediate control was necessary. The 'base' system was established, which looked after six squadrons on three separate but associated stations. This did not apply to No. 8 or No. 100 Group, which were speciality groups.

The following list indicates the geographical location of the Lancaster squadrons and, for interest's sake, a relevant piece of squadron information for further reading. There are many, many sources of concise squadron histories available, which is why this book will not go into such particulars for each squadron.

No.	Code	Location/s	Further reading
7	MG, XU	Oakington, Cambs	1944 Lancaster B.VI
9	WS	Waddington, Lincs	Flt Sgt George Thompson VC
		Bardney, Lincs	
12	PH, GZ	Wickenby, Lincs	Flying Officer D. Garland VC
			Sergeant T. Gray VC
15	LS, DJ	Mildenhall, Suffolk	Famous Lanc LL806 J for Jig
35	TL	Graveley, Hunts	1917 attached to Cavalry Corps
44	KM	Waddington, Lincs	Squadron Leader J. Nettleton VC
		Dunholme Lodge, Lincs	
		Spilsby, Lincs	
49	EA	Scampton, Lincs	Flight Lieutenant R. Learoyd VC
		Fiskerton, Lincs	
		Fulbeck, Lincs	
50	VN	Skellingthorpe, Lincs	Flying Officer L. Manser VC
		Swinderby, Lincs	
57	DX, QT	Scampton, Lincs	Wesel raid, Rhine crossing
		East Kirkby, Lincs	
61	QR	Syerston, Notts	Flight Lieutenant W. Reid VC
		Skellingthorpe, Lincs	

		Coningsby, Lincs				Hemswell, Lincs	
75	AA, JN	Mepal, Cambs	Sergeant Pilot RNZAF J. Ward VC	186	XY	Tuddenham, Suffolk	Operation Exodus
83	OL	Scampton, Lincs	Flight Sergeant John Hannah VC			Stradishall, Suffolk	
		Wyton, Hunts		189	CA	Bardney, Lincs	EE136 *Spirit of Russia*
		Coningsby, Lincs				Fulbeck, Notts	
90	WP, XY	Tuddenham, Suffolk	Operated Boeing B-17 Flying Fortress	195	JE	Witchford, Cambs	Initially Hawker Typhoon squadron
97	OF, ZT	Coningsby, Lincs	Marker squadron, Friedrichshafen			Wratting Common, Cambs	
		Woodhall Spa, Lincs		207	EM	Bottesford, Leics	Avro Manchester to squadron service
		Bourn, Cambs				Langar, Notts	First raid 24/25 February 1941
		Coningsby, Lincs				Spilsby, Lincs	
100	HW, FZ	Grimsby (Waltham), Lincs	Japanese forces at Endau	218	HA, XH	Methwold, Norfolk	Flight Sergeant A. Aaron VC
		Elsham Wolds, Lincs				Chedburgh, Suffolk	
101	SR, MW	Holme-on-Spalding Moor, Yorks	*Airborne Cigar* or ABC	227	9J	Balderton, Notts	Temporarily No. 19 SAAF Squadron
		Ludford Magna, Lincs				Strubby, Lincs	
103	PM	Elsham Wolds, Lincs	ED888 Pm-M2 140 trips	300	BH	Faldingworth, Lincs	First Polish-manned bomber squadron
106	ZN	Coningsby, Lincs	Sergeant N. Jackson VC				No. 405 to 434 are Royal
		Syerston, Notts					Canadian Air Force squadrons
		Metheringham, Lincs		405	LQ	Gransden Lodge, Beds	KB700 first Canadian Mk X, *Ruhr Express*
109	HS	Wyton, Hunts	Squadron Leader R. Palmer VC	408	EQ	Linton-on-Ouse, Yorkshire	Returned Canada for Tiger Force
115	KO, IL	East Wretham, Norfolk	Service trials of Gee	419	VR	Middleton St George, Durham	Pilot Officer RCAF A. Mynarski VC
		Little Snoring, Norfolk		420	PT	Tholthorpe, Yorkshire	Returned Lancaster aircraft to Canada
		Witchford, Cambs		424	QB	Skipton-on-Swale, Yorkshire	Wangerooge raid
138	NF, AC	Tuddenham, Suffolk	Special Operations Executive	425	KW	Tholthorpe, Yorkshire	Mandrel operation
149	OJ, TK	Methwold,Norfolk	Fight Sergeant RAAF R. Middleton VC	426	OW	Linton-on-Ouse, Yorkshire	Post-war Korean airlift
150	IQ, JN	Hemswell, Lincs	Operation Manna	427	ZL	Leeming, Yorkshire	First RCAF squadron to fly CF-104
153	P4	Scampton, Lincs	Berchtesgaden raid, April 1945	428	NA	Middleton St George, Durham	Flew aircraft to Canada
156	GT	Warboys, Hunts	One of the original four PFF squadrons	429	AL	Leeming, Yorkshire	Disbanded in England
		Upwood, Hunts		431	SE	Croft, Durham	Flew aircraft to Canada
166	AS	Kirmington, Lincs	Gardening (minelaying) raids	432	QO	East Moor, Yorkshire	Disbanded in England
170	TC	Dunholme Lodge, Lincs	Operation Dodge	434	IP, WL	Croft, Durham	Flew aircraft to Canada

			460 to 467 are RAAF squadrons
460	UV, AR	Breighton, Yorkshire	W4783 at Australian War Museum
		Binbrook, Lincs	
463	JO	Waddington, Lincs	PD329 recorded attack on Tirpitz
467	PO	Scampton, Lincs	R5868 second-highest number of raids
		Botesford, Leics	
		Waddington, Lincs	
514	A2, JI	Waterbeach, Cambs	Gee-H-equipped blind-bombing squadron
550	BQ	Grimsby (Waltham), Lincs	EE139 *The Phantom of the Ruhr*
		North Killingholme, Lincs	
576	UL	Elsham Wolds, Lincs	First Op Berlin 2/3 December 1943
		Fiskerton, Lincs	
582	6O	Little Staughton, Hunts	Captain SAAF E. Swales VC
617	AJ, YZ, KC	Scampton, Lincs	Wing Commander G. Cheshire VC
			Wing Commander G. Gibson VC
		Coningsby, Lincs	Operation Chastise
		Woodhall Spa, Lincs	Known as the Dambuster Squadron
619	PG	Wood Hall Spa, Lincs	Wing Commander S. Birch destroyed V1
		Coningsby, Lincs	
		Dunholme Lodge, Lincs	
		Strubby, Lincs	
622	GI	Mildenhall, Suffolk	LL885 100+ raids
625	CF	Kelstern, Lincs	Flying Officer David Mattingley DFC
		Scampton, Lincs	
626	UM	Wickenby, Lincs	RAF Wickenby
630	LE	East Kirkby, Lincs	Lincolnshire Aviation Heritage Centre
635	F2	Downham Market, Norfolk	Squadron Leader I.Bazalgette VC
			Operational trials Lancaster B.VI 1944

No. 1 Group: 'Swift to Attack'

No. 1 (Bomber) Group formed at Abingdon on 1 May 1936. It was responsible for the Central Area of the Air Defence of Great Britain. It had three stations: Abingdon, Bircham Newton and Upper Heyford. Its ten squadrons were equipped with the Hawker Hind. Just prior to start of hostilities, the eight stations and seventeen squadrons were equipped with Bristol Blenheims or Fairey Battles.

The group proceeded to France in the summer of 1939 as the Advanced Air Striking Force (AASF), Nos 71 to 76 inclusive wings. Despite a gallant effort, the AASF left France in June 1940 to reform at Hucknall, Notts. By 1941 the group was converting to Vickers Wellingtons and the headquarters had moved to Bawtry Hall, South Yorkshire.

By August 1942, No. 103 Squadron was fully operational on the Handley Page Halifax heavy bombers. By November, Nos 460 and 103 squadrons were operating Lancasters. During the summer of 1943, the group switched from the Battle of the Ruhr to the Battle of Hamburg. By November, the group had performed four major attacks on Berlin in nine days. One day, 15 February 1944, saw over 130 Lancasters drop their bombs on Berlin.

March 1944 saw twenty-one aircraft fail to return from Nuremberg. The Prime Minister of Australia, the Rt Hon John Curtin, on a visit to Station Binbrook, was presented with Lancaster W4783 G for George. It is now in the War Museum in Canberra, Australia. It had logged ninety operational sorties. In the spring the group was generally softening resistance, and during one May night the group lost twenty-eight aircraft over the military centre of Maily-le-Camp.

However, in June the group broke all records by dropping over 15,000 tons of bombs with a low loss rate. Perhaps the tide of war was turning in preparation for the invasion of Europe. No. 101 Squadron played a historic role through prolonged patrols spent electronically jamming the enemy's defences. No. 460 Squadron set an all-time record for a squadron by dropping 1,867 tons of bombs in August 1944.

The group cut the sea wall at Walcheren, Zeeland, Netherlands, in October and flooded the German defences. Bases and sub-bases continued to be formed, sometimes allocated to other resources.

No. 3 Group: 'Nothing Without Labour'

No. 3 (Bomber) Group was formed on 1 May 1936 at Andover, Hampshire, with the headquarters moving to Mildenhall, Suffolk, early the next year. It was responsible for the western area of the Air Defence of Great Britain. The Vickers Wellington replaced such aircraft as the Virginia and Heyford in the group. The first squadron to receive the Wellington was No. 99 Squadron in October 1938. The second bombing operation of the war was carried out by 3 Group Wellingtons against some German warships.

Two squadrons were sent north and one of them, No. 115 Squadron, was the first squadron to bomb a mainland target, Stavanger airfield. A raid was carried out on Italy from the south of France in early June 1940, but the squadrons were quickly withdrawn due to the imminent collapse of France. Later in the year, the first four-engine bomber, the Shorts Stirling, joined the group, followed by the Lancaster in 1942.

The first thousand-bomber raid was on the night of 30/31 May 1942 against Cologne. A new technique was also adopted in 1942: a flare force guided by radar lit up the target for the main bombing force. Aircraft were drawn from all squadrons and were located under the administrative control of airfields in No. 3 Group. On the night of 3/4 November 1943, No. 3 Group led a blind bombing attack on Dusseldorf using the G-H radar bombing aid. The following year, No. 3 Group attacked flying bomb sites during the summer. The build-up to the D-Day invasion was preceded by attacks on railway junctions and marshalling yards.

During the final push for Berlin, No. 3 Group bombed the town of Wesel in preparation for the crossing of the Rhine. Just prior to VE Day, the group were involved with Operation Manna, dropping food to the citizens of the Netherlands.

No. 5 Group: 'Undaunted'

No. 5 (Bomber) Group was formed on 1 September 1937 at Mildenhall, Suffolk, and moved its headquarters to Grantham, Lincolnshire. The initial allocation at Grantham was ten squadrons of Handley Page Hampdens on five stations. It is interesting that the future Air Officer Commanding-in-Chief of Bomber Command, Air Vice-Marshall A. T. Harris, was at one time in command of No. 5 Group. The Hampdens lasted until the winter of 1940/1, when the group started to convert to Avro Manchesters.

The group was unique in that it pioneered the art of minelaying; in fact, it had been responsible for all minelaying from the air. The group was involved in some of the more specialised and dramatic attacks of the war. For example, the breaches of the Dortmund–Ems Canal, the destruction of the Möhne and Eder dams, the sinking of the *Tirpitz* and the shuttle raids flying between England and North Africa.

In the spring of 1941 the group was involved in the daylight attacks on the Scharnhorst and Gneisenau of the German Navy at Brest. A year later the group had started to reequip with the Lancaster and the first operation was minelaying in the Heligoland Bight. The Augsburg MAN diesel engine factory was attacked in April at very low level, and unfortunately casualties were high. Cologne was attacked by a thousand-bomber raid, and No. 5 Group contributed 162 aircraft.

During October the group made three raids that were most important to the war effort, raiding Genoa, Milan and the Schneider armament works at Le Creusot. The most famous of all raids took place in May 1943: the Dams raid on the Möhne and Eder dams by No. 617 Squadron, led by Wing Commander Guy Gibson. The group also played a full part in the Battle of Berlin. Spring 1944 was devoted to softening up targets in advance of the planned May invasion.

June saw the group fly more than 5,000 sorties, and the first Tallboy dropped, which blocked the Saumur Tunnel. The group also took part in the attack on Wesel to permit the crossing of the Rhine, and in March dropped the heaviest bomb yet, the 22,000 lb Grand Slam. No. 5 Group was selected to the Tiger Force to be deployed against Japan. By December 1945, this well-known group was disbanded.

No. 6 Group: 'Initiative and Skill'

No. 6 Bomber Group (RCAF) was formed on 25 October 1942, with the headquarters moving to Allerton Park, Yorkshire, in December. The cost of No. 6 Group was borne by the Canadian government, except for RAF and local personnel attached to the group. January 1943 saw the initial transfer of six stations with their established RCAF squadrons. They were Leeming (Nos 408 and 424 squadrons), Middleton St George (Nos 419 and 420 squadrons), Dishforth (Nos 425 and 426 squadrons), Croft (No. 427 Squadron), Dalton (No. 428 Squadron) and Skipton-on-Swale, which was still being built. The squadrons were flying Handley Page Halifaxes or Vickers Wellingtons prior to later conversion to the Lancaster.

The eventual seven operational stations were organised as bases and each had sub-stations with operational squadrons. The largest base was No. 62 (Beaver) Base at Linton-on-Louse, with No. 408 and No. 426 as resident squadrons. The two sub-stations were East Moor, with Nos 415 and 432 squadrons, and Tholthorpe, with Nos 420 and 425 squadrons. The other two bases with their own sub-stations were No. 63 Base at Leeming and No. 64 Base at Middleton St George. No. 61 Base, later renamed No. 76 and associated with the RAF, was established as the training organisation and supported several heavy conversion units.

Many RCAF squadrons were formed and added to the group later, and there was constant movement of all squadrons from base to base. The only exception was Mynarski's squadron, No. 419, which remained at Middleton St George until the end of the war. Worthy of mention are the two attacks on Duisburg, sixteen hours apart, when the group put up over 500 aircraft. The previous week, the night of 6 October 1943, the group bombed Dortmund with close to 300 aircraft. The group overall had a great history of serviceability.

Eight squadrons were earmarked for the Tiger Force, and some Lancasters were ferried back to Canada in preparation. Four squadrons remained active in Great Britain for a short time. By the end of August 1945, the 'Canadian Bomber Group' had come to an end. Canadian airmen – both at home in the British Commonwealth Air Training Plan and home defence, and abroad with the RAF and RCAF – can be proud of their contribution to the war effort.

No. 8 (PFF) Group: 'We Guide to Strike'

There seems to be a confusing start to this famous group. Initially founded in September 1941 with headquarters at Brampton, Cambridgeshire, as No. 8 (Bomber) Group, it was not until after No. 8 (PFF) Group was formed in January 1943 that it was disbanded. No. 8 (Bomber) Group never became operational. No. 8 (PFF) Group originally started as the Pathfinder Force (PFF) in August 1942 with headquarters at Wyton, Huntingdonshire. It comprised specially chosen squadrons from each of the groups.

No. 1 Group	No. 156 Squadron	Vickers Wellington
No. 2 Group	No. 109 Squadron	Vickers Wellington & de Havilland Mosquito
No. 3 Group	No. 7 Squadron	Shorts Stirling
No. 4 Group	No. 35 Squadron	Handley Page Halifax
No. 5 Group	No. 83 Squadron	Avro Lancaster

The idea was that these handpicked squadrons and crews from each group would be under the direct command of Air Chief Marshall Harris, Air Officer Commanding-in-Chief, Bomber Command. The (PFF) group eventually transitioned to the Avro Lancaster and de Havilland Mosquito as the aircraft of choice. By the end of 1941, Bomber Command wanted to have specialist squadrons (an idea first used by the Luftwaffe) to initiate the bombing stream. No. 3 Group had been doing it in limited capacity using the new Gee apparatus.

The elite PFF group was not without its detractors; they were not opposed to the idea, but the elite connotation was, for some, not very acceptable. However, actions speak louder than words. The PFF group so improved the accuracy of the bombing raids that it became the recognised method for pinpointing the target for the main force. Group Captain D. C. T. Bennett then assumed command in January 1943 for the entire length of its existence.

The use of the blind bombing aid Oboe and highly visible marker aids of different types increased the efficiency of the group. The group continued to grow throughout the war and consisted of nineteen squadrons just prior to VE Day. Its contribution to the success of Bomber Command is immeasurable, but the PFF squadrons paid a high price for their dangerous role.

Bomber Command: 'Strike Hard, Strike Sure'

Bomber Command was a direct descendant of the First World War strategic bombing forces. Unlike the deterrent bomber forces of the Cold War Era – the famous RAF 'V' bomber force of the Avro Vulcan, Handley Page Victor and Vickers Valiant – the Lancaster was the most important part of the RAF's Second World War strategic offensive bomber force. The strategic part was provided by Bomber Command headquarters, founded at Uxbridge, Middlesex, in July 1936. By March 1940 it had moved permanently to High Wycombe, Buckinghamshire.

The policy and strategic bombing philosophy was in the hands of Bomber Command, subject to the overall aims of the war effort. Initially, as the threat grew, Bomber Command was the junior player in the build-up of arms. The UK being an island, it was the Navy that got the first priority, followed by the defensive air force. In the early years, the striking power of Bomber Command was limited to leaflet dropping, defensive patrols and a disastrous attempt at daylight raids on the heavily protected German Navy.

Bomber Command initially lagged in manpower and advanced aircraft, but was continuing to grow when the Lancaster arrived on the scene in 1942. It also had a new Commander-in-Chief, Air Marshall A. T. Harris. The tables were turning, with night-time area bombing done by larger and larger numbers of heavy bombers. The PFF, incendiary bombs, Oboe and H2S all contributed to the growing accuracy and destructive power of Bomber Command. Guidance to Bomber Command from the chiefs of staff in 1943 read, 'Your primary object will be the progressive destruction and dislocation of the German military, industrial and economic system and the undermining of the morale of the German people to a point where their capacity for armed resistance is fatally weakened.'

The gloves were off, and Sir Arthur Harris was given, it seems, a free hand to conduct the bombing campaign as he saw fit. How was he going to do this? The only thing that would shut down the offensive war would be bad weather, but was that the case everywhere? And were there any gaps that could be exploited? The weather proved the key factor in how daily events would unfold.

The commander-in-chief (C-in-C) would attend a morning conference and briefing in the operations room at command headquarters. The meteorological officer would give a briefing on the expected weather conditions over enemy territory and the home bases. The intelligence officer then briefed on what target objectives were available in the weather-suitable area. The targets would be on a priority list, which had them grouped under such headings as rail transport, oil, airfields and industrial areas, etc.

Once the targets were selected and their nature understood, the number of aircraft and type of bomb load were calculated and decided upon. The number of available aircraft varied daily as per maintenance serviceability, attrition from last operation and delivery of new aircraft off the production line. The deputy C-in-C was responsible for the planning details, while the senior air staffing officer was responsible for the operational side. The C-in-C made a decision about 'H hour', the time over the target, considering such variables as the weather, distance to target,

hours of darkness and coordination of effort with other operations. The groups concerned were now given 'warning orders' of the impending raid.

Routes, aiming points, enemy defence activity and electronic countermeasure details were all planned and sent out to the groups as operational orders. Upon acceptance by the group, there was room for negotiation; the orders would be passed on to the various stations. The individual squadrons would then be passed their details for the planned raid. A further confirmation would be made by Bomber Command during the afternoon and the operational side would continue to prepare itself for the planned departure times – the HQ work was done and now it was the turn of 'the pointy end', the squadrons and their aircraft (which included the Avro Lancaster in ever-growing numbers), to get the job done.

Previous page: No. 626 Squadron at RAF Wickenby, photographed during 1944. (RAF Wickenby Memorial Collection)

Above: Lancaster B.III NG347 QB-P *Piccadilly Princess* of No. 424 Squadron. (Canadian Forces Joint Imagery Centre)

A Lancaster of No. 424 (Tiger) Squadron RCAF, Skipton on Swale, performs engine runs at dispersal during the summer of 1944. (Canadian Museum of Flight)

Above: A fine air-to-air study of Lancaster B.I R5852, OL-Y, of No. 83 Squadron. (Via Martin Keen)

Left: A Lancaster of No. 44 Squadron flies across its home base at RAF Waddington. (Via Martin Keen)

KB732 VR-X *X-Terminator* of No. 419 (Moose) Squadron RCAF. A
Canadian-built Lancaster, KB732 completed eighty-four operations,
more than any other in RCAF service during the Second World War.
(Canadian Forces Joint Imagery Centre)

Aussie, a suitably named Lancaster serving with No. 460 Squadron RAAF. No. 460 Squadron suffered the highest loss rate of any Lancaster Squadron in No. 1 Group. (Art Sewel)

Left: A Lancaster B.III of 619 Squadron, RAF Coningsby, on a test flight, 14 February 1944. (Via Martin Keen)

Right: Hellzapoppin, JB405 PH-H, with her air and ground crew at RAF Wickenby. JB405, a Lancaster B.III of No. 12 Squadron, was lost during operations to Mailly-le-Camp on 3 May 1944 with only the rear gunner, Sgt S. Johnson, surviving to become a POW. (RAF Wickenby Memorial Collection)

Air and ground crew from No. 419 Squadron RCAF suitably mark the completion of 1,000 Canadian Lancaster sorties. (Canadian Forces Joint Imagery Centre)

A No. 434 (Bluenose) Squadron B.X, *S for Smitty*, photographed late in the war. (Canadian Forces Joint Imagery Centre)

No. 424 (Tiger) Squadron RCAF
celebrate the Squadron's 2,000th sortie.
(Canadian Museum of Flight)

AN EASTER EGG
FOR HITLER
TIGER SQDN.
2000TH SORTIE

SK-75

3

THE LANCASTER OPERATIONS

The Lancaster was designed to drop bombs and this it did very successfully for the duration of the war. This operation was not without losses, which varied depending on weather at the target and at home base, intensity of anti-aircraft (AA) fire, fighter activity, mid-air collisions and the ever-present plain bad luck. The development of radar by Germany, both ground and airborne, contributed greatly to the operational losses. Later in the war, radar-guided AA fire and radar-guided, ground-controlled night fighters, with their own on-board radar, added to the effectiveness of the German defences. However, by then the tide of war was changing. It was a matter of too little, too late, with dwindling resources. The bombing campaign had taken effect.

However, in spite of these operational losses the Lancaster flew more than 156,000 sorties and dropped over 600,000 tons of bombs. The bombs varied in size, from 4 lb incendiary bombs, sea mines and 250 lb bombs, to the mighty *Grand Slam* at 22,000 lbs. Mention should be made of specialty bombs, such as the rotating, skipping bombs used in the famous Dambuster Raids. Initially operations were flown during the day, quickly switching to night raids due to the heavy losses. Towards the end of hostilities, with diminishing fighter resistance, daylight raids resumed with long-range fighter escort. The raids were conducted at all altitudes, from 'on-the-deck' penetration raids to mid- and high-level saturation bombing. The number of aircraft varied from squadron level to the all-out massive assault of the thousand-aircraft raids.

The large raids were an opportunity for the Luftwaffe night fighters, as, in spite of diversionary raids, it was difficult to disguise the intended track of such an armada of aircraft. It was only due to the rugged double-spar construction that the Lancaster could take such aggressive defensive manoeuvres against the enemy fighters and survive to bomb another day. The threat of mid-air collision was always present as the aircraft dived, twisted and turned, and went to maximum speed to either avoid the searchlights or pursuing night fighters; this all happened in the middle of the night.

The bombing campaign of the first half of the war had been carried on with a collection of aircraft that would eventually be mostly replaced by the Lancaster. Bomber aircraft such as the Armstrong Whitworth Whitley, Bristol Blenheim, Fairey Battle, Handley Page Hampden and Short Stirling carried on the bombing campaign until development overtook them and they were assigned training and other duties. The Whitley was assigned to Coastal Command, the Blenheim to night-fighter duties, the Battle to air-gunnery schools and target tug duties, the Hampden to torpedo bombing with Coastal Command, the Stirling to minelaying, troop carrying and glider tugging, and the Wellington took part in the thousand-bomber raids in 1942 before relinquishing major duties to the Lancaster.

Sir Arthur T. Harris assumed the post of Commander-in-Chief of Bomber Command in February 1942, coinciding with the introduction of the Lancaster to Bomber Command. **The end of December 1941 saw the** delivery of three Lancasters to No. 44 (Rhodesia) Squadron at Waddington with the instructions to have eight crews fully operational by the end of January 1942. Wartime did not allow for the luxury of long conversion courses; the Lancaster was needed yesterday. It flew its first operational flight against Germany on 3 March 1942. This was a 'gardening' flight to lay mines against the German Navy and shipping.

Air Chief Marshall Sir Arthur Harris, KCB, OBE, AFC, was soon to change the direction of the bomber force. The present mining operations to support the Navy were displaced to second priority in favour of massed strategic bombing that was designed to destroy the industrial structure and demoralise the general population. Opposition to this bombing policy was centred on the theory that bombing targets should be restricted to military installations only. Many great minds and books have debated this issue, and this book will not be one of them. Instead the focus will be on the history of the raids in which the Lancaster took part.

Arthur Travis Harris was born in 1892, and, going against his parents' wishes, he emigrated to Rhodesia to make his fortune in colonial Africa. The First World War intervened, and he found himself as a bugler in the Rhodesia Regiment. In 1915 he returned to England and gained his pilot's wings at the historic Brooklands Aerodrome. The aerodrome was now famous by its association with aircraft development through Vickers Aircraft Company, and would in future be known for the sport of motorcar racing. By November 1915 he had been commissioned by the Royal Flying Corps and assumed duties in home defence against the raiding Zeppelins, and was subsequently posted to France and the Western Front. Returning to Britain in 1917, he was given command of No. 44 (Home Defence) Squadron before moving to No. 191 Squadron for night fighters. He was awarded the Air Force Cross in 1918.

Harris began his association with Bomber Command when he was assigned a bomber squadron in the North-West Frontier Province of India. It was during this assignment that Harris became an outspoken critic of the equipment and working conditions of the men. Perhaps it was then that Harris assumed his style of aggressive leadership, with total loyalty to his troops. The intervening war years saw command of a bomber squadron, staff college, desk jobs with Operations, Intelligence and Planning, overseas assignments and, as an air commodore, he took command of No. 4 Bomber Group in 1937. He had absolute faith in his bomber force and believed that the war, when it ultimately came, would be won by his group – end of discussion. Some of his superiors did not agree.

In September 1939, Harris assumed command of No. 5 Group and its seven squadrons. They operated Handley Page Hampdens and were assigned the immediate task of attacking German shipping and laying sea mines. The sea mines served two purposes – disrupting the German shipping, both the Navy and merchant ships, and causing valuable resources be diverted to minesweeping the shipping lanes. In 1940 he was promoted to Deputy Chief of the Air Staff and moved to London. He emphasised the fact that the operating units were the backbone of the RAF and they were to be given every possible aid to do their assigned tasks. The 'tail was not going to wag the dog' in Harris's Air Force.

Harris saw first-hand the destruction caused by the Luftwaffe as the bombs rained down on London. He was a witness to the challenges of fire suppression and the morale of the general population as they went about their daily lives amid the chaos and aftermath of a bombing raid. 7 September 1940 saw the start of nearly two months of continuous bombing of London, the Blitzkrieg. It is said that Harris stated, while standing on the Air Ministry roof during one of these raids, 'They have sown the wind, and so they shall reap the whirlwind' – a rough interpretation from Hosea in the King James Bible. There was no doubt now on the future bombing policy of the soon-to-be-nicknamed 'Bomber Harris'.

On 10 March 1942, the first operation over Germany by Lancasters occurred – a raid on Essen. The Harris mandate had begun, as had his ensuing controversy. The mandate would continue, his ears deaf to the controversy. The background on the mandate was the Butt Report of 1941. Bomber Command had no way of verifying crew claims of targets bombed and damage done, and it was decided to mount cameras triggered by the bomb release, which would then record the event.

Lord Cherwell was commissioned to do a report on over 600 photographs taken during the bombing operations of June and July 1941. David Bensusan-Butt, a civil servant in the War Cabinet Secretariat, was tasked with producing a report. What he reported was a shock, though probably not so much to those involved, who were well aware of the failures of the present system:

One in three attacking aircraft got within five miles, eight kilometres of target

Over Germany it was one in four, over the Ruhr it was one in ten

Full moon it was two in five, new moon it was one in fifteen

These figures refer to aircraft attacking the actual target, not the total sorties. Post-war analysis revealed that in 1941 the actual number of aircraft reaching the target was dismal compared to the effort and sacrifice. The answer would be technology and visual target marking, which eventually improved accuracy. Lord Cherwell produced a paper which was circulated in March 1942. He stated that the deficiencies of the RAF bombing campaign could be mitigated by the use of area bombing rather than precision bombing. The political and military issues of the two approaches were thus solved – sort of. The area bombing solved the accuracy problem, but there was still criticism of the resources allocated to Bomber Command, with suspicions over what was really being achieved. It was in this environment that Harris assumed control of Bomber Command.

The way to silence the critics, Harris thought, was to mount a show of strength as much for the home audience as for the unsuspecting enemy. Barely three months after he assumed command, a veritable armada of aircraft left Britain for Cologne. This attack included all kinds of aircraft to make up the intimidating force of 1,000. It included aircraft drawn from the training units and any available type of bomber, past or present, serviceable enough to fly the mission. The point was made and would be made several times more before Harris was finished.

Prior to Harris assuming command there was a continual build-up of resources until the outbreak of war in September 1939. At that time Bomber Command consisted of light bombers supplemented by medium bombers: Hampdens, Whitleys and Wellingtons. The main area of concern was the Fall of France and the evacuation of the troops at Dunkirk. Daylight bombing of the invasion ports gradually changed to night operations. Technology was advancing rapidly on both sides of the conflict and these bombers were becoming obsolete. Well-defended searchlights and some night fighters were the expected defences.

With the Fall of France, the occupying force concentrated on fortifying their positions in Western Europe with defensive measures. This consisted of Ground Controlled Intercept (GCI) night fighters under the guidance of a radar system which extended from Denmark through Holland and Belgium to France. The night fighter was assigned to a particular box and controlled by one GCI station. All the boxes joined to form a formidable electronic wall. A searchlight belt was constructed to preserve the Ruhr industrial area.

On 20 August 1940, Sir Winston Churchill made his famous 'The Few' speech, renowned for his remarks about the gallantry of the fighter pilots; but included in that speech were the words, 'On no part of the Royal Air Force does the weight of the war fall more heavily than on the daylight bombers who will play an invaluable part in the case of invasion and whose unflinching zeal it has been necessary in the meanwhile on numerous occasions to restrain.'

Heavy bombers such as the Avro Manchester, Handley Page Halifax and Short Stirling joined Bomber Command in 1941. Although an improvement, Command still lacked striking power. The Manchester and Stirling in particular were a disappointment as heavy bombers due to lack of power preventing the carrying of heavier bomb loads. Something new was needed to improve the productivity of the bombing campaign. That something turned out to be the four elements that made the formidable bomber force. They were the leader, Harris; the new aircraft, the Lancaster; the new technology, Gee; and the new target identification technique using flares, the forerunner of the Pathfinders.

First, Harris assumed command of Bomber Command in February 1942. Command would confirm its focus, concentrated striking power by groups of aircraft proceeding to an illuminated target. Saturation of defences was the name of the game en route to the target. Secondly, the Lancaster arrived in squadron service and the bombing productivity started to improve. Thirdly, the navigational aid Gee became widely available, giving accurate tracking up to 350 miles from the squadron's home station. Fourthly, No. 3 Group was assigned to lay flares on the target, followed by incendiaries for the main stream of aircraft to bomb on.

Aircraft would no longer plan their own route to the target, but common routes would be planned at command headquarters with group input, and with the experience of the thousand-aircraft raid the target saturation was planned at ten aircraft per minute. The accuracy of the navigation to the target and its positive identification remained an issue. In August 1942 the Pathfinder Force was established and the accuracy started to improve. The force comprised specially chosen squadrons within each group who marked the target for the following aircraft. By 1943, the force became No. 8 (PFF) Group under the command of Air Vice-Marshall D. C. T. Bennett.

The Telecommunications Research Establishment (TRE) concentrated on the development of devices to counter the expanding radar network protecting Germany. Two of the inventions were called Mandrel and Window. Mandrel jammed the Freya ground radar, and Window was a batch of metal foil strips, cut in specific lengths to match frequencies of the ground radar and released in large clouds to obscure and confuse the enemy radar. Other inventions included H2S, which was a self-contained ground-mapping radar set to identify the target. Oboe was a twin-beam navigation aid used in blind bombing. Monica 1 and Boozer were passive radar devices that warned of approaching aircraft.

The method eventually adopted was to mark the target with flares using H2S or Oboe and the Pathfinders would use visual markers to guide the way for the main bomber stream. Sky markers hung about 5,000 feet over the target and illuminated it. The bad aspect of this is that all became a focal point for the fighters. Three basic colours were used for marking – red, green and yellow. It was not unknown for spoof coloured markers to be placed out in the country to try and draw the main force away from the real target.

Oboe enabled the target to be marked regardless of weather, but it was preferable that thick cloud was avoided so that the bombing force could see the ground markers. Moonlight was no longer needed and the rising bomber-loss rate was slowed as operations could now take place in the dark days of the month. The tide of fortune was no longer going out, and in early 1943 it could be said that the tide of the aerial bombing campaign was on the turn.

Procedures and technical developments continued to improve bombing accuracy, and hence the destructive impact on the industrial regions of the enemy. Raid reports were initiated for each sortie and, in combination with the camera images, gave a more complete understanding of the actual success or failure of the raid. This definitely encouraged the crews to greater effort as it showed them exactly where their bombs had landed. Inaccuracies could be rectified and the knowledge applied to future raids. The photo interpreter became a very important part of the team.

The idea of flak evasion was discouraged as it caused more problems than it was worth. The final run up to the target could now be done on a steady, accurate course. It also reduced the risk of collision. The bomber stream could be up to 150 miles long for the 400 aircraft. The target was planned at ten aircraft per minute passing overhead. The average height was 20,000 feet approximately and vertical separation was provided for aircraft unable to continue the raid and returning against the stream.

The bomber aircraft types were further divided by altitude and grouped within the stream: the higher-flying Lancasters would be separated from the medium-altitude Halifaxes, which in turn would be separated from the lower-flying Stirlings and Wellingtons. This was designed to prevent the lower-flying aircraft being hit by incendiary bombs from the aircraft above. The stream itself was orchestrated on a time-over-target basis, and the concentration rate was upped to take advantage of the slower response time of the night fighters.

By 1944, the concentration of bombers had risen at times to forty or fifty aircraft per minute over the target. The danger of collision rose accordingly. To prevent this, the navigation lights were left on until closer to enemy territory, streams were separated by five to eight miles laterally, the height band was increased slightly and careful search procedures were instated at turning points.

In the constant game of aerial chess, the visual element came to the fore again. Due to all the confusion caused by Window, the German Observer Corps were called upon to assist in the plotting of the bomber stream and calling in the night fighters, who were increasingly operating on a freelance basis. The stream would be identified as to direction and altitude and the probable or actual target. Some of these fighters were operating at up to 300 miles from home base, and this contributed to the slower response rate than the radar-guided response of previous local squadrons.

As 1943 progressed, it was found that varying speed (and thus type of aircraft), irregular assignment of the aircraft stream altitude and Mosquito diversionary raids contributed to a lower loss rate. It was also necessary to keep the stream width narrow to get the most number of aircraft under the cover of Window. So the aerial game of chess continued, with the Luftwaffe varying between defending the target or attacking the main stream en route to or returning from the target. The deep-penetration raids into Germany were taking their toll. Ghost dummy runs at targets en route would be altered at the last minute to confuse the defences as to the real target.

Additional technical developments such as Fishpond, which worked in conjunction with H2S to give a picture of aircraft in the vicinity, were quite disappointing. The problem was, and would remain, that it was unable to identify aircraft as friend or foe. However, the bombing campaign was evolving into an all-weather capability. H2S, together with Gee and the blind landing system, now gave the aircraft of Bomber Command the capability of operating in low cloud or poor visibility. The poor-weather capability would also apply to the target area, which would make it harder for night fighters to intercept the bombers or return to their home base.

What exactly were these technical innovations, and how did they work to assist Bomber Command in its bombing campaign? Who designed them and where were they developed until suitable for operational use? TRE and scientists inside and outside of the organisation worked as a team as these technical innovations were developed. There is absolutely no doubt that the three systems contributed to the operational success of night-time blind bombing, which by itself is a challenge without the additional complications of searchlights, flak and night fighters. The word flak comes from letters in the German word *Flugabwehrkanone*, meaning anti-aircraft cannon. The British term is AA, for anti-aircraft, or the slang 'archie'.

Oboe worked on the principle of a transponder-carrying aircraft that retransmitted signals from two Oboe transmitters, which could be seen by a remote operator and guided to stay on the required path. The 'Cat' transmitter would send dots or dashes depending on its error from the curved track. The operator would give instructions to the aircraft to remain on the plotted course, which was only 105 feet wide. It was a very accurate system but it was limited to one aircraft at a time and it was susceptible to enemy electronic jamming.

Two Oboe transmitters were used at the same time: one transmitter to provide the curved path and the second one to mark the position of the target. The target was located at the intersection of the two curved paths centred on each transmitter. These transmitters were called the 'Cat' for the planned aircraft track and the 'Mouse' to indicate the point where the bombs were released. There was a network of Oboe stations in Southern England that could be used in pairs as 'Cat' and 'Mouse' to define the target position. Oboe was practically limited to the Ruhr Valley, and it was not until late 1944 that it was established on the Continent and the range allowed deeper Oboe penetration into Germany.

Developed by a team from TRE and Standard Telephones and Cables Ltd, Oboe was reputed to be the most accurate of the bombing systems. It had three restrictive limitations in that it was line-of-sight based (not good for deep penetrations of Germany), the aircraft followed a predictable curved path and it could be jammed by defensive radar. It was successfully used on Pathfinder missions by the de Havilland Mosquito, which enjoyed a fast cruising speed and the ability of higher-than-normal altitudes.

'Gee-H' took the basic principle of Oboe and reversed the transmitter and receivers – the aircraft transmitted to two ground receivers. The aircraft was now vulnerable to electronic detection. The system could theoretically manage up to eighty aircraft. Gee-H should not be confused with Gee, which operated on a different principle.

Gee was another TRE invention to facilitate night-time blind landings that developed into a navigation system. It measured the time delay between two signals to give a fix relative to the required track. An A-type scope display would indicate the two signals received from spaced stations. The operator could distinguish which signal was received first by the position of the two blips and therefore know which one was closest to the aircraft. By turning away from the closer one, the correct track would once again be intercepted.

Gee stations were built as a 'Master' with three 'Slave' transmitters at 120 degrees from each other. More than one 'Master' was built, and the resulting overlay of lines formed a grid – hence the name, Gee for the G in grid. It was a time-delay chart superimposed on a geographical chart. A collection of Gee stations was known as a 'chain'. Although the Gee system could be jammed at the longer ranges over Germany, it still remained a viable navigation system when approaching England. The system eventually developed the capability of changing operating frequencies en route to stay away from the jamming; the cat and mouse game continued. Gee consisted of a receiver and oscilloscope in the aircraft.

The Rebecca/Eureka system is a blind homing/approach aid used by the navigator to obtain the relative location of ground beacons. It was also used to locate Eureka, which was a ground beacon used by the Allies and Resistance groups to enable supplies to be delivered to specific locations. The Eureka beacon and aerial could be airdropped to be assembled in the drop zone.

H2S, another TRE development, on the other hand, did not require any ground support beacons like Oboe and Gee and was totally self-contained in the aircraft. It was the first airborne ground-scanning radar system. It was especially vital on raids to Berlin and other targets beyond the range of Oboe and Gee. The operator could identify targets at night and in cloudy conditions outside the normal navigation range of the other two systems. It did, however, have the drawback of having the aircraft's radar transmitter identifiable by the enemy's NAXOS radar detector, installed in night fighters. The radar image of the ground was presented to the operator on a Plan Position Indicator scope.

The ground-based defensive radar was the start of the electronic game of who could trump the other's radar. These radar installations could detect approaching aircraft and enable the defensive network to respond to the threat. The challenge then became jamming the enemy's radar to render it ineffective. The long-range Freya and short-range Wurzburg radars were the main German defensive network, controlling the searchlights, flak and night fighters.

The Freya radar was jammed by using a device called Mandrel. The fighter controller's radio frequencies were jammed by transmitting sound from the aircraft's engine bay. The sound was deafening and destroyed all hope of communication. This was called Tinsel. Another option was German-speaking Women's Auxiliary Air Force radio operators transmitting countermanding instructions which caused confusion among the night fighters; this was called Corona.

Each side tried to find ways to disrupt the other's communication and radar network. The struggle went on in the technical laboratories. F/Lt Bill Pearson, bomb aimer, said, 'It seemed that every week a new electronic device would show up with the instructions to "try this" and report back.' This ebb and flow of technical supremacy was a matter of life and death for the aircrews.

A major contribution to the success of bombing raids was the invention of Window, called 'chaff' in North America. Bundles of metallised strips cut in lengths corresponding to certain radio frequencies were dropped and formed large, slowly drifting and descending clouds that confused the radar sites. Despite its success, the British held back using Window because of the Germans finding the strips on the ground and realising what was affecting their radar sets. However, the continued increase in Bomber Command losses forced it to be made available to save aircrew lives. It was first used by the RAF in an attack on Hamburg on the night of 24 July 1943. The defences were rendered useless. The radar screen portrayed a force fifteen times greater than it really was, the radar controlled searchlights could not remain steady on a target aircraft and the ground controllers were unable to control the night fighters. The Hamburg raid had an astonishingly low loss rate of 1.5 per cent.

The Window advantage would not continue, as the corresponding German laboratories worked out that by calculating the relative speeds of the different radar echoes it was possible to differentiate the aircraft from the drifting Window. Something else was needed, and that was No. 100 Group. It was responsible for all electronic countermeasures and flew cover with the bomber stream. 100 Group also flew spoof and decoy missions using Window and other devices to represent a large bomber force and so divert some of the fighters away from the main bomber route. A few hours before D-Day, a small force of Lancasters flew back and forth across the English Channel and diverted attention away from the real attack on Normandy.

Offensively, RAF night fighters were equipped with Serrate airborne radar on intruder missions into Germany. This device tracked the Luftwaffe radar as night fighters looked for the RAF bombers. The hunter now became the hunted. TRE and the myriad scientists behind the scenes saved many lives with their innovative solutions and dedication to having the trump card in the electronic card game.

In spite of and in addition to these electronic devices, the best way of identifying the target was by visual means. It was too easy for the following aircraft to bomb the fires in the darkness below, which may or may not be the assigned target. Copying a German model, the Pathfinder Force (PFF) was established. The idea was that they would use the latest navigational aids – Oboe, Gee, H2S – to positively identify the target and use flares to guide the main force to the target. The PFF job was deemed to be so hazardous that a full tour consisted of only fifteen trips in addition to a first tour of thirty.

The PFF was in three main sections: the illuminators to drop white markers along the attack vector, the visual markers to drop coloured flares on the target and the fire starters to back up the visual markers by starting long-lasting fires with incendiary bombs. Other marking techniques included sky markers, utilising flares attached to parachutes, and offset markers. The offset makers would be a short distance from the target and the main force would be given a course and timing/distance to fly to the target. This was to preclude the defence forces starting fires in open country or non-critical areas to divert the bombing from strategic industrial, military or transportation areas. The game of 'cat and mouse' was not only electronic, it had a visual component to it as well.

The gallantry of the PFF is legendary, and its contribution to the war effort greatly exceeded the sum of its parts. The sustained Battle of the Ruhr was one of its main successes. Targets such as Duisburg, Oberhausen, Essen, Witten, Gelsenkirchen, Hagen, Bochum, Dortmund, Hagen, Hamm and Mulheim surrounded the general area of the Ruhr Valley. Essen was a prime target because of the Krupp armament works, and it had been the subject of many raids. On the night of 25 July 1943 it was accurately marked by eight Oboe-equipped Mosquitos, and the main-stream bomber force of 600 inflicted more damage on the works than all the previous raids. This raid caused a complete stoppage of the Krupp works – something never achieved before.

A further development of the PFF was the master bomber. This special aircraft and crew would circle the target and give directions by radio to the PFF on where to mark the target before guiding the main force to the bombing location. This was an extremely hazardous job as the circling aircraft was prone to be 'coned' by searchlights and subject to accurate flak attacks. In the event of 'creepback' – bombers dropping their bombs too early leading up to the target – the target would be remarked under the direction of the ever-circling master bomber and 'deputies'.

The approximate range of Oboe was 250 miles and the range of Gee was 300 miles, which covered the western portion of Germany and ensured the crews were aware of their position when initially over enemy territory. The Oboe stations were positioned close to the North Sea and English Channel to give deeper coverage into enemy territory. Two of the 'Mouse' stations were Trimingham and Great Yarmouth in Norfolk, and two of the 'Cat' stations were Kingsdown and Walmer in Kent. The 'Cat' stations covered the northern half of France, Luxembourg, Belgium and most of the Netherlands.

The open weight of the Lancaster for fuel and bombs was approximately 21,000 lbs. Greater distances meant more fuel was needed and thus less carrying capacity was available. The direct route was preferred, but due to the searchlight, radar and gun defences this was not always available. The whole raid was a compromise, with fuel holding the priority. However, in spite of careful planning, a particularly strong westerly wind on the return journey could have the crews making an emergency landing away from base at an east-coast runway, or, worse, ditching in the Channel. Taking a few of the more common targets and using Lincoln as a departure station, the distances were as follows, with the number of main force attacks on the target:

Raids	Target	Distances	Flying time	
		(round trip, miles)	(straight line)*	
28	Essen	684	6.0	
24	Berlin	1168	8.5	
22	Cologne	712	6.0	
18	Duisburg	664	6.0	
18	Stuttgart	1048	7.5	
17	Hamburg	872	7.0	
16	Hannover	866	7.0	
13	Mannheim	934	7.0	
12	Bremen	776	6.5	
11	Nuremberg	1130	8.0	(see chapter 4)
2	Konigsberg	1720	10.0	(see bomb aimer, chapter 4)

*After consulting some logbooks, it seems the actual flight time was 2 to 2.5 hours longer on average than the straight-line distance, due to diversion around known defences, evading night fighters and tactics en route.

The following is a list of Lancaster aircraft that flew over 100 operational sorties:

Mark	Serial	Squadron	#	Remarks
Lancaster I	R5868	83 'Q', 467 'S'	137	RAF Scampton
Lancaster I	W4783	460 'G'	[90]	Australian War Museum
Lancaster I	W4964	9 'J'	106	'Johnnie Walker nose art
Lancaster III	DV245	101 'S'	119	Shot down (SD)
Lancaster I	DV302	101 'H'	121	Scrapped (SCR)
Lancaster I	ED588	97, 50 'G'	116+	Failed to Return (FTR) Konigsberg
Lancaster III	ED860	156, 61 'N'	130	Beyond Repair (BR)
Lancaster III	ED888	103 'M', 576 'V2/M2', 103 'M2'	140	Record Holder SCR!
Lancaster III	ED905	103/106 'X', 550 'F'	100+?	Press on Regardless
Lancaster III	EE136	9 'R', 189	109	Spirit of Russia
Lancaster III	EE139	100 'R', 550 'B'	121	Phantom of the Ruhr
Lancaster III	EE176	7, 97 'N/O'	122	Ground training BOAC
Lancaster III	JB138	61	123	Released 1946
Lancaster III	JB663	106 'A'	111	Released 1946
Lancaster I	LL806	15 'J'	134	Released 1945
Lancaster I	LL843	467, 61	118	SCR 1947
Lancaster I	LL885	622 'J'	113	SCR 1946
Lancaster I	ME746	166	116	SCR 1946
Lancaster I	ME758	12 'N'	108	Released 1945
Lancaster I	ME803	115 'A4-D, KO-L, IL-C'	105	Released 1946
Lancaster III	ND458	100 'A/A2'	123	SCR 1947
Lancaster III	ND578	44 'Y'	100+?	Released 1945
Lancaster III	ND644	100 'N'	115	FTR Nuremberg
Lancaster III	NE181	75 'M'	101	Released 1947
Lancaster III	PA995	550 'V'	100+?	FTR Dessau

The following is a chronological list of Lancaster and other relevant operations after the Lancaster joined Bomber Command in December 1941 and became operational in March 1942:

Date	Sqn	Comments
1942		
3 March	44	Sea mines (gardening), Lancaster first operation
10 March	44	First Lancaster raid on Essen
13 March		Cologne first Gee attack
17 April	44/97	Day attack on Augsburg
30 May		First thousand-bomber raid, target Cologne
1 June		Second thousand-bomber raid, target Essen
		Second massive raid two days later managed to get 956 aircraft airborne. Thirty-one aircraft FTR.
25 June		Third thousand-bomber raid, target Bremen
		The third massive raid got 960 aircraft airborne. Forty-four aircraft FTR.
15 August		Pathfinder Force formed
18 September		PFF first operational mission, Flensburg
17 October		Le Creusot
		Dusk raid on Schneider Works and transformer and switching station at Montchanin, Lancasters from Nos 9, 44, 49, 50, 57, 61, 97, 106 and 207 Squadrons. Ninety-four aircraft, one FTR
24 October	5 Group	First daylight attack on Italy, Milan and Le Creusot, France. Eighty-eight Lancasters from UK bases, fourteen FTR
28 November	106	Two 8,000 lb bombs used on Turin, Italy
20 December	109 (Mosquito)	First operational use of Oboe
1943		
28 January		Pathfinder Force re-designated No. 8 Group (PFF)
30 January	105/139	First daylight attack on Berlin to coincide with speeches at tenth anniversary of regime
30 January	7/35 PFF	First operational use of H2S by Stirlings/Halifaxes
25 February		Allied air forces began round-the-clock bombing, 2,000 sorties in forty-eight hours
5 March		Battle of the Ruhr begins, target Essen
		Typical Operational Plan
16 May	617	The Dambuster Raid. Möhne, Eder, Soepe and Schwelm dams attacked at night with special bombs. Nineteen Lancasters performed the operation with W/Cdr Guy Gibson receiving the VC for his role as master bomber

18 June		Radar became official nomenclature for RDF, etc.
20 June		First shuttle bombing operation. Target was Friedrichshafen, with aircraft proceeding on to Algiers
24 July		Battle of Hamburg begins, 74 per cent built-up area destroyed over five days along with the dockyard. First use of Window, immediate 30 per cent loss reduction
August		Bomber Command Tactical School opened
17 August		First attack on Peenemunde research and development station with 600 heavies
15 September	617	First operational use of 12,000 lb HC bomb against Dortmund–Elm Canal on a low-level raid. Five Lancasters lost out of eight with only two bombs on target
22 September		First use of 'spoof' technique used by Bomber Command, target was Hanover with spoof target Oldenburg
22 October		Operation Corona begins, jamming and bogus instructions to enemy fighters begins
November		First emergency runway, Woodbridge, becomes available
3 November		First Gee-H attack by thirty-eight Lancasters of Nos 3 and 5 Group against Mannesmann Steel Works at Dusseldorf
8 November		Formation of 100 (Bomber Support) Group to provide electronic countermeasures
18 November		Battle of Berlin begins
19 November		The RAF Fog Intensive Dispersal Operation (FIDO) in use. Thirty-five Halifaxes landed at Graveley. Fifteen stations eventually became equipped with the system, allowing aircraft to recover in restricted visibility due ground fog and low cloud

1944

February		New tactics – shorten stream, two attacks on same target during one day, more heavy bombers on diversionary raids, enter Germany through France
24 February		Beginning of Combined Bomber Offensive. Raid on ball bearing industry at Schweinfurt following a daylight raid by the USAF
6 March		Rail centres in northern France are targeted in preparation for invasion of France in June
30 March		Heaviest Bomber Command losses in a single attack, target Nuremberg. Ninety-five aircraft FTR out of 795 aircraft
April		Manston and Carnaby opened as emergency runway
11 April		Famous attack by Mosquitos, Gestapo HQ in The Hague
22 April		First use of 30 lb liquid-filled incendiary

5 June	617	Diversionary operations by the use of Window in the English Channel away from the location of and prior to the Normandy landings on 6 June. By D-Day thirty-seven rail centres had been extensively damaged
8 June	617	First operational use of 12,000 lb Tallboy deep-penetration bomb used on the Saumur railway tunnel
August		Rumours of upward-firing guns on night fighters
27 August	5 Group	First major daylight raid, target Homberg in the Ruhr
14 October		Largest bomb tonnage in one night, Duisburg, 4,547 tons
12 November	617/9	Battleship *Tirpitz* destroyed by Tallboy bombs

1945

3 March		Luftwaffe sends fighters to stations in England to attack departing and returning bombers
11 March		1,079 aircraft dropped 4,661 tons on Essen in blind bombing
12 March		1,107 aircraft dropped 4,851 tons on Dortmund
14 March	617	22,000 lb Grand Slam bomb, Bielefeld Viaduct
27 March	9/617	Target Farge U-boat pens, Tallboys and Grand Slams
25 April	1, 5, 8 Groups	359 Lancasters attacked Hitler's chalet and Berchtesgaden
25 April	4, 6, 8, 100 Groups	Lancasters attack coastal gun batteries at Wangerooge Island
26 April		First British POWs repatriated, Operation Exodus
29 April	1, 3, 8 Groups	Supply drops to civilians in Holland, Operation Manna
1 May		Hitler's death reported by Hamburg Radio
2 May		Surrender of German forces in Italy
2 May		Bomber Command's last offensive action
7 May		Unconditional surrender of Germany, Rheims
8 May		VE (Victory in Europe) Day, Prime Minister Winston Churchill announces German surrender in House of Commons

Air Chief Marshall Sir Arthur Harris, KCB, OBE, AFC, has stated, on many occasion, words to the effect that the Lancaster was the greatest single factor in winning the war because of its performance; it could lift a 22,000 lb bomb, it could absorb punishment both from enemy fire and evasive manoeuvres and most importantly it could bring the crews home against all odds. He referred to the aircraft as 'that shining sword in our hands'. The double waist-high wing spars were an important part of its robustness, but its long bomb bay was its crowning glory, enabling it to carry ordnance of all shapes and sizes, sometimes with necessary modification to the bomb doors.

To get the Lancaster ready for a raid it took a great many people, including the aircrew, flying control officer and assistant (usually a WAAF), parachute packer (WAAF), oil-tanker driver, petrol-bowser driver/operator, armourers to load bombs, tractor driver for bomb load (often WAAF), many mechanics (as necessary, but could be eight or so), and radar/wireless specialists (as many as mechanics at times). What started all this activity around the aircraft in the squadrons?

Bomber Command would issue the instructions for the raid, which would follow the chain of command to the group and then the squadron, followed by the flight and finally to the particular aircraft's bomb load. Every station had its own ammunition dump/storage facility to supply the bombs for the raid. Orders were issued and the bomb loading began. It was important for the pilot to open the bomb doors hydraulically prior to engine shutdown, otherwise it was a laborious task by hand pump. The Lancaster had a very flexible capacity for loading different types and sizes of bombs in the one load. However, it had to be done in a standard pattern depending on the bombs involved.

The bombs were loaded on trolleys which were then towed in 'trains' to the aircraft dispersal areas. These areas were adjacent to the 'Peri', perimeter track, which was the taxiway at the edge of the airfield joining all the runways. It was a very exposed area for the task of uploading the bombs into the aircraft, pleasant on a summer's evening and not so on a January night. Working around the bomb-loading team, or getting in their way, were the engineers, the fuellers, the armourers and the radio countermeasures team. That was one aircraft; consider that often there were two squadrons on the same station preparing for the raid. Not long into the six years of the war, by necessity, a system was worked out to make it as efficient and as safe as possible. The weight and size of bombs became larger, requiring special handling procedure and equipment, not always available and serviceable, which complicated and delayed the bomb loading.

A great many bombs were left over in armouries after the First World War. These thin-skinned bombs were not very effective as they had no penetrating power before exploding. It quickly became apparent that new weaponry was required. This resulted in two main families of bombs being developed. The first was the thin-skinned, cylindrical high-capacity (HC) bombs, weighing 2,000, 4,000, 8,000 and 12,000 lbs, which were designed for their high blast effect and were combined with incendiary bombs to light the ensuing rubble of fire. The HC bombs were used for area or saturation type bombing. These bombs had an unfortunate design weakness in that they were liable to explode during a take-off crash.

The second family of bombs were the thick-skinned, slightly tapered, rear-finned medium-capacity (MC) bombs, designed to have penetrating power before exploding. These were used on specific tactical targets. They suffered from some fusing problems and supply issues. They came in 500, 1,000, 4,000, 12,000 and 22,000 lbs types.

There were also specialty bombs designed for specific purposes, like rolling bombs for dam destruction and high-tensile steel bombs for battleships, railway tunnels and the reinforced concrete of submarine pens. The mainstay of Bomber Command was the 4 lb magnesium incendiary bomb. Its drawback was the lack of precise aiming and susceptibility to tailfin damage. It was also a slow and laborious process to load the small bomb container (SBC). The main concern, however, was the shower of incendiaries spreading out from the SBC and causing danger for aircraft at lower altitudes.

By 1944 this SBC problem had been cured by the use of clusters, although they themselves suffered drawbacks. The cluster containers were extremely fragile and easily damaged, both while transporting from the factory and in the installation of ordnance. By 1944 the 500 lb and 750 lb clusters were available in small quantities, followed by the 1,000 lb cluster in the autumn. The clusters enabled faster and easier loading of large quantities of incendiary bombs. In spite of constant upgrading and modifications to the cluster it never reached a satisfactory level of operation. The difficulties were associated with hang ups on the bomb rack, fuse problems and general ground handling.

The variety of bombs in use complicated the handling of these weapons. It was important that the bomb-handling aspect be mechanised to achieve a quicker turnaround of the aircraft. Ideally there should be no time gap between the introduction of new ordnance and the equipment to handle it, and this was always a struggle to achieve. Ingenuity at the local squadron and station level very often saved the day. The ammunition dump itself became an inefficient bottleneck, due to oversupply at times causing handling or retrieval problems.

The trolleys were towed by Fordson and David Brown tractors. The trolleys were given alphabetic designations. For example, the type-B trolley could handle four 500 lb bombs and the type-D could carry one 4,000 lb HC bomb. The trolleys had a very low frame and adjustable chocks on the carriage to hold the bombs during transit to the aircraft. They were very hardy but took a lot of abuse and required brakes and tyres from time to time, which were in short supply. It took until the summer of 1944 for the trolleys to be equipped with hydraulic winches, which was a great improvement over the slow manual operation.

Arriving at the aircraft, the bombs were winched into position. This secured the carrier via the guide rollers to the bomb housing in the bomb bay. Like everything mechanical during the war, there were resources made available to 'build a better mouse trap'. Release slips, girdles, crutches, SBCs and clusters were all continually modified through experience, mostly incidents and accidents, to come up with the perfect solution for safe bomb storage and timely release. The matter of pyrotechnics was another challenge. Armoured chutes for photoflash and unarmoured chutes for normal pyrotechnics were designed and implemented in the body of the aircraft, made easier by the fact that the Lancaster was not pressurised like the modern aircraft.

The release of the bombs on target was the next procedure involving the loaded bomb bay. The bomb aimer controlled the release of the bombs on his panel. When to release the bombs was calculated by using a bombsight, which took many factors into account and calculated the correct time to release the specific type of bomb; different bombs required different release points to achieve an accurate hit on target.

The Mk II Course Setting Bomb Sight (CSBS) was in general use in Bomber Command during the initial few years until 1942. It was an open-sight type and suitable for night-time bombing. It required accurate winds to be effective and the run-in to the target to be straight and level. In 1942 the Mk IXA bombsight became operational, incorporating the moving target vector. Harris had two further requirements for his bomber force, and these were that the bomber should be able to take evasive action up to and including bomb release, and that the number of settings be kept to a minimum for the bomb aimer to ensure the concentration on accurate release time.

The Mk XIV met these requirements and was in effect a higher level of automatic bombsight, requiring a different computer for each aircraft type. By January 1944 the Mk XIV equipped the majority of heavy bombers. By July 1944 the American version of the Mk XIVA, the T1A sight, was appearing in Canadian-built Lancasters. It only required ten seconds of stabilised flight prior to bomb release. It required the wind speed and direction to be entered. It consisted of the computer on the port side of the bomb aimer's compartment and a stabilised optical graticule head.

In parallel, the Automatic Bomb Sight (ABS) continued to be developed. It required a long run-up to the target straight and level, exposing the crews to accurate AA fire. A major development was a more sophisticated, and hence complicated, manual computer which calculated its own wind and even had automatic bomb release. This bombsight was known as the Stabilised Automatic Bomb Sight (SABS) Mk IIA. It was connected to a Bombing Direction Indicator (BDI), which the pilot followed to bring the sight on to the target. The MK XIV was thought of as the area-bombing sight and the SABSIIA as the precision sight. These two bombsights were the major sights used and with modifications and maintenance performed what they were designed for with the wartime technology available.

In August 1943, Harris made the decision to equip No. 617 (Dambuster) Squadron RAF with the SABS Mk IIA and to train the squadron to use the sight to carry out precision attacks on selected targets. The SABS Mk IIA was allocated to Nos 83 and 97 squadrons RAF for a trial period from June to September 1944. The units were installed on aircraft to back-up initial markers installed by Mosquito aircraft. It was being qualified on the SABS bombsight that caused F/Lt W. (Bill) E. Pearson to end up in a prisoner-of-war camp. See the story in chapter 4 under 'Bomb Aimer'.

The bomb doors are opened, the target sighted and the bomb load is ready to be released. The bomb aimer would use the Automatic Bomb Distributor (ABD) to drop a stick, a series of bombs dropped sequentially with a timed interval between each one. The type VI can drop a stick of sixteen bombs to create relatively evenly spaced craters. A contact arm on the ABD moves automatically over contacts marked one to sixteen. There is also a holding position marked H. In order to release the mixed bomb load in any desired sequence, a pre-selector was introduced in to the circuit. The type VII could release a stick of thirty-two bombs. The system could be, and was, overridden by the bomb aimer manually by arresting the movement of the contact arm during mixed loads of HE and incendiary bombs. As with previous technical systems, the ABD was constantly under modification to reduce the workload of the bomb aimer when approaching the target.

The development of pyrotechnics was a constant race to stay ahead of the enemy. There was a concerted effort by the enemy to duplicate the colours and type of the marker pyrotechnics to set up decoy locations away from the actual industrial target. Between the beginning of the Lancaster era and the end of the war there were over forty different types of flares used. Initially the recce flares were dropped to illuminate the area, first individually and then in an SBC carrying four flares. Large quantities were also dropped to further mark the target area by creating concentrated fires. The 'Pink Pansy' was a special HC 4000 lb bomb case filled with a substance to give an initial flash that was a brilliant pink colour.

The blind bombing of targets using Oboe required another technique. The target was marked with coded flares of different colours and visual effects to provide an aiming point above the clouds. This was called sky marking. It did allow the raids to continue on nights when normal visual target identification was impossible. In January 1943, on a Berlin raid, target indicator (TI) bombs were first used. The TI had good ballistic properties for stability and then burst open at a pre-determined height to release a shower of ground pyrotechnic candles. These candles were ignited upon ejection to fall as a brilliant cascade or alternatively set to lie dormant on the ground for a short time. A barometric fuse was set to burst the bomb at a particular height above sea level.

TI bombs had a double role as a guide to approaching aircraft or indicating the aiming point. Initially it was the 250 lb bombs. The TIs could also be coloured to give a spot of red or green and placed as a route marker for the bomber stream. The TIs could also be hung beneath a parachute to give longer time as a sky marker. As the enemy became more adept at setting decoy markers it was decided that one solution was to totally overwhelm the marked target by using a 1,000 lb TI. This bomb had teething problems, however, such as a lack of stability and coming apart prematurely.

An important part of the crew debrief and raid report was to accurately pinpoint the aircraft at time of bomb release. It was a three-part process. A camera was installed in the Lancaster in a system which deployed a bright photoflash with a timing fuse on bomb release. The photo was then examined for accuracy of bombing. The photo was proof of where exactly the bombs were dropped, a silent watchdog on the performance of each bomber crew. The photos could illustrate a bombing timeline and could be used to assess the actual damage caused.

Minelaying or 'gardening' was the first operational trip of the Lancaster after being released to operational service. Over 49,000 mines were laid by Bomber Command to disrupt enemy shipping. A parachute was used to slow down the vertical descent rate prior to entering the water. Some of the different types of mines used were impact mines, acoustic mines, oscillating mines and single/double contact mines. A variety of fuses were developed to avoid premature detonation by minesweeping countermeasures, such as period and mechanical delay, electric arming clocks and sterilisers. The Lancaster carried six 1,500 lb mines in its bomb bay.

The Lancaster was equipped with eight Browning .303 guns for defence, two in the nose, two in the mid-upper and four in the rear-gunner position. A dorsal turret was tried, the FN (Fraser Nash) 64, but due to having a periscopic sight and no way for the gunner to determine the relative direction of the guns it was removed in favour of H2S radar. A limited number of Lancaster aircraft had a single .5-inch gun fitted if they did not have any specialised equipment in the dorsal position.

The German night fighters had larger-calibre guns and heavy protective armour. This rendered the Lancasters outgunned at normal engagement range and unable to penetrate the fighter's armour. Harris always maintained that the defensive armament of the heavy bombers was insufficient. He concluded that if turrets were to be worth carrying they should have uninterrupted field of view for the gunner, guns of sufficient calibre to damage night fighter, easy escape routes and a means of heating turret components and the gunner himself! In the later stages of the war a Rose turret, .5-inch calibre, was fitted to tail guns in some No. 1 Group aircraft.

Visibility for the rear gunner was of prime importance because most attacks by night fighters were from behind and below the aircraft. The Luftwaffe enjoyed some success in late 1943 with the 'Schrage Musik' upward-firing night fighter. Armament was removed along with the Perspex cupola. Heating was now of utmost importance for the guns and gunner, minus thirty degrees Celsius now being the normal temperature en route. Once again it was not until 1944 that gun heaters, special cold-temperature lubricants and eventually heated suits for the mid-upper and rear gunners became available.

Automatic Gun Laying (AGL) turrets were introduced as a blind-firing method, using on-board radar to track the attacking fighter. It was first introduced on a trial basis to No. 460 Squadron at Binbrook (see Sewell in chapter 4), and No. 49 Squadron at Fiskerton. The main problem was the identification of friend from foe. It required the whole bomber force to be equipped with transmitters that displayed on the gunner's sight. Gunners were hesitant to trust the new system and perhaps fire on their own aircraft. It was difficult to keep serviceable and reduced the line of sight when it was not working.

The normal operational sequence for belting ammunition was seven ball type, two incendiary and one tracer. The subject of tracer ammunition was an ongoing discussion – to use it or not? It tended to encourage the gunner to 'hosepipe', firing in the *direction* of the fighter instead of using the sight for accuracy. This could easily occur during the danger of an imminent attack. Just before the war ended, Harris directed that only incendiary bullets be employed, as the ball ammunition was useless against the night-fighter armament and the incendiary had a better chance of igniting a fuel tank or fuel pipe.

The corollary of having massed aircraft raids was the recovery at home base or, if the weather did not permit, a diversion to a suitable recovery airfield. A large number of aircraft would arrive in the dark at home station, often very close to a large number of aircraft proceeding to another station just outside the circuit. The density of air traffic was a concern, along with fuel shortages, not to mention the possibility of minor or major damage to the aircraft or injury to the crew.

Flying Control was initially responsible for three main areas: the orderly control of aircraft taking off and landing at home station, the expeditious handling of aircraft diverting to a more suitable airfield and, finally, the assistance to aircraft in distress. Flying Control had to control all three areas simultaneously, as they were all interrelated and part of the 'big picture'. The original Flying Control officers only became involved when the aircraft was having difficulties, but the job description slowly changed and they found themselves being responsible for the orderly flow of local air traffic departing and landing at the station. It followed that standard operating procedures were established for Bomber Command to supersede local procedures.

The necessity of operating two squadrons from the same airfield compounded the problem. In 1942 the average number of aircraft landed per hour was ten, corresponding to one every six minutes. This was not acceptable, so between new radio telephone (R/T) procedures and improved landing and airfield aids, including lighting, the number increased safely to an aircraft every two minutes, thirty per hour. However, the one factor that threw everything into disarray was the fickle British weather. The waves of snow, sleet, rain and clouds that were driven by the wind from the Atlantic were a constant worry to the Bomber Operations staff. Dewar recalled that he 'had set up a system of lights in [RAF Station] Wickenby to tell Flying Control when the aircraft had touched down, passed mid-runway and had turned off the runway [in low visibility]'.

Dewar also recounted the story about the 'most exciting day of my life. Earlier in the day I was in the radio room of the Watch Tower when one of the radios went on fire. I quickly grabbed it and threw it out the window. I was upstairs with the new guy on station having a cup of tea. The station was on stand down when the phone rang and it was group to say that thirty-six Consolidated B-24 Liberators were diverting due weather at home base to Wickenby. Between the lack of radios, no receiver, using the Tannoy, American R/T procedures and pilots' accent we managed to get all of them down and parked on out-of-use runways. In the confusion of darkness and many manoeuvring aircraft I had to run out on the balcony and fire a red flare with the Very pistol to get the aircraft to stop taxiing.'

In the early years of the war, operations were based on the fact that the aircraft would return to their home base. The raid would be cancelled if the weather was not suitable. The aircraft and crew would be deemed to be in 'distress' if in fact they had to land at another airfield. There was no co-ordination between bases and no standard procedure, so diversion to another airfield became a high-stress manoeuvre with a share of landing accidents. The answer to this confused state lay in communication and coordination between Flying Control at each airfield with each other and a group's Flying Control. The diversion in case of weather was pre-planned so crews could familiarise themselves with where they were going. By 1944 there was a published 'Bomber Command Diversion Schedule', and together with 'Standard Landing Procedures', established in 1942, the diversion of aircraft became more orderly.

The weather became a less decisive factor in the scheduling of operations. Subsequent to the weather briefing, the Central Flying Staff at Bomber Command, in consultation with the groups, would allocate the diversion airfields based on the weather forecast for their area. This way the returning aircraft would already be aware of the diversion airfield and the airfields could prepare for the possible eventuality of having to cope with extra aircraft. Provisional diversions were made for 95,000 sorties, with 20,000 actual diversions occurring.

Petrol diversions were also planned to get aircraft deeper into Germany with greater bomb loads. After the liberation of France, sorties would be planned at low level, avoiding the North Sea and the German defences by routing through the south coast of England, across the English Channel and at low level across France to avoid the enemy radar. The returning aircraft would land in Southern England to refuel before continuing on to home base.

The ever-present winter fog was addressed by the invention of Fog Intensive Dispersal Operation (FIDO), which consisted of pipelines of petrol each side of the runway with multiple burner cans to heat up the surrounding air and disperse some of the fog and increase the cloud ceiling. The designated emergency airfields – Carnaby, Manston and Woodbridge – with longer runways and special facilities for recovering damaged aircraft and wounded crew had FIDO, as did about a dozen other airfields. Between the weather and petrol diversion procedures and emergency airfields, the fatal and non-fatal accident rate among returning aircraft continued to decrease.

Perhaps the sorties of Bomber Command could be summed up by the title of the 1966 film *The Good, The Bad and The Ugly*. An example of the Good would be the daylight raid on Augsburg, the Bad would be the raid on Nuremberg and the Ugly would be all the other dangerous 'routine' sorties. Of course, none of this would apply if you were one of the unfortunate ones that did not survive your tour of duty. There were 55,573 crew declared killed or missing in action.

The following statistics are for relative information only and not to be accepted as totally accurate; they were gathered from many sources that often disagreed, but taken in context will give an idea of the quantities involved in events that happened over seventy years ago. In many cases

they have been rounded off to the nearest hundred. Wartime, by its very nature, would not lend itself to accurate bookkeeping, the emphasis being to get the job done and update the records later. The statistics themselves were often not adequately described or defined, leading to apparent discrepancies. Some random statistics follow:

1942	35,338 aircraft despatched	1,450 missing	45,561 tons dropped
1944	166,844 aircraft despatched	2,770 missing	525,518 tons dropped
1939–45	657,674 tons dropped on Germany		955,044 total tons dropped
1942	35,637 tons on industrial towns		12 tons on oil targets
1944	184,688 tons on industrial towns		48,043 tons on oil targets

Highest number of sorties despatched, day	1,189 (16 November 1944)
Sorties despatched on one target, day	1,107 (12 March 1945, Dortmund)
Highest tonnage dropped on one target, day	4,851 (12 March 1945, Dortmund)
Sorties despatched on one target, night	1,047 (31 March 1942, Cologne)
Heavy bombers despatched on one target, night	970 (14 October 1944, Duisburg)
Highest tonnage dropped on one target, night	4,547 (14 October 1944, Duisburg)
Highest number of aircraft missing, night	96 (30 March 1944, Nuremberg)
Air combat claims destroyed	1,191 (probable 310, damaged 897)
Aircraft type destroyed	JU88, 333 Bf110, 198 ME262, 5
Bomber Command crew lost or missing in action	55,573

The monthly average of Bomber Command sorties started with 1,900 in 1939 and built to a crescendo of 16,800 by 1945. Similarly, the monthly total tons of bombs and sea mines dropped grew from 1,600 in 1939 to an enormous 46,200 in 1945. These figures were not achieved without great personal loss and sacrifice. The loss rate was 4.1 per cent in 1942, 3.7 per cent in 1943, 1.7 per cent in 1944 and 0.9 per cent in 1945. The introduction of Radio Counter Measures (RCM) in 1944 had an initial dramatic effect on losses until Germany introduced its own RCM. However, by then the tide of aerial combat had turned, with the Allies in Continental Europe in June and the subsequent occupation of France and Belgium taking away the early-warning radar capability. These are the average losses for the year, but some catastrophic losses still occurred, such as the nearly 60 per cent loss rate of the daylight Augsburg raid on 17 April 1942.

What were the results for all this effort? The raids are generally credited with creating restrictions in the movement of raw material to production facilities and disrupting industrial planning. An inordinate amount of people were required for defence purposes rather than production purposes. The psychological effect of night-time bombing by the Lancaster, in addition to the casualties, is very difficult to quantify. Suffice to say it was not a positive experience and therefore it must have had an effect on the population and defence forces.

It is interesting to note that the 9,000 tons of bombs dropped on the Italian cities of Genoa, Turin and Milan had a far greater effect on the civilian citizens, causing a general population exodus. Their leader, Mussolini, encouraged an additional nightly exodus, leaving military personnel only in the city. The raid on the Italian Navy base of Spezia added to the general feeling of malaise. So per ton of bombs delivered the Bomber Command thinking was that it had a greater effect in Italy than in Germany and consequently less tonnage was required.

The number of heavy bombers available gradually grew over the course of the conflict. It grew from 44 to 262 during 1942, 313 to 776 in 1943, 818 to 1,381 in 1944 and eventually to 1,625 by VE Day. Lancaster production was up and running in England and, although affected by enemy bombing, managed to keep ahead of the attrition rate. The 430 from Victory Aircraft in Canada helped also. The total attrition rate of all Bomber Command aircraft since Harris assumed command was 8,000 out of 336,000 sorties or 2.4 per cent. It is interesting to note that the incendiary bombs dropped were 26 per cent of the total tonnage dropped. The incendiaries, as well as the marker pyrotechnics, played an important role in marking targets, as well as starting fires in general.

The Lancaster is an inanimate machine; without its supporting crew it is nothing. Unless it was maintained, repaired, armed and refuelled, and the crew fed, housed and kept healthy, the whole effort would be for nought. Then it was up to the bravery and skill of the Bomber Command crews that produced the destruction statistics that contributed to the Allies winning the other battles in the air, on and below the sea and on the ground, which ultimately won the Second World War. Who were these men, what did they do and where did they come from?

Armourers preparing to select the 'mix' ordered for the next operation from the station bomb dump. (Canadian Museum of Flight)

Right: Aircrew of Nos 431 (Iroquois) and 434 (Bluenose) squadrons RCAF are briefed on their target for the evening, at RAF Croft. (Canadian Forces Joint Imagery Centre)

Left: Lancaster R5727 was built in the UK and then flown to Canada to act as the pattern aircraft for the Victory Aircraft-built B.X (see KB700 in chapter 1). Noteworthy here is the rarely photographed, and short-lived in active service, FN-64 ventral (belly) turret. (Canadian Forces Joint Imagery Centre)

With the cowlings and spinner removed from engine no. 3, ground crew service this No. 419 Squadron RCAF Lancaster at RAF Middleton St George. While the stories in this book relate to the experiences of the aircrews, they all in turn recognise that the contribution of the hard-working ground crews was critical to every sortie flown. (Canadian Forces Joint Imagery Centre)

11 January 1945. Despite heavy snowfall, Lancaster operations must continue at this Bomber Command airfield. (Canadian Forces Joint Imagery Centre)

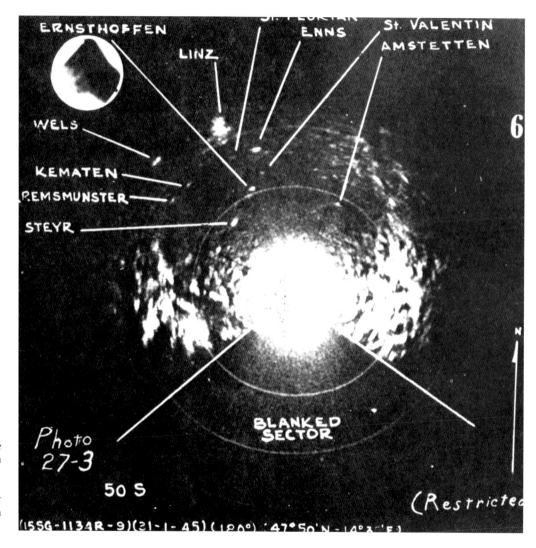

Right: H2S image. H2S was the first operational airborne ground-scanning radar system and was widely used on Lancaster aircraft. (Via Martin Keen)

Opposite: With 'Ops on', a No. 115 Squadron Lancaster crew arrive at their RAF Witchford dispersal. (Canadian Museum of Flight)

Aircrew arrive at their Lancaster's dispersal courtesy of a Ford WOT1 crew bus. (Canadian Forces Joint Imagery Centre)

The Krupp works at Essen, Germany. These were totally destroyed by Bomber Command raids. (Via Martin Keen)

Right: A view of Germany after VE Day in May 1945. (Canadian Museum of Flight)

Below: A member of the WAAF assisting in the Flying Control Room at RAF Dunholme Lodge. (Via Martin Keen)

Right: The aircrew of a No. 115 Squadron Lancaster leave their aircraft at dispersal and head for debriefing. (Canadian Museum of Flight)

Left: Returning from a raid on Dortmund, Germany, aircrew from No. 115 Squadron collect mugs of tea before undergoing debriefing by intelligence officers. (Canadian Museum of Flight)

Left: One of the 7,377 Lancasters that served during the Second World War. ED413, a B.III, served with Nos 57, 630 and 207 squadrons, No. 1651 HCU and No. 44 Squadron before being struck off charge in January 1945. (Bomber Command Museum of Canada)

Right: Celebrating the end of hostilities in Europe, May 1945. (Canadian Forces Joint Imagery Centre)

Above and right: With the end of the war in Europe, Canadian Lancaster squadrons in the United Kingdom returned home either for disbandment or for further action in the forthcoming Pacific Tiger Force against Japan. Pictured here is one such squadron, ready for departure from RAF Middleton St George in May 1945. (Canadian Forces Joint Imagery Centre)

This page and the next two pages: A selection of nose art applied to Canadian Lancaster B.Xs of No. 428 (Ghost) Squadron RCAF for their journey home. The aircraft are pictured here on 8 June 1945 at RCAF Yarmouth in Nova Scotia, where the squadron was disbanded on 5 September 1945. Lancaster KB843 NA-D *Dolly* was the last RCAF aircraft and last No. 6 Group bomber to land from combat duty in the Second World War. (Anthony Walsh)

4

THE LANCASTER CREW

What made the Lancaster, an inanimate object, come alive? It was people. The RAF hierarchy comprised people from the leaders in Bomber Command down through the chain of command, to group, to station, to squadron, to flight, to crew. It was people who maintained, repaired, refuelled, and armed the aircraft. It was the station people in catering, hospital staff, transport, construction engineering and a thousand other jobs. These people were all part of the vital effort to support the Lancaster, as were the local community providing supplies and of course the people who designed and built the aircraft. The list goes on and on, all necessary to provide a serviceable aircraft so that the operational sorties could be accomplished. The Lancaster sat, a lifeless object in the darkness at dispersal, until brought to life by all these people. The aircrew were the last link in the long human chain.

The Lancaster had a normal crew of seven, supplemented or replaced at times by observing crews and equipment specialists. Each crew member volunteered for aircrew duties. They stayed and worked as a crew most of the time as they completed their tour of thirty sorties. Postings, illness, training and special equipment assignments, such as the Stabilised Automatic Bomb Aimer Sight (SABS), could change the normal crew complement for a few sorties or permanently. The crew was a tight operating unit and the leader, the pilot, was often referred to in endearing terms such as 'my pilot', 'the skipper' and 'the old man' by the interviewed veterans. The pilot spoke of his crew as 'my crew', 'the lads' and 'the gang' at various times and also specifically by name, nickname or as 'the Nav', 'the tail gunner', and so on.

The impression left with the author was that these men, from all different backgrounds – rich, poor, suburban, rural, colonial – through the duress of war, formed a lasting bond that time would never diminish. Letters, reunions and now social media maintained this bond over the years. This comradeship grew from a close working relationship and the fact that each member of the crew realised that they all depended on each other, not only to get the job done but for their very own survival. Through the shared terrors, relief and joy of a successful sortie, and the occasional beer, it's no wonder their friendships lasted. Often spread throughout the world, the crew never forgot those days of Bomber Command during the passing years. Remembrance Day, 11 November, each year is an especially poignant time for the crew. The memories of former friends and crews who didn't make it are recalled with sadness.

The Lancaster had seven crew positions. The lone pilot flew the aircraft assisted by the flight engineer, who sat on his right and looked after the aircraft systems. The flight engineer also had a panel of instruments aft of his seat on the starboard wall of the fuselage. The navigator sat immediately aft of the pilot, facing the port wall behind a blackout curtain. He had a table for his charts and in later years the special navigation equipment such as Gee. Further aft sat the wireless operator, facing forward. The radio rack separated him from the navigator.

The bomb aimer and nose (front) gunner was a step down and forward of the cockpit. The mid-upper gunner sat in a suspended seat from the fuselage roof aft of the wireless operator. The tail (rear) gunner was at the end of the fuselage aft of the tailplane spar. Most gunners had a hydraulically driven Frazer Nash turret, although there were other makes later, such as Martin, which enabled their guns to move and follow the path of the attacking fighter.

The pilot and flight engineer were the ones who flew to the assigned location, to drop the bombs and return safely to home base. The Lancaster was a war machine and as such needed specialists to carry out its mission. The air gunners were its defence and the bomb aimer was its offense. The navigator was both – offensive to get it to the target to fulfil its mission, and defensive to get it back to base to do it all again another day. The wireless operator was the ears of the aircraft, keeping in touch with other aircraft in the bomber stream and Bomber Command, plus passing back enemy information and weather reports.

A civilian volunteered for service and so began the journey of training to convert them to a way of life that perhaps he or she had never been aware of before. The vast majority had had no previous exposure to military life nor family military experience to guide them. It was quite a shock at the beginning, but most accepted the routine, rules and regulations, and there were always the rebels to provide the hijinks and humour to soften the transition to military life.

A full medical, health and dental check enabled the person to continue with basic training at an Initial Training Wing (ITW) after the initial recruiting interview. The military life is based on a rank hierarchy, so the recruit was instructed in how to obey commands. This was achieved through such activities as physical training, marching, saluting and the inevitable barrack and parade inspection. These all led to the military decision of what the candidate was most suitable for. There were four career paths at that stage: flight engineer, pilot, air gunner and wireless operator/air gunner. Most flight engineers were trained in Britain, but 1,900 graduates came from Canada after July 1944.

Psychological and aptitude tests sent the most successful graduates overseas to Canada for flying training. The pilot went to an Elementary Flying Training School (EFTS). The course was eight weeks in length and gave the new pilot fifty hours on such aircraft as the Tiger Moth, Fleet Finch and Fairchild Cornell. Successful trainees then went on to a Service Flying Training School (SFTS) for more advanced instruction. This was also where the pilot group was divided into fighter pilots and bomber, coastal and transport pilots. The course varied from ten to sixteen weeks and seventy-five to a hundred hours. The fighter pilots would train on the single-engine North American Harvard, a real rudder airplane, due to the powerful radial engine; the multi-engine airplanes used for training were the Avro Anson, Cessna Crane and Airspeed Oxford. Performance on the SFTS would decide if a candidate would proceed with further pilot training or become a bomb aimer/navigator. This selection process also depended on present wartime requirements, much to the disappointment of would-be pilots.

The pilot went on to an Advanced Flying Unit (AFU) and the bomb aimer/navigator path led to an Advanced Observer School (AOS) for five weeks of aerial photography, reconnaissance and air navigation, and then to an Advanced Flying Unit (AFU). After 1942 the duties of the air observer were divided between the bomb aimer and navigator, thus abolishing the observer category.

Navigators specialising in bombing spent eight weeks at a Bombing & Gunnery School and twelve weeks at an Air Observer School. Navigators specialising as wireless operators trained for twenty-eight weeks at a Wireless Training School and twenty-two weeks at an Air Observer School. Bomb aimers spent five weeks at an ITS, eight to twelve weeks at a Bombing & Gunnery School and six weeks at an Air Observer School. Bomb aimers also learnt map-reading and observation skills to assist the navigator. Wireless operators spent twenty-eight weeks at a Wireless Training School followed by six weeks at a Bombing & Gunnery School. The air gunner went through twelve weeks of ground training and actual air-to-air firing practice.

At the very beginning of the war Britain looked to the colonies to help set up the Empire Air Training Scheme to train aircrew. Britain did not have the room to accommodate both training and operational facilities, being in the range of enemy fighters and bombers. Canada offered this opportunity to Britain as it certainly had the space, with larger capacity to manufacture aircraft (Lancaster and Hurricane are examples which are part of the BBMF). Canadian industry had ready access to parts from the USA and, perhaps most importantly, Canada had decent proximity to Britain. The Canadian Prime Minister, William Lyon Mackenzie King, believed that the British Commonwealth Air Training Plan (BCATP) would be 'the most essential military action that Canada could undertake'. It would be a significant contribution to the war effort without Canadians being in the front lines. That would change, as more than 72,000 went overseas.

The BCATP agreement was signed by the United Kingdom, Australia, New Zealand and Canada on 17 December 1939. This commitment so early in the war was one of the major decisions which contributed to the ultimate success of the air war. The participants agreed on training requirements and their share of the costs. The United Kingdom paid in materials which Canada did not have. By 31 March 1945 the plan had cost £118,529,430 for 151 schools, more than 100 airfields and emergency landing fields and 104,113 ground personnel, men and women, to train 131,553 Air Force crew.

That produced an astonishing 2,100 fully trained aircrew per month, approximately. The exhaustive classroom curriculum and schedule turned out crews at a fast rate; only the strong would survive. This meant the calibre of aircrew reaching England was extremely high, contrary to what you would expect in a fast-paced training environment. Twenty-nine EFTS and all ten Air Observer Schools were run by local companies, airlines and flying clubs.

To this day, when flying in Canada you can see the familiar triangle shape of the wartime runways, built to ensure the novice trainees could always land into wind on initial training. Some locations have developed into major airports, and some are as they were left in 1945. In all, 856 trainees of the BCATP were killed or seriously wounded, and the Commonwealth War Graves Commission maintains the graves of those Commonwealth trainees who died on Canadian soil.

Canadians took great pride in welcoming the trainees into the community and the social fabric of the area changed. The schools entertained the community and the community in turn entertained the trainees. Morale for the war effort was very high, although tinged with sadness at each graduating ceremony as the trainees left for an uncertain future in the vagaries of war. There also was a demographic change in the local area, as some Canadian wives, nearly 4,000, left the area to join their husbands after the war ended, in addition to the servicemen some married returning to Canada after release from the Air Force.

Nationality	Graduates
Royal Canadian Air Force (RCAF)	72,835
Royal Australian Air Force (RAAF)	9,606
Royal New Zealand Air Force (RNZAF)	7,002
Royal Air Force (RAF), which included	42,110
Poles	448
Norwegians	677
Belgian & Dutch	800
Czechs	900
Free French	2,600
Total	131,553
[Naval Fleet Air Arm	5,296]

It is interesting to look at the number of RAF and RCAF aircrew trained by the BCATP, as many are featured in the four museums in Britain and Canada described in this book.

	RAF	RCAF
Pilot	17,796	25,747
Navigator (Bomber)	3,113	5,154
Navigator (Wireless)	3,847	421
Navigator	6,922	7,280
Bomb Aimer	7,581	6,659
Wireless Operator/Air Gunner	755	12,744
Air Gunner	1,392	12,917

All this RCAF station construction, which came at the end of the Great Depression, put many communities back on the map. Apart from requiring local materials and labour, there was also an influx of station personnel who would be spending their wages in the local area. The local newspaper in Yorkton, Saskatchewan, predicted the SFTS would bring in a thousand people to run the station, with a monthly payroll of $100,000.

Upon completion of basic military training – how to march, parade and salute – the airmen and officers would proceed to their respective trade training. Depending on their progress and Air Force requirements, their trade could be changed mid-course. Upon graduation they were now ready to get 'crewed up' and start training as a seven-man unit.

How were these individuals assigned to a crew? Simple: the different crew positions were all put in a large hall with pots of tea and biscuits and told to sort themselves into individual crews. Crews mostly stayed together, but sometimes sickness or crew leave on other crews meant they would fill in as necessary. By staying together they would all hope to reach their operational tour of thirty trips at the same time.

A few personal stories told to me in person – those of Pearson, Sewel, Blackman and Plenderleith – along with personal family records or museum archives, will illustrate just what these young men went through in the prime of their lives. These are stories that perhaps have not been told in seventy years. The interviews brought back a flood of old memories to the interviewees, but through it all there was a sense of pride, accomplishment and even humour.

Bomb Aimer

The rest of the crew got the Lancaster safely to the vicinity of the target; now it was the turn of the bomb aimer to deliver the ordnance accurately. Initially area bombing was the norm, but as bombsights and the aerodynamics of bombs improved and the Pathfinders were added to the operation, the ability to deliver bombs to a specific target became possible.

The bomb aimer's crew position was in the very nose of the aircraft, a cold position at the best of times. Returning from a raid on Stuttgart, his thirteenth op, on the night of 21 February 1944 in Lancaster LL785-Freddie, Flt Lt W. (Bill) E. Pearson asked the skipper if he could come up to the cockpit to get warm. As he climbed the stairs, something happened. 'I saw a flash of a red light and then there was a loud crash and the whole bomb aiming compartment was destroyed – we had been involved in a mid-air collision.' The whole crew were very fortunate to survive the accident; the other aircraft crashed, and when asked about it Pearson said, 'Lucky. Just plain lucky.'

Pearson was born in Regina, Saskatchewan, and two days before the attack on Pearl Harbour he volunteered to serve in the RCAF. Initial Training School (ITS) was in Edmonton, Alberta, followed by gunnery training on the Fairey Battle and navigation training on the Avro Anson in Lethbridge, Alberta. He returned to Blatchford Field (Edmonton) for some navigation training but mainly bombing training. By December 1942 he had his observer wings and commission and in January 1943 he boarded the *Queen Elizabeth* in New York and sailed to Greenock, Scotland, where he boarded a train for Bournemouth.

Pearson then went to the Advanced Flying Unit (AFU) at Penrhos, north Wales, and flew Bristol Blenheims. He said, 'I never felt so cold in all my life up there next to the Irish Sea.' Next he went to the North Luffenham permanent base to get crewed up and start the Operational Training Unit (OTU) on the Vickers Wellington bomber. Pearson's first crew consisted of English, Australian and Canadian aircrew, the mix not an uncommon one.

He recounted, 'The base was going to be taken over so they moved us to Bruntingthorpe just outside of Leicester. Our first OTU trip was a nickel raid, dropping leaflets on our own, single aircraft (Op), to Rennes, France. This is when I had my first mishap in the air. I had relieved the pilot, I could hold it straight level after some basic Link training, while he had a pee and when he came back we exchanged seats, I unplugged my intercom and stepped down. The escape hatch release on a Wimpy is on the right side, it is a lever with a red knob on it. I must have inadvertently kicked it and I stepped out in to space. I caught myself on both sides but I was not plugged in so I could not tell anyone. I just screamed my head off and the Wireless Operator heard me and pulled me up.'

The crew were then posted to No. 1654 Wigsley heavy conversion unit to transition to the Lancaster, where they picked up a flight engineer to make up the crew of seven. Pearson said, 'This is where the engineers became indoctrinated – ours became indoctrinated bloody fast. We did an overshoot one day and he lifted the flaps before the undercart [landing gear] and now that was some sinking feeling. He got a certain amount of you know what from the rest of the crew, he never forgot that.'

The crew were then posted to No. 207 Squadron RAF up in Lincolnshire and the pilot, Johnny Kirkup (RAF), went on a 'second dickie'

familiarisation trip and never came back. The crew were now headless, but resisted attempts to split them up. Dave Pearce, recovering from a bail-out injury, was assigned as the skipper. Pearson said, 'They went to Balderton, Newark on Trent, to do some circuits and bumps, bombing runs and cross countries with the new skipper before being posted to No. 9 Squadron RAF, code WS, at Bardney, Lincolnshire. Wing Commander Cheshire VC, he had many other decorations also, joined us for a few circuits. While we were at Newark we saw a Wimpy (Vickers Wellington) with the rear turret removed and a stove pipe stuck out the back. I guess they were doing some secret testing on a jet engine from a guarded hangar at the far end of the field.'

The second trip at No. 9 Squadron RAF 'was to Leipzig where we got shot up by an Fw [Focke Wulf]. We had just started our bombing run, dropped our bombs and cleared target. The elevator was damaged, the mid-upper gunner, an Aussie, was wounded and I had to help the engineer take the strain [to maintain level flight]. We diverted to an emergency runway in the South of England. An engineer pushed down on the left elevator and it snapped. The navigator Jim got the DFC on that trip. All his charts went out the back and he remembered enough of the numbers to get us home. That was our baptism of fire.'

The crew were assigned Berlin as a target very many times, which brought them up to March 1944, the infamous Nuremberg raid; more on that later. Pearson said, 'We were now the senior crew on 9 Squadron with eight trips.' Leave was every six weeks and lasted seven to ten days. F/O Dave Pearce got married and completed his tour of thirty trips. 'I had about twenty-five trips around the same time and my only claim to fame is Lancaster WS-J completed 110 trips and I had two trips in that baby,' laughed Pearson. The station commander, Wing Commander Porter, needed a crew and Pearson's crew all needed a few more trips after Pearce left to complete their thirty trips. However, Porter had been tagged to the Pathfinder Force and the crew were all sent on end-of-tour leave. 'To me that was a slap in the face as we all wanted to be in on D-Day,' said Pearson.

The crew decided to do another tour as Pathfinders, and they went to RAF Station Coningsby. Pearson said, 'We did most of our work with 97 Squadron aircraft and we were assigned to be master bomber on 54 Base Nos 83 and 97 Squadron. We did some eight to ten trips there and we had some interesting trips. We even had a daylight trip with a bunch of B-17s and marked [the target] with our methods. We got another leave and I came back a day early because I was broke. I flew a couple of trips with different crews and then one day they did not have any qualified visual bomb aimers.'

Pearson paused and said reflectively, 'This was my thirty-seventh-and-a-half trip, I flew more than half of it. They said, you will volunteer for this won't you Pearson? The skipper was Squadron Leader Sparks, he had just returned from a bail out and walked back through the Pyrenees. I met the rest of the crew for the first time climbing into the aircraft, OL-C PB249. It was one of the longest raids of the war, Konigsberg, East Prussia [the city was annexed by Russia and is now called Kaliningrad]. We were deputy one on that trip and we had the markers for marking. Our aircraft on that trip had the Semi-Automatic Bomb Sight (SABS). We went over, I dropped a marker that I think was pretty good and had just started to peel away when we got nailed by flak. I think we were down between seven and eight thousand and I think that it was heavy flak that knocked out the port engines, inner and outer. They went on fire and I kicked out the escape hatch, buckled on [the parachute] and hesitated, thinking [that] maybe they will get those fires out. Suddenly there was a guy pushing me, it was the Wireless Op. I went out, he went out and Squadron Leader Sparks followed me out.

'I got coned part way down and they were peppering at me and I landed on a cobbled road near a potato patch on the outskirts of Konigsberg. I didn't even get my harness off before I got bayonets in my face. I was a POW pretty quick. After some local confinement I was sent to an interrogation camp near Frankfurt, I think, for a couple of weeks. It is where they send all the aircrew. Then I was sent to Stalag Luft 1 at Barth, Pomerania, up on the Baltic coast. The Russians released us on 30 April, 1 May & 2 May when they came through. The date [shot down] was 29 August 1944. I was flown back to England in a B-17 late May 1945. I was 185 [lbs] when I was shot down and 138 [lbs] when I weighed in.

'Squadron Leader Sparks was in the same camp, he eventually got there at a different time. He was captured about the same time because I was under guard in a local municipal hall being looked over by the locals when a Luftwaffe car drove up with Squadron Leader Sparks sitting in the back seat with a guard on each side. They brought me outside and shone a light in his face and asked me if I knew this guy. I said, "No, but good luck guy."'

This is a record of the aircraft shot down over Konigsberg that night:

29/30 August 1944 Konigsberg
JB593 LL790 LM237 LM267 LM583 LM656 ND331 ND982 PB249 (Pearson)
PD258

In many ways, the bomb aimer was the eyes of the operation. He helped the navigator, when they were flying in visual conditions, to pinpoint their position and guided the pilot in the last few miles to the 'bombs-away' point. Pearson mentioned during an interview that he 'had enough training and skill to keep the aircraft straight and level when returning from ops over England to allow the pilot to go back and take a pee'. Together with his duty as the nose gunner on the twin Browning .303 machine guns, the bomb aimer was a very busy member of the crew.

The bomb aimer's compartment was a step down from the cockpit and access was forward on the starboard side to the sighting window. To use the bombsight would require the bomb aimer to lay flat on his stomach over the forward escape hatch. The control panel for setting up the bomb-release sequence was on the right-hand side of the fuselage, with the bombsight next to the front window. The bombs were released with a handheld switch. The cry of 'Bombs gone!' was the most welcome sound to the crew, as they could immediately take evasive action to get out of the area.

The basic bombsight at the beginning of hostilities was a Course Setting Bomb Sight (CSBS) that went through redevelopment as the speed, altitude and manoeuvrability of the new bomber aircraft increased. The four main input settings were wind direction and velocity, bomb's terminal velocity and the altitude of the target above sea level. Any manoeuvring, to avoid flak or fighters, would require the bombsight parameters to be reset. This meant that the aircraft would have to fly straight and level for some time approaching the target – not a recipe for longevity.

The solution started to reach the squadrons by the spring of 1942: it was the Mk XIV stabilised-vector bombsight. The four main parameters were entered into the computer and repeaters supplied the altitude, airspeed and course of the aircraft. The computer automatically updated the 'aim point' and could recalculate this point in ten seconds of level flight after radical manoeuvring or curved-descent attack, which made it harder for the fighters.

The bombsight consisted of two main parts: the sighting head by the window and the computer on the left-hand side of the fuselage. They were joined by two cables which carried the information from one to the other. There was a stabilisation gyro to maintain the sighting mechanism at the correct attitude. A collimator handle allowed the bomb aimer to check the track of the aircraft and drift angle by sighting ground objects.

At that time the instruments were rudimentary, but they were a precursor to what would develop in the post-war years.

Pilot

The pilot was the crew leader during operations, regardless of rank. He was the man who coordinated the seven-man crew, and he was the man who would 'get them home'. A lot rested on his shoulders – very often young shoulders – and he had to develop leadership skills in a hurry to shape the crew into an effective one. The men all depended on each other: with the objective of surviving thirty trips there was no room for failure, although a few did get a second chance.

I interviewed F/O Bill Blackman when he was ninety-five years old and living in an assisted-living facility. Although he was bright and energetic, his memory at times was incomplete, and no wonder. We were talking about things that happened seventy years ago and were not often discussed. When Blackman first applied to be a pilot with the RCAF, he was told, 'We are not accepting married men for aircrew at the moment, so you are five-thousandth on the waiting list.' Blackman got his call-up in 1941 and took his EFTS training on the Fleet Finch and de Havilland Tiger Moth. This was followed by SFT on the North American Yale and Harvard near London, Ontario. Blackman received his wings from the famous First World War fighter ace RCAF Air Marshal William 'Billy' Bishop VC on 3 April 1944.

By May, Blackman was in England training on the Airspeed Oxford. He laughingly said, 'I was to be a fighter pilot but I had no killer instinct, I was a little older than the others at twenty-four.' Blackman then went to No. 12 OTU on the Vickers Wellington before No. 1668 HCU for the Lancaster at RAF Bottesford on the Leicestershire–Lincolnshire border. Blackman's first trip on the Lancaster with No. 195 Squadron RAF was on 19 February 1945 to Wesel, Germany. Other targets that he mentioned were Datteln, Altenberge,

Gelsenkirchen, Bremen and the Scholven Buer synthetic oil plant.

Blackman was then sent on a Gee-H course at RAF Feltwell, East Anglia. The basis of Gee-H was picking up a radar arc that was displayed on an oscilloscope and being at the correct altitude and speed until reaching a predetermined location from a second beacon. Blackman said that 'you had three minutes to be at the correct height and speed before the bomb doors opened and the bombs dropped automatically'. The reported accuracy was 150 yards at 300 miles. Early May he went to The Hague in aircraft HK753 on Operation Manna. Blackman stayed in the RCAF in telecommunications and returned to Germany after the war to inspect RCAF radar facilities.

F/L David Walsh's story is unique in many ways. Late, last and first of first would adequately describe him. His son Anthony Walsh was able to provide logbook information and images to complete his dad's story. Walsh was stationed at Middleton St George with No. 428 'Ghost' Squadron RCAF flying the Lancaster. He completed twenty-eight missions before the end of the war, mostly in Lancaster KB843 NA-D. Targets included Dresden, Nuremberg, Hanover, Hamburg, Dortmund, Dessau and Bremen.

His son Anthony proudly wrote the following story about his father:

His Lancaster was the last RCAF aircraft and last Group 6 bomber to land from combat duty in the Second World War for the commendable reason for which I honour him [that is diverting on the return flight from a bombing mission, back over alerted territory to locate crew members in the North Sea who were seen parachuting from two Lancs that collided on the way to Wangerooge, the last raid of the war, a daylight raid]. The collision was seen by my father ahead and below to the left, who then had his navigator mark the spot. By a minor miracle they found the spot in the evening haze and saw six yellow Mae Wests with lots of marker dye in the water. Low on fuel, my dad loitered over the spot having called rescue, until a Consolidated PBY Catalina [flying boat] was in visual range.

Dad departed as soon as the PBY confirmed they had his location locked in. Unfortunately my dad and crew learnt subsequently that the rescue recovered only six bodies, all having succumbed to injuries and/or hypothermia in the many hours in the cold North Sea. Now critically low on fuel, dad made it to the closest coastal emergency base RAF Carnaby [East Riding of Yorkshire], landing at 2036 hours, thus was the last bomber to land in European war. Two days later they repositioned NA-D back to Middleton St George much further north.

That explains the late and the last. What a great story to commemorate and honour the crews of Bomber Command, at various times criticised by those who did not understand the importance of the bombing campaign.

F/L Walsh started his military career the same way as P/O Shelson: both went overseas with the Canadian Army before re-mustering to aircrew. He joined the RAF on 21 August 1942 and was sent to Canada for training on 4 May 1943. During his stay in Canada he transferred to the RCAF. Returning to England, he flew the Vickers Wellington and Handley Page Halifax before attending No. 6 Lancaster finishing school at RAF Dishforth, Yorkshire. Walsh was posted to No. 428 Squadron RCAF at Middleton St George on 29 November 1944.

Now for the first of first. F/L Walsh flew KB843 NA-D back to Canada in the first wave of returning Lancasters for the Pacific War Tiger Force. His was the first Lancaster to land back in Canada at Gander, Newfoundland. The final leg of the flight was to Yarmouth, Nova Scotia, on 8 June 1945, and F/L Walsh never flew as a pilot again. He became an engineer.

About fifteen years ago, a friend asked me to join him for lunch at an Air Crew Association (ACA) luncheon. This was long before I ever thought of writing a book. I very quickly became aware that the room was full of Second World War aircrew, a generation removed from me, who were reliving some of the memories of that exciting but terrible time. One of the attendees was Ken Brown. I had heard of the Dambuster Squadron and knew generally about what they did, but had never researched further and so did not know Brown's connection.

Ken Brown joined the RCAF as a pilot in 1940, and although recommended for fighters he was posted to Coastal Command on the Armstrong Whitworth Whitley, where there was most need. Posted to a Lancaster HCU prior to joining No. 44 Squadron RAF, he so impressed his instructor, the famous Mickey Martin, on evasion tactics in fighter affiliation exercises that when Martin went to No. 617 Squadron RAF he recommended Brown to the commanding officer, Wing Commander Guy Gibson VC DSO* DFC*. So Flight Sergeant Brown joined the elite ranks of the special Dambuster Squadron.

He set about low-level training for an as-yet-unknown target. Assigned a cross-country trip at 125 feet above ground, he climbed to 250 feet to avoid men on a hangar roof. Reprimanded by Gibson, he was instructed to repeat the exercise and this time the men had to dive to avoid being killed. On the CO's carpet he was told, 'I didn't mean THAT low.' Another location used was the Derwent Dam, Derbyshire – at night, at sixty feet above the dark water. Finally, it was revealed that the target was three dams in Germany – the Möhne, the Sorpe and the Eder – to be hit with the special rotating, bouncing bomb designed by Barnes Wallis.

Departing 17 May 1943 at 00.12 hours, F/Sgt Brown in Lancaster ED918/G, squadron code AJ-F, lifted off from the runway at RAF Scampton, Lincolnshire, and into the history books. Brown was on the third wave of aircraft, to inflict further damage needed to any of the dams. For his bravery that night, F/Sgt Ken Brown was awarded the Conspicuous Gallantry Medal (CGM) and subsequently received his commission as an officer. The CGM was awarded to non-commissioned officers (NCOs) who had shown exceptional gallantry in the face of the enemy. It is second only to the Victoria Cross and is the NCO equivalent to the DSO.

Ken Brown CGM gave a speech to the Bomber Command Museum of Canada on the occasion of the fiftieth anniversary of the Dams raid in 1993, here is an excerpt:

We arrived at the Möhne Dam. It had been breached by that time. The gunners were still fairly active. We thought we'd leave them alone and we went over to the Sorpe Dam. The Sorpe was of a different construction altogether. It was an earthen dam, where you have a solid core and earth on either side – very difficult to breach. This was one thing that they never really took a hard look at with such a dam. But our tactics were to run parallel with the dam and drop our bomb in the middle so that it would explode, wash out the front of it, crack the wall and the water would do the rest. But we needed more than one.

The only problem was the whole damn valley was full of fog. When we arrived there, they told us that there would be a church up on top of the village. We found that all right – but just the spire of the church. So I tried to position myself from the spire. I didn't do too well. I got behind the dam on the first run. When I found myself at ground level, behind the dam I had to climb up roughly eighteen hundred feet. It didn't do my nerves any good at all. Because I was on top of the trees, I had to do a flat turn. I couldn't move the wing down to get around. I had to stand on the rudder to get around and then we were down in the valley again. Well we did quite a number of runs on the dam, before we were able to clear enough of the fog away with the propellers constantly going through it. And I must say, according to the historians today, it was a near perfect drop. And I didn't even write them about it. However, we were pleased with it and as far as the explosion was concerned, the waterspout went up to about a thousand feet and so did we. I think we ended up about eight hundred.

There was one thing that sort of bugged me. When we went to the Möhne

Dam, one of our aircraft [flown by Flight Lieutenant John Hopgood] had been shot down there. And I felt we owed the fellow a visit. So I went back. All the other aircraft had left. But as soon as we came over the Möhne, they were throwing 20mm at us. I think there was some that was 37mm. But I figured that we owed that fellow a visit. So we came real low, below the towers, straight on at them. And I heard this fellow's story about three weeks ago in Germany, and he said – No. I won't try his German. Anyhow, we opened up at about five hundred yards and carried in over the tower and the rear gunner depressed his guns and we raked the thing as we went through. Well, there was no firing coming from that tower when we left. We figured we'd done him in, however the fellow got the Iron Cross. So we weren't that successful.

The worst was really yet to come. It was then daylight or just breaking. We had to go across and up the Zuiderzee. There was no horizon – the mud from the Zuiderzee and the sky were all one. So I started across, strictly on my altimeter with my head below the cockpit top at fifty feet and I hung onto it. I'd been told by a famous Wing Commander in the RAF, 'Never, ever pull up. If you're low, never pull up.' So I hoped he was right – because all hell broke loose within a matter of fifteen minutes.

Searchlights, even though it was light, caught us from the starboard side and straight on. There was a lot of light flak immediately in front of us. The cannon shells started to go through the canopy, the side of the aircraft was pretty well blown out, and there was only one thing to do. That was go lower, so I put her down ten feet. We came across and actually their gun positions were on the sea wall. So they were firing slightly down at us and I guess they couldn't believe we were lower than what they could fire. So in this turmoil with the front gunner blazing away at them, I just got a glance, for a moment, and I could see the gunners either falling off because they were hit from our guns or rather they were jumping off to save their skin.

I pulled up over top of them and we all gave a great sigh of relief. I think I've never had a bowel movement that ever gave me greater relief. We figured we had it made at this stage of the game. I called each of the crew members and I was really surprised to find that no one had been hit. There was a great deal of damage.

The loss of aircraft and life on the raid was very heavy: eight out of nineteen aircraft failed to return. Only three of the fifty-six crew posted missing in action ever returned. A high proportion of the participating crews received gallantry awards. W/C Gibson was awarded the Victoria Cross for his leadership by example that night in the face of determined enemy opposition, which included flying alongside the aircraft delivering bombs to draw defensive fire away from them. A very stark reminder of the quantity of casualties of Bomber Command is the fact that neither W/C Gibson VC nor any of his crew survived the war.

Flight Engineer
Initially flight engineers were taken from the ranks of the ground crew already established at RAF stations. However, with the rate of heavier bombers being produced, supply soon outstripped demand. The 'second pilot position' was being replaced by a crew member more familiar with the aircraft systems: the flight engineer. The auxiliary equipment on a four-engine bomber was far greater and more complicated than that of the previous two-engine bomber. The decision was made to train direct-entry flight engineers from scratch. Initially, from 1940 to 1942, Britain did all the training until joined in 1943 by Canada, Australia, South Africa and India in order of numbers. The RAF trained nearly 18,000 flight engineers of all nationalities, and 1,900 were trained by the RCAF in Canada.

No. 4 School of Technical Training was established at St Athan, South Wales, and was one of the larger stations at that time. The camps, East Camp and West Camp, were divided by the airfield. West Camp was home of No. 19 Maintenance Unit and East Camp was used for training. The training time for a flight engineer was approximately six months, in addition to the basic technical work. The successful graduate was awarded the flight engineer's half-wing 'E' brevet and given the rank of sergeant.

The job specification for the flight engineer included responsibility for the technical maintenance of the aircraft both in the air and on the ground. Before each flight the engines, instruments and all equipment had to be tested, although they were possibly checked also by the pilot and navigator, responsible for calculation of the fuel load considering distance of raid and bomb load. During flight the flight engineer was to operate the engines efficiently (at least one air mile per gallon was the aim), maintain instrument readings and to assist in an emergency. He was also to relieve the pilot at the flight controls for short periods and make inflight emergency repairs. Notwithstanding the aforementioned, the flight engineer was an extra pair of eyes and spent a lot of time scanning the skies for threats.

During training the candidate would learn about fuel, engine, electrical, pneumatic and hydraulic systems. Flight controls and instrument panels would also be studied. Non-academic courses included the pre-flight inspection, hypoxia training in a decompression chamber and a 'maker's course' at an Avro factory to gain an insider's knowledge on how the Lancaster was built. The final assessment consisted of a written and oral test. Next step was a posting to an HCU to meet the rest of the crew, who had been together for some time.

Sgt John H. Crammond completed his course and was posted to No. 1661 HCU at RAF Winthorpe, Lincolnshire, for the Shorts Stirling aircraft. After forty-five flying hours he was assigned to No. 5 Lancaster Finishing School at RAF Syerston, Nottinghamshire. After eleven hours of Lancaster I and III training he was posted to No. 44 Squadron at RAF Dunholme Lodge, Lincolnshire, where he completed his first operational trip to Beauvoir, France, on 16 June 1944. Railway yards, bomb sites and Army support featured regularly in his logbook. Under 18 July 1944, Caen, 3.35 day, he had written, 'German Army – Most helpful [trip] of war.'

On 26 (10.40 night) and 29 (11.40 night) July 1944 he made the long trip to Konigsberg on the Baltic Sea. The trip of the 29th was the same raid on which F/L Pearson got shot down. On 19 September 1944 Crammond witnessed the target, Monchengladbach, being marked by Wing Commander Gibson's PFF de Havilland Mosquito. Wing Commander Gibson VC DSO* DFC* was killed in action that night and is buried in Steenbergen, Netherlands.

Navigator

The navigator sat facing the port fuselage wall aft of the pilot. A screen curtain separated the navigator at night to prevent the chart-table light from attracting the attention of an enemy night fighter. The table would be covered in charts, pencils, protractors and a computer to plot and check the course. The H2S set with its cathode ray tube was also installed at the navigator station, sometimes to be operated by a special equipment operator.

Navigation prior to the electronic age had always caused problems. What with bad weather, night-time flights and evasive manoeuvres due to flak and enemy fighters, it was a formidable task to get close to a destination. At the beginning of the war, initial track setting used low-frequency beacons, which were good for the first 200 miles, and then the navigation procedure switched to dead reckoning (DR), supplemented by visual position confirmation and celestial navigation, weather and competency allowing.

The basis of DR was the mathematical calculation of a future location from the present location. The accuracy of the present position and wind speed/direction was crucial to the calculations. The main problem with DR was that the navigation track errors magnified as the flight progressed, unless there was some opportunity to update the present position accurately. The war hastened a solution to the compounding error problem, and it was the invention of Gee, Oboe and H2S.

P/O Donald M. Currie completed his navigator training at No. 2 Air Observer School in Edmonton, Alberta, through the British Commonwealth Air Training Plan. Subsequently posted to No. 1 Air Flying Unit at Wigtown, Scotland, for further training, he was then assigned to the Pathfinder Navigation Training Unit at Warboys, Cambridgeshire. Upon completion of specialised Pathfinder training he was sent to No. 635 Pathfinder Force Squadron at Downham Market, Norfolk. The Pathfinder Lancasters carried two navigators, an observer navigator and a plotter navigator.

The observer navigator, P/O Currie, kept track of their position by using Gee and H2S and passed these fixes on to the plotter navigator every six minutes. The pure DR navigation was now being updated by non-visual means via the Gee box and H2S. It was now possible to navigate to the target and perform the bombing run totally 'blind', i.e. with no reference to geographical features. The final run-in to the target would be marked with the PFF target indicator (TI) flares and coloured indicators. Some of these would be barometric markers, which would remain at different selected heights above the target and the clouds.

During his wartime training, P/O Currie took extensive comprehensive notes of his specialised Pathfinder navigator training. These notes included information on systems that were designated restricted and were not carried on the aircraft in case they should fall into the enemy's hands. I found P/O Currie's navigation school notes, which had been donated by him to the archives of the Bomber Command Museum of Canada in Nanton, Alberta. They are very comprehensive and one page is included as an example of the level of development of navigation procedures during that time. His notes included information on the electromechanical Air Position Indicator,

including vectoring and resetting over target, estimated time of arrival and timing calculations, day and night flash photography, DR procedures, taking shots of the stars and explaining the working relationship between the two navigators. Curries donated examples of flight logs kept and filed by the navigator after each trip to the BCMC.

The all-important Gee and H2S procedures to assist navigation are mentioned, plus the bombsight and bomb-panel operation. The then-sensitive information on PFF pyrotechnic Tis and their codes are mentioned, plus the operation of blind bombing using H2S. The notes give a great insight to what was going on inside the aircraft, with the navigators getting the aircraft to and from the target on the designated track. It has been mentioned by several sources that some navigators never came out from behind the blackout curtain until they were safely back at home base.

Wireless/Air Gunner

The wireless operator's station was just in front of the main spar, in the rear part of the cockpit section. In addition to his official duties related to the radio equipment, the W/Op was also expected to have a working knowledge of the navigator's equipment, understand the aircraft's electrical and intercom systems, and administer first aid as necessary. As well, he was generally on duty in the astrodome in the event of contact with enemy fighters and over the target. The astrodome was a dome-shaped piece of Perspex which protruded above the aircraft's fuselage in order that the navigator could take shots of the stars. It also provided an excellent viewpoint.

P/O Jack W. Shelson was born in Toronto and volunteered to serve in the RCAF. Turned down by the RCAF for medical reasons, he went overseas with the Canadian Army to serve his 'King and Country'. He subsequently re-mustered to the Air Force and trained as a wireless operator/air gunner at

No. 2 Radio School, Yatesbury, Wiltshire. He successfully completed Course No. 158 at No. 1 (O) Advanced Flying Unit on the Avro Anson. Subsequent service saw him crew on the Handley Page Halifax and Vickers Wellington prior to his first trip on the Avro Lancaster with B Flight, No. 419 Squadron RCAF at Middleton St George on 3 June 1944.

Shelson was operating radar coverage on the night of 12 June 1944. He departed Middleton St George, 'Goosepool', at 22.10 in VR-Z, twenty-six minutes later than P/O Mynarski in VR-A. The No. 419 Squadron RAF raid was on the railyards at Cambrai. Shelson returned; Mynarski did not. As described in chapter 1, P/O Mynarski won the VC for his heroic actions that night and, unfortunately, entered the history books posthumously. Shelson completed his tour and had started a second one when the war ended.

He took his Northampton war bride, Margaret Barrett, back to Canada, where he was honourably discharged. Shelson was not alone. Nearly 45,000 war brides and 21,000 children came to Canada, some during the war, most after. The Canadian forces had spent a very long time in Britain during the war and relationships were inevitable. It was a brave woman that left Britain for the unknown of Canada. The locations could vary from cities such as Montreal, where one had to learn a new language, to the isolated wilderness of northern British Columbia, where one had to learn a new way of life.

One of the famous aircraft in No. 419 Squadron RCAF was VR-X, nicknamed *X-Terminator* because of its nose art. It was the thirty-third Lancaster built in Canada at the Victory Aircraft assembly line in Malton, Ontario. Arriving in Britain in April 1944, it was assigned to No. 419 Squadron RCAF; it was coded VR-X and replaced the original VR-X, which had been lost on a railyard raid at Louvain on 12/13 May 1944. Coincidentally, Shelson was on the same raid in VR-V. *X-Terminator* was almost Shelson's personal aircraft for June 1944 as he completed eleven trips in it. At 05.20 on 7 June 1944 Shelson returned with the aircraft from a diversion, and by that night it had become the first Canadian-built aircraft to shoot down an enemy aircraft.

On the night of 7/8 June, VR-X was on a raid to the railway junction at Acheres, France, when it was attacked by an enemy fighter. The rear gunner, Sgt Mann, and mid-upper gunner, Sgt Burton, managed to shoot down the attacking Ju 88. Both gunners received the DFM for their 'displayed notable determination' to destroy the enemy aircraft. The aircraft claimed a second enemy fighter, an Fw 190, on 28/29 July 1944 during a raid on Hamburg. It flew its last raid on 25 April 1945 to Wangerooge, a Frisian island, completing eighty-four operations, more than any other Canadian-built Lancaster.

VR-X returned to Canada in June 1945 and reached its final destination at Pearce, just east of Fort Macleod, Alberta. It was finally 'struck off strength' in May 1948 and broken up for scrap. In retrospect, perhaps this aircraft should have been the Lancaster kept in the National Collection.

By chance, the author discovered that his cousin Flt Sgt John Plenderleith served on the Lancaster. It all started for John at the airfield in Stobo Castle, Scotland, where the City of Edinburgh No. 603 Squadron RAF would come to practice. John lived in Stobo and the sight of aircraft flying around motivated him to join the RAF on 12 July 1943. Posted to No. 4 Radio Signals School at RAF Madley, Herefordshire, and then to Avro Ansons at RAF Mona, Wales, John then went on the Vickers Wellington OTU at RAF Husbands Bosworth, Leicestershire, and then to the Lancaster HCU at RAF North Luffenham, Rutland, before being assigned to No. 626 Squadron RAF at RAF Wickenby, Lincolnshire.

The station picket post issued the crew blankets and they proceeded to their billet to find it occupied. Returning to the post, the clerk said, 'Oh, have they not cleared it out yet? They didn't come back.' John thought at the time that 'this was a fine beginning to things'. The war was now coming to an end, and John took part in Operation Manna during April 1945, operating Lancaster UM-A2. This was dropping sacks of food into drop zones in Holland. In May 2015, John and his son Brian went to Holland to celebrate the food drop's seventieth anniversary. John turned ninety on 5 May 2015.

Air Gunner

Flt Sgt Art C. Sewel was born in Highgate, a suburb of London, England. At the outbreak of war Sewel contributed to the war effort by building wooden mock-up models of the Miles Magister aircraft to serve as decoys on false air fields. In the air cadets at Reading, Sewel volunteered for the RAF as soon as he turned eighteen. He completed basic training in Blackpool and was assigned 'somewhere in the Cotswold area for radio operator training'. Sewel just 'could not get [his] Morse Code speed up to the required eighteen words per minute so was transferred to flying gunnery school'.

The gunner's position was a cold and lonely one. The mid-upper and rear guns were outside the heated fuselage. In fact, for better visibility the rear gun had no centre panel in front of the gunner. It was only in the later years of the war that the gunner had an electrically heated suit. The initial gunners suffered from frostbite and hypothermia due to the extreme cold temperatures at cruising altitude. 'You daren't touch anything [with your bare hand], it would take your skin off,' remembered Sewel. The only connection with the rest of the crew was through the intercom (internal communication system).

Sewel recalled that 'condensation due the extremely cold temperatures was a big problem until they finally installed muzzle caps'. Generally, the gunners did not fire their guns at night until positively under attack by an enemy fighter, to avoid the tracers giving their position away. The guns were extremely noisy, with the casings going overboard. The soft leather helmet was not very good at protecting hearing.

Sewel learnt to 'oil, clean and strip the Browning .303 machine guns. The guns were too heavy for us to get in and out so that was the armourer's job. They put the ammunition in ducts that ran along the side of the aircraft and under my feet. I took my training in Wellingtons at No. 27 OTU Lichfield, Staffordshire which had the same turret as the Lanc. We actually used [gun] cameras to fire at drogues pulled by another aircraft.' Sewel mentioned that late in 1944 he took training on the Automatic Gun-Laying Turret (AGLT), which was a radar-based system to allow a target to be tracked and fired on in total darkness, the target's range being accurately computed as well as allowing for lead and bullet drop. The system was referred to by the codename 'Village Inn'.

Sewel's logbook shows he graduated from No. 12 Air Gunnery School at Bishops Court, Downpatrick, Northern Ireland, on 2 October 1943. Subsequently he was posted to No. 1481 Gunnery Flight, Ingham, Lincolnshire, which was part of No. 3 Bomber Air Gunnery School. During April 1944 he was on the Handley Page Halifax, and by May was at the Lancaster Finishing School at Hemswell, Lincolnshire. Crewed up with an Australian pilot, P/O G. P. Finemore, the crew comprised four Australians (pilot, navigator, wireless operator and mid-upper gunner) and three Englishmen (tail gunner, flight engineer and bomb aimer). They were stationed with No. 460 Squadron RAAF at Binbrook, Lincolnshire. Sewel was young at nineteen and the pilot, Finemore, was old at twenty-nine!

Sewel's first operational trip was just after the D-Day landings on 12 June 1944, to Gelsenkirchen in the northern part of the Ruhr area. When asked about his first operational trip he said, 'It was a bit scary. You had to concentrate on what you were doing. We weren't afraid. [You were] so involved with what you were doing it took all the fear out of you. The last thing you saw [as a tail gunner] was the White Cliffs of Dover – just wondering if you would be back or not.' The tide of the war was changing.

Says Sewel: 'Most of our targets were railway junctions [to prevent movement of supplies to the front lines], airports and manufacturing centres.' In support of the advancing armies, raid names such as Rheims, Ligescourt, Vierzon, Oisement, Dijon and Tours appear in his logbook. Of one such occasion Sewel said, 'On one bombing run we were flying over the target with our bomb doors open when we received a call to abort the attack. Our troops had advanced further than expected and we would have been bombing our own troops!'

Sewel commented on the fact that the Lancaster was one of the few bomber aircraft able to perform violent evasive manoeuvres due to its strength of construction. The rear gunner was responsible for communicating evasive manoeuvre direction to the pilot in event of a fighter attack from behind. Over Abbeville 'our aircraft got caught in the blue master searchlight. The other searchlights quickly locked on to us and during the escape manoeuvre the pilot had great difficulty pulling out of the steep dive and he [the pilot] used the trim to help him, putting the aircraft into a loop before recovering the aircraft to level flight.' The violent tactic had jammed a 500 lb bomb in its rack, which fell on to the bomb doors and was only discovered after landing. Sewel later discovered, to his chagrin, that the manoeuvre had jammed the belt feed for his guns. That had been over enemy territory. Lucky. The target that night, 22 June 1944, was Reims, which the crew continued on to bomb.

Sewel recounted the action: 'Flak hitting the aircraft gave a zinging noise as the pieces hit the fuselage. Our survival was probably due to keeping our eyes open, working as a crew, following the briefing instructions, and a bit of luck and skill. I knew every aircraft by silhouette, British and German, and I think that is what got me through the interview process and tour.' Sewel's tour-completing thirtieth raid was on 23 October 1944 to Essen – he in fact did thirty-two trips in total. Sewel then worked in Flying Control until the end of the war.

I brought Art Sewel up to see Bill Pearson and the two had a good chat over lunch. I listened with interest as the nonagenarians recounted their experiences of the Second World War and the Lancaster. When we were leaving, Pearson said, 'You seem like a nice young chap, Art; why don't you come back and share my 100th birthday party!' That is indicative of the indomitable spirit of the young men who made the Lanc so successful.

The Night Operation (Op)

The Lancaster became the night owl of the RAF bomber force due to the unavailability of long-range fighter escorts as the goals moved deeper into Germany. To cut losses, the decision was made to have bomber streams of all aircraft types – in very large numbers on occasion – attack targets at night and leave before sunrise. It also had a psychological effect on the German population, with disturbed sleep patterns affecting work production.

The crews were always under nervous tension during pre-flight preparation, between notification of the raid and the actual departure. Once underway, the anxiety sometimes disappeared temporarily only to return as the target neared. The tension was always present and each crew member dealt with it in his own way, some better than others. The mess and local pub were the scene of many hijinks as crews let off steam to cope with the situation. The station's daily routine also continued, which was not conducive to proper rest after a long night airborne. Even training trips were subject to attack from marauding enemy aircraft looking for easy targets over the English countryside. The stations themselves were subject to attack from both fighter and bomber aircraft.

Pre-Departure

A fairly typical day started with a flight roll call, and the crew were advised of the results of the previous night raid and whether another operation was scheduled for that night. Group HQ would send the Op message to the intelligence section, who decoded it and sent the information to all the relevant sections. The station would be locked down to prevent any inadvertent leak of the Op information. Another Op would mean that the whole station became very active. This included the cooks, administrative staff, mechanics, armourers, fuel-truck drivers, photo section, electronics personnel and all the support staff, including the very important meteorologist.

The crew would inspect their aircraft at the dispersal point with the ground crew and take it for a test flight if necessary. The briefing would be held several hours before the first departure to allow for fuelling, arming the guns and loading the bombs required. The Ruhr Valley, a trip of under five hours, would allow less fuel load and a large bomb load. A longer trip deep into Germany or Italy would require a larger fuel load and a reduction in bomb load. A full fuel load would give an approximate range of 2,500 miles with 7,000 lbs bomb load.

Clear weather was critical over the target area until the advent of H2S, although Gee and Oboe were of great assistance in locating the target. To help with the DR navigation, an aircraft would be dispatched on the initial route to check the weather and especially the winds. The weather at home base upon return was a major concern. After surviving the flak and fighter activity, the single Lancaster pilot had to face the English weather to land. Landing aids were primitive during the 1940s, and unfortunately fog and low cloud were prevalent during a large portion of the year, not surprising as England is an island nation. The factories were operating at full capacity and contributed to an industrial haze, further restricting visibility. Extra fuel was carried to allow diversion, if needed, to other stations experiencing better weather.

Ground Preparation

Many reported that the crew briefing was the start of the heightening tension and the uneasy feeling in the stomach. The crew gathered, quite often more than one squadron, and were briefed on the upcoming target; weather conditions; expected flak and fighter activity; type of bomb load and delivery instructions; number, type and source of other aircraft; and were given secret signals by specialists introduced by the station commander. The navigator then plotted the course with the expected winds to give the flight duration, fuel used and estimated time of arrival at the target.

The pilot next met with all the crew to go over the details of the entire raid so everyone was aware of how and when things were going to happen. Everything was planned down to the smallest detail, but planning and reality sometimes were quite different. In spite of all this planning, it was not unusual for aircrew to go through 'lucky' rituals and carry lucky charms, for many crew realised it would be luck that got them through the mission.

A final meal of the obligatory egg and cup of tea and the crew was on its way to the locker room to pick up their parachutes, Mae Wests and, for the gunners, their kapok 'Taylor Suits'. The crew reached their aircraft at the dispersal point many ways, walking if close during the dry summer months, cycling using the station bikes or driving in an enclosed van. A final check with the ground crew, a last cigarette and nervous pee and all climbed aboard to make their scheduled take-off time. The uneasy feeling had now turned to a knot in the stomach. There was no getting around this feeling, and it seemed to make no difference to the crews whether they were on their first or second tour.

Everyone proceeded to their crew station. Those in the front had to scale the main wing spars, which constricted the passageway and caused a few skinned shins. That was nothing compared to the gymnastics that the rear gunner went through in his warm suit to get over the tailplane spar and close the rear doors of the turret. The emergency parachute was hung inside the fuselage.

Pre-starting check was followed by communication with the ground crew, clearance to start and the engine-start sequence of the four engines. Engine warm-up, magneto check and propeller check were followed by the take-off throttle position to check boost and rpm. The airfield was a noisy place until all had departed.

Taxi/Take-Off

Chocks away, and the Lanc would join the stream of aircraft on the perimeter track to the runway, steered with the outer engines as much as possible. The visibility over the nose was restricted for the pilot as he taxied in the dark. Pre-take-off check followed by a green light from control, and the throttles were advanced to take-off position. Leading the throttles on one side corrected the swing until the flying controls took effect. The flight engineer held the throttles in the take-off position during the take-off run. Forward pressure on the control column raised the tail up and, when approaching 100 mph, back pressure was applied to the control wheel and the heavily laden aircraft lifted off.

Safely airborne, the brakes were applied to stop the main wheels spinning, undercarriage retracted and above 500 feet the flaps were retracted in five-degree increments. Beyond the 125 mph safety speed, the throttles were brought back to the climb setting. A climb was initiated at 165 mph until cruising altitude was reached, where the speed was increased to 200 mph. The radio operator picked up the latest winds from the 'windfinders', the first aircraft in the stream, and passed them forward to the navigator for course adjustments.

En Route

Although the aircraft were in a bomber stream, sometimes of up to 1,000 aircraft, each navigator plotted his own course to the target. Constant outside vigilance by the rest of the crew allowed the navigator and wireless operator to attend to their respective duties inside the aircraft. The vigilance was not only for attacking fighters; collision avoidance with other bombers was no less important. Lights-out work within the bomber stream was extremely hazardous.

Constant updating of position by visual assistance from the bomb aimer – and, in later years, Gee and Oboe – kept the aircraft on course. The gunners and bomb aimer would inform the pilot of any fighter activity directed at them and call out the evasive action. The corkscrew evasive manoeuvre was standard for the Lancaster as it could take the stresses of twisting, turning and diving.

Target

Amid the confusion of flak guns, searchlights, fighter aircraft, clouds and other bombers, the crew had to remain calm and steady to deliver the bombs on target. Approaching the target, the bomb aimer confirmed his bomb-dropping settings and opened the bomb-bay doors. Following the Pathfinder's coloured flares and TI markers, he released the bombs on target. 'Bomb doors open – master switch on – bombs fused and selected,' followed by, 'Bombs gone – bomb doors closed – let's get the hell out of here.' The pilot adjusted trim for the weight reduction, closed the bomb doors and maintained course for the important photoflash to confirm their drop accuracy. That completed, the navigator passed a new course to the pilot for clearing the target area.

Return

The crew were on their way home after having survived the gruelling task of bombing the target. The unspoken question in the aircraft was, would they survive the journey home to celebrate? The odds were not in their favour, for now the journey home could involve wounded crew, damaged aircraft (perhaps even loss of one or more engines), uncertain navigation due to equipment damage, loss of hydraulic pressure, deteriorating weather conditions, loss of communication and the ever-present danger of flak and night fighters. Cloud and darkness were the crew's best friends at this time. Time passed agonisingly slowly as the aircraft headed for England with the unforgiving sea ahead of them. Fatigue could not be allowed to interfere with the constant visual scan in the night sky for enemies. Now was the time for the aircraft captain to show his leadership qualities and keep the crew sharp and alert.

Landing
All being well, they would return to their own station, be correctly identified and join the traffic pattern for the landing. Eyes were still vigilant because it was not unknown for an enemy fighter to join the circuit and shoot the bomber down when it was most vulnerable, during the landing approach. Initially flying at 140 mph, the flaps were lowered in increments, speed reduced and the undercarriage selected down to cross the 'hedge' and runway threshold at 95 mph for touchdown at 90 mph. The flight engineer brought back the throttles to idle as the pilot applied the brakes. Now light, the aircraft could be taxied on the two inner engines to the hardstand.

Interrogation
The whole crew would be debriefed by the intelligence officer over a cup of tea as to flak, fighter activity and anything witnessed on the raid. These were the last things anybody wanted to talk about when minds were set on getting out of flying gear, maybe grabbing some breakfast and getting some sleep. 'A fried egg for breakfast; that was part of our payment,' chuckled tail gunner Sewel.

Log Book
A flight-time logbook was kept individually by all the crew and submitted to the flight commander monthly for examination. Very often notations were added to the basic entries such as 'lost one engine, rear gunner injured, crash landed', which turned the book into a living history account of wartime experiences. It is an invaluable source for the archivist, historian and author.

There were five general outcomes to a wartime operational trip:

The crew survived the trip and returned safely to home base

The crew survived the trip and returned with injuries or casualties

The crew were shot down, all/some survived; survivors became POWs held in a 'Stalag Luft' or escaped and returned home, casualties were buried locally and some were later reinterred at a War Cemetery or Commonwealth War Graves Commission site

The crew went missing, their fate – some, not all – discovered after the war ended

Unfortunately, abandoning a Lancaster was not an easy proposition. The hatch in the bomb aimer's floor was quite small and presented a real challenge when in bulky flying gear, and if the aircraft was not flying straight and level any exit was highly unlikely. The alternative was to clamber over two main wing spars to the rear-entrance door. The rear gunner could leave his turret, by turning it hydraulically or by using, as Art Sewel called it, 'a manually geared dead man's handle' so that he could fall out backwards. Alternatively, he had to clamber over the tailplane spar to reach the main entrance door. Ergonomically the Lancaster was not well designed for egress, but this was the 1940s and such things had low priority in wartime.

Decorations

Decorations were awarded for gallantry and meritorious service during the war and are a visible reminder to us of the valour and sacrifice made by the wearer. Unfortunately some are awarded posthumously, as in the Victoria Crosses awarded to P/O Mynarski and S/L Bazalgette, to whom the Canadian Warplane Heritage Museum and the Bomber Command Museum of Canada dedicated their Lancasters respectively.

The Victoria Cross (VC) is awarded to a soldier, sailor or airman, regardless of rank, of the British or Commonwealth forces, for most conspicuous bravery, some daring or pre-eminent act of valour or self-sacrifice, or extreme devotion to duty in the presence of the enemy. It is the rarest of all British decorations and takes precedence over all other orders and medals.

As recounted in chapter 1, P/O A. C. Mynarski VC RCAF was a Lancaster mid-upper gunner detailed to attack Cambrai on the night of 12 June 1944. The aircraft caught fire after a night-fighter attack; both port engines had failed and the fuselage was an inferno. Ordered to abandon the aircraft, Mynarski attempted to help the trapped tail gunner before jumping himself. His attempts were unsuccessful, but before exiting the aircraft he turned and saluted his doomed friend. By now Mynarski's clothing and parachute were alight, and he fell, a burning human torch, to die shortly after from his terrible injuries. His friend, P/O Brophy, miraculously survived the uncontrolled crash to tell the story.

S/L I.W. Bazalgette VC RCAF was the master bomber marking the V-1 flying bomb site at Trossy St Maximin on 4 August 1944 when his aircraft was hit by enemy fire. Despite his aircraft being on fire, he pressed on to mark and bomb the target and tried to bring his aircraft and crew back to safety. With only one engine running, he ordered his crew to abandon the burning aircraft. Two wounded crew were unable to leave the aircraft, so Bazalgette attempted to land his stricken aircraft in a field. He avoided a French village by supreme effort, but the aircraft exploded on touchdown and all three were lost.

Lancaster aircrew awarded the Victoria Cross

A/S/Ldr J. D. Nettleton	44	Lancaster Mk I, R5508 'B'	17 4 42	Augsburg
A/W/Cdr G. P. Gibson	617	Lancaster Mk III ED932 'G'	16 5 43	Dams raid
A/F/Lt W. Reid	61	Lancaster Mk III LM360'O'	3 11 43	Dusseldorf
P/O A. C. Mynarski	419	Lancaster Mk X KB726 'A'	12 6 44	Cambrai
A/S/Ldr I. W. Bazalgette	635P	Lancaster Mk III ND811 'T'	4 8 44	Trossy St Maximin
A/S/Ldr R. A. M. Palmer	109P	Lancaster Mk III PB371 'V'	23 12 44	Cologne
F/Sgt G. Thompson	9	Lancaster Mk I PD377	1 1 45	Dortmund
Capt E. Swales	582P	Lancaster Mk III PB538 'M'	23 2 45	Pforzheim
Sgt N. C. Jackson	106	Lancaster Mk I ME669 'O'	26 4 45	Schweinfurt
W/Cdr G. L. Cheshire	617	Lancaster	various	various

The Distinguished Service Order (DSO) is awarded to commissioned officers in the British armed forces who have been mentioned in dispatches for bravery, for meritorious or distinguished service in the field or before the enemy. The Distinguished Flying Cross (DFC) is awarded to British officers and warrant officers for acts of valour, courage or devotion to duty performed while flying in active operations against the enemy. After 1942 it was awarded to Commonwealth forces too. The Air Force Cross (AFC) is awarded for acts of valour, courage or devotion to duty while flying, though not in active operations against the enemy. The Conspicuous Gallantry Medal (CGM) is awarded to NCOs who had shown exceptional gallantry in the face of the enemy. It is second only to the VC and is the NCO equivalent to the DSO. The Distinguished Flying Medal (DFM) is awarded to aircrew NCOs for acts of valour, courage and devotion to duty while flying in active operations against the enemy. The Air Force Medal (AFM) is awarded to NCOs for acts of valour, courage or devotion to duty whilst flying, though not in active operations against the enemy.

If you have ever wondered why some veterans have more than one decoration on their clasp, the answer is that campaign stars and medals were awarded for different campaigns. A typical Bomber Command set of decorations could have the Air Crew Europe Star, the France and Germany Star and the War Medal, among others.

It is only recently that a Bomber Command clasp has been presented to those aircrew involved in the bombing campaign – far too late to honour our veterans who survived the carnage and gave their youth for our freedom. Wing Commander A. J. Wright DFC RAF (Ret) stated in a letter to the *Oxford Times*, 5 March 2015, that 'many eligible BC veterans or their next of kin did not apply because they considered the clasp to be an insult to the memory of the fallen [55,805 aircrew and 1,400 ground staff] ... we believe that a campaign medal would have been more honourable and worthy award than the clasp awarded to aircrew only'.

Nuremberg

30 March 1944 will be forever etched in Bomber Command history, the day when an incorrect weather forecast (clear and cloudy at the wrong places and times) combined with plain bad luck. Debate has continued seventy years on as to why so many night fighters were gathered to attack the bomber stream. Was it espionage? A deliberate leak to avoid compromising double agents? Perhaps just coincidence, bad planning or, once again, plain bad luck?

The raid happened at the end of the Battle of Berlin, which had not fared well during the winter of 1943/4. Berlin was beyond the range of the ground-based navigation aids and the long transit across enemy territory exposed the bombers to the night fighters for long periods of time. In spite of new measures and countermeasures, the Bomber Command losses per raid continued to slowly increase. German night-fighter radars, upward-pointing guns and coordinating radar tactics were beginning to gain the upper hand, for now.

The choice of the target and route were predicated on a weather forecast – certainly not an exact science in 1944, and still a challenge in 2015. The long, straight route to Nuremberg from the German border was forecast to be cloudy with the target area clear on arrival. The weather forecast was tragically wrong. The bombers left to rendezvous over the North Sea. The first aircraft from No. 101 RAF Squadron left from Ludford Magna, Lincolnshire, at 21.35. After crashes and turn-backs, the bomber armada numbered 726 heavy bombers. An hour later, the leading aircraft reached the start of the long leg over Germany to the final turning point at Nuremberg.

Revised winds were calculated and passed back by the leaders – a very important task as the end of the route would be flown using established winds to calculate the DR headings. This information should have kept the sixty-eight-mile stream on the planned route. The wind changed and the stream drifted over one of the night fighter holding beacons. There were 300 fighters held at two beacons which were, as it happens, on each side of the bomber stream. The cloud cover disappeared early and the contrails of the bombers in the cold, clear air were clearly seen in the moonlight.

Just after midnight the losses started, and in one hour the stream lost fifty-nine Lancasters and Halifaxes; that equates to a crew and aircraft shot down every minute. The inaccurate winds caused the main stream to be north and east of where it should be. Once again the weather played a deciding factor in the disaster: the target was cloud-covered. The PFF could not accurately find Nuremberg, and only some of the PFF aircraft had cloud markers. The plan was to drop 3,000 tons of high explosives and 70,000 incendiaries. Some 15 per cent of the bombers targeted Schweinfurt in error; more damage was done there than in Nuremberg.

Ninety-six (the number varies depending on criteria) bombers failed to return, and 545 airmen died; that was more airmen than in the entire Battle of Britain. Operation Grayling was definitively the worst night in the history of Bomber Command.

The Lucky: F/L Bill Pearson, the bomb aimer mentioned above, was on the Nuremberg raid. Flying with No. 8 Squadron RAF from Bardney, Lincolnshire, he departed at 22.08 in Avro Lancaster LL785 WS-F. Pearson said to me, 'That aircraft was our lady luck. It was the first paddle prop Lanc on the Squadron and we could get two to three thousand [feet] more altitude than the main force.' The pilot was F/L Pearce, and the trip took eight hours. Pearson told me 'there was fierce fighter activity'.

The Unlucky: P/O Chris Panton, flight engineer, was on the same Nuremberg raid. Flying with No. 433 (Porcupine) Squadron RCAF from Skipton-on-Swale, North Yorkshire, he departed at 21.49 in Handley Page Halifax HX272 BM-N. The pilot was P/O Nielsen. Panton was shot down by a Luftwaffe Bf 110G over Friessen, near Bamberg, Germany. HX272 was the seventy-sixth aircraft shot down on this disastrous night. Three crew, including the pilot, abandoned the exploding aircraft and survived; Chris Panton did not. He was hours away from completing his thirtieth and final trip to finish his tour.

The Lincoln Aviation Heritage Centre was created in memory of P/O Chris Panton. See chapter 6 for further details.

Left: Bomber Command veterans Art Sewel and William Pearson, photographed in early 2015. (Gordon Wilson)

Opposite top left: The air and ground crew of Flt Lt Pearson's Lancaster. (William Pearson)

Opposite bottom left: Flt Lt William (Bill) Pearson, bomb aimer, 1943. (William Pearson)

Opposite far right: Flt Sgt Art Sewel, air gunner, 1943. (Art Sewel)

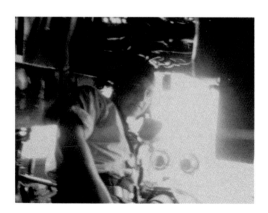

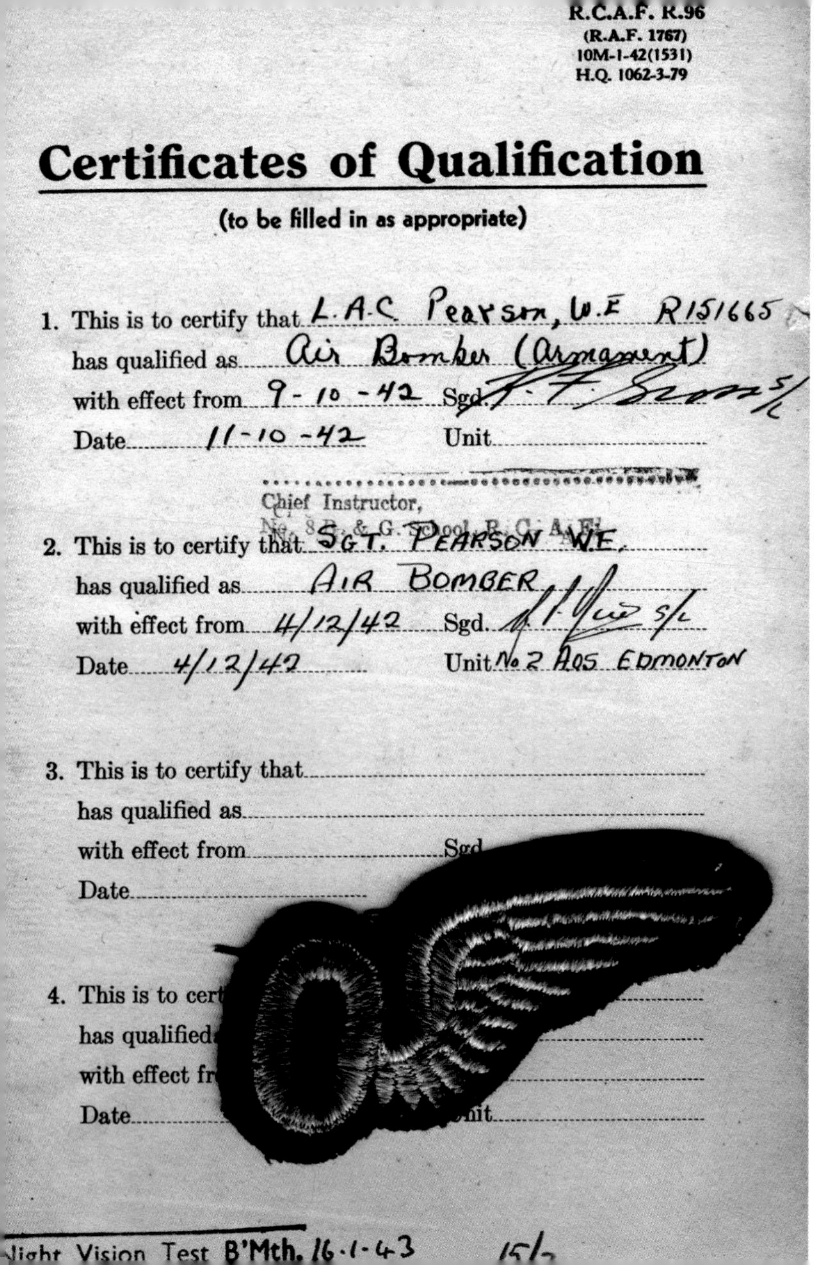

Certificates of Qualification

(to be filled in as appropriate)

1. This is to certify that L.A.C Pearson, W.E R151665
   has qualified as Air Bomber (Armament)
   with effect from 9-10-42 Sgd. F.F. Broms S/L
   Date 11-10-42 Unit

   Chief Instructor,
   No. 8 B. & G. School R.C.A.F.

2. This is to certify that SGT. PEARSON W.E.
   has qualified as AIR BOMBER
   with effect from 4/12/42 Sgd. S/L
   Date 4/12/42 Unit No 2 A.O.S EDMONTON

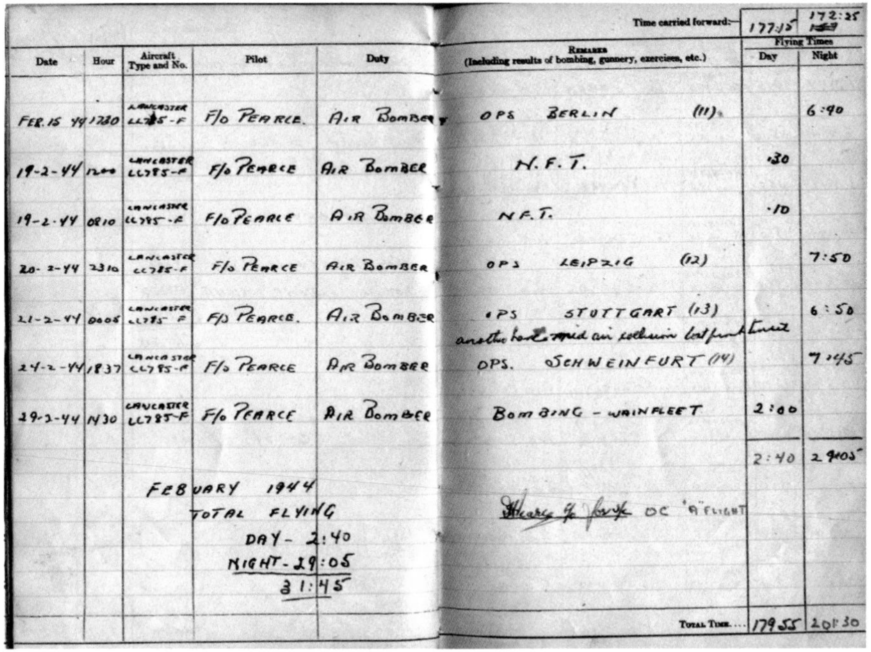

3. This is to certify that
   has qualified as
   with effect from Sgd
   Date

4. This is to cert
   has qualified
   with effect fr
   Date

Night Vision Test B'Mth. 16.1.43 15/2

Above and next seven pages: Flt Lt W. (Bill) E. Pearson's logbook. (Gordon Wilson)

Left: Flt Lt W. (Bill) E. Pearson's certificate of qualification and aircrew badge. (Gordon Wilson)

83 Sqdn (P.F.F.)   RAF CONINGSBY

Time carried forward:- | 239.05 | 332.2

Date	Hour	Aircraft Type and No.	Pilot	Duty	Remarks (Including results of bombing, gunnery, exercises, etc.)	Day	Night
Aug 21	11.20	Lancaster T	P/o Duncan	Air Bomber	Local Flying	.50	
21	22.30	Lancaster -K	P/o Duncan	Air Bomber	Cross Country + Y Runs		3.20
23	15.35	Lancaster T	P/o Duncan	Air Bomber	Cross Country + Y Runs	1.95	
24	11.15	Lancaster T	P/o Duncan	Air Bomber	High Level Bombing S.A.B.S 37ˣ	2.25	
25	13.00	Lancaster Q	P/o Duncan	Air Bomber	Y Runs	1.55	
25	21.00	Lancaster S	P/o Duncan	Air Bomber	OPS - DARMSTADT (36)		7.5
27	11.45	Lancaster H	P/o Duncan	Air Bomber	Y Runs	1.25	
27	18.00	Lancaster T	P/o Duncan	Air Bomber	S.A.B.S + Y Runs	3.30	
28	16.00	Lancaster N	P/o Duncan	Air Bomber	Y Runs + Gee Bombing	1.55	
29	11.40	Lancaster W	P/o Duncan	Air Bomber	Acceptance Test + Y Runs	2.50	
29	18.00?	Lancaster C	S/Ldr. Sparks	Air Bomber	OPS - KOENIGSBERG (37)		6.0
					SHOT DOWN. P.O.W. STALAG LUFT I		

Date	Hour	Aircraft Type and No.	Pilot	Duty	Remarks (Including results of bombing, gunnery, exercises, etc.)	Time carried forward:— 211:30	312·4
						Flying Times	
						Day	Night
15·7·44	2214	LANCASTER NE 167 /Y	W/C PORTER	AIR BOMBER	OPS — NEVERS RAILWAY YARDS (31) CONTROLLER		7·15
17·7·44	1025	LANCASTER NE 167/Y	W/C PORTER	AIR BOMBER	BOMBING & W/T CONTROL	2·10.	
18·7·44	1047	LANCASTER NE 167/Y	W/C PORTER	AIR BOMBER	AIR TO SEA FIRING & AIRTEST	·55	
20·7·44	1019	LANCASTER NE 167/Y	W/C PORTER	AIR BOMBER	CIRCUITS + LANDINGS	·55	
20·7·44	2312	LANCASTER N.E 167/Y	W/C. PORTER	AIR BOMBER	OPS COURTRAI (RAIL YARDS) CONTROLLER (32)		3·25
24·7·44	10·15	LANCASTER NE 167/Y	W/C PORTER	AIR BOMBER	N.F.T	·35	
25·7·44	1000	LANCASTER NE 167/Y	W/C PORTER	AIR BOMBER	LOCAL FLYING	1·50	
26·7·44	1013	LANCASTER NE 167/Y	W/C PORTER	AIR BOMBER	H.L. BOMBING	1·40	
26·7·44	1420	LANCASTER NE 167/Y	W/C PORTER	AIR BOMBER	OBSERVING T.I. TEST 18000	1·50	
26·7·44	2115	LANCASTER NE 167/Y	W/C PORTER	AIR BOMBER	OPS — GIVORS — BADEN RAIL JUNCTION — ELECTRIC STORMS CONTROLLER. (33)		9·00
					TOTAL TIME....	221·25	332·2

1654 CONVERSION

Date	Hour	Aircraft Type and No.	Pilot	Duty
		COMMENCED	1654 CON. UNIT AUG.	
15-8-43	0958	LANCASTER R 5690	P/O McGREGOR	AIR BOMBER
17-8-43	0900	LANCASTER W 4260	P/O McGREGOR	AIR BOMBER
17-8-43	1200	LANCASTER W 4260	SGT KIRKUP	AIR BOMBER
17-8-43		LANCASTER W 4902	P/O McGREGOR	AIR BOMBER
19-8-43	1655	LANCASTER W 4260	P/O McGREGOR	AIR BOMBER
19-8-43	1730	LANCASTER W 4260	SGT. KIRKUP	AIR BOMBER
23-8-43	1645	LANCASTER W 4296	P/O SUTTER	AIR BOMBER
24-8-43	1425	LANCASTER R 5733	SGT KIRKUP	AIR BOMBER
24-8-43	2200	LANCASTER R 5733	P/O SUTTER	AIR BOMBER
24-8-43	0219	LANCASTER R 5733	SGT. KIRKUP	AIR BOMBER
25-8-43	0124	LANCASTER W 4260	SGT KIRKUP	AIR BOMBER
26-8-43	1430	LANCASTER W 4260	P/O SUTTER	AIR BOMBER
30-8-43	13.35	LANCASTER E 3704	SGT. KIRKUP	" "
3-9-43	1620	LANCASTER R 5759	P/O GUMBLEY.	" "
8-9-43	1512	LANCASTER ED.826	F/S. KIRKUP	" "
1-10-43	1600	W	W/O PLAYER	" "
1-10-43	1615	LANCASTER	F/S KIRKUP	" "
1-10-43	2025	R 5747	W/O PLAYER	" "

			Time carried forward:—	137:50	62:50

UNIT. WIGSLEY

REMARKS (Including results of bombing, gunnery, exercises, etc.)	Day	Night
9 1943.		
FAMILIARIZATION	2:35	
FAMILIARIZATION	1:25	
CIRCUIT & LANDING	:10	
CHECK CIRCUIT	:10	
CHECK CIRCUIT	:30	
LOCAL FLYING	1:35	
THREE ENGINED LANDINGS	1:00	
CROSS COUNTRY - BOMBING - FIRING YDS—230ˣ (2)	3:50	
NIGHT FAMILIARIZATION		2:20
CIRCUITS & LANDINGS		:30
CROSS COUNTRY-BOMBING ERROR 279ˣ (4)		2:50
COMBAT MANOEUVRE.	1:05	
CROSS COUNTRY-BOMBING. 269ˣ (4) ERROR	5:15	
FIGHTER AFFIL.	:55	
" "	1:05	
LOCAL FLYING	:10	
" "	:25	
SEARCHLIGHT AFFIL ERROR 227ˣ (2)		3:25
(ALL BOMBING CONVERTED TO 10,000' G.K.)		
TOTAL TIME....	158:00	71:55
	310	

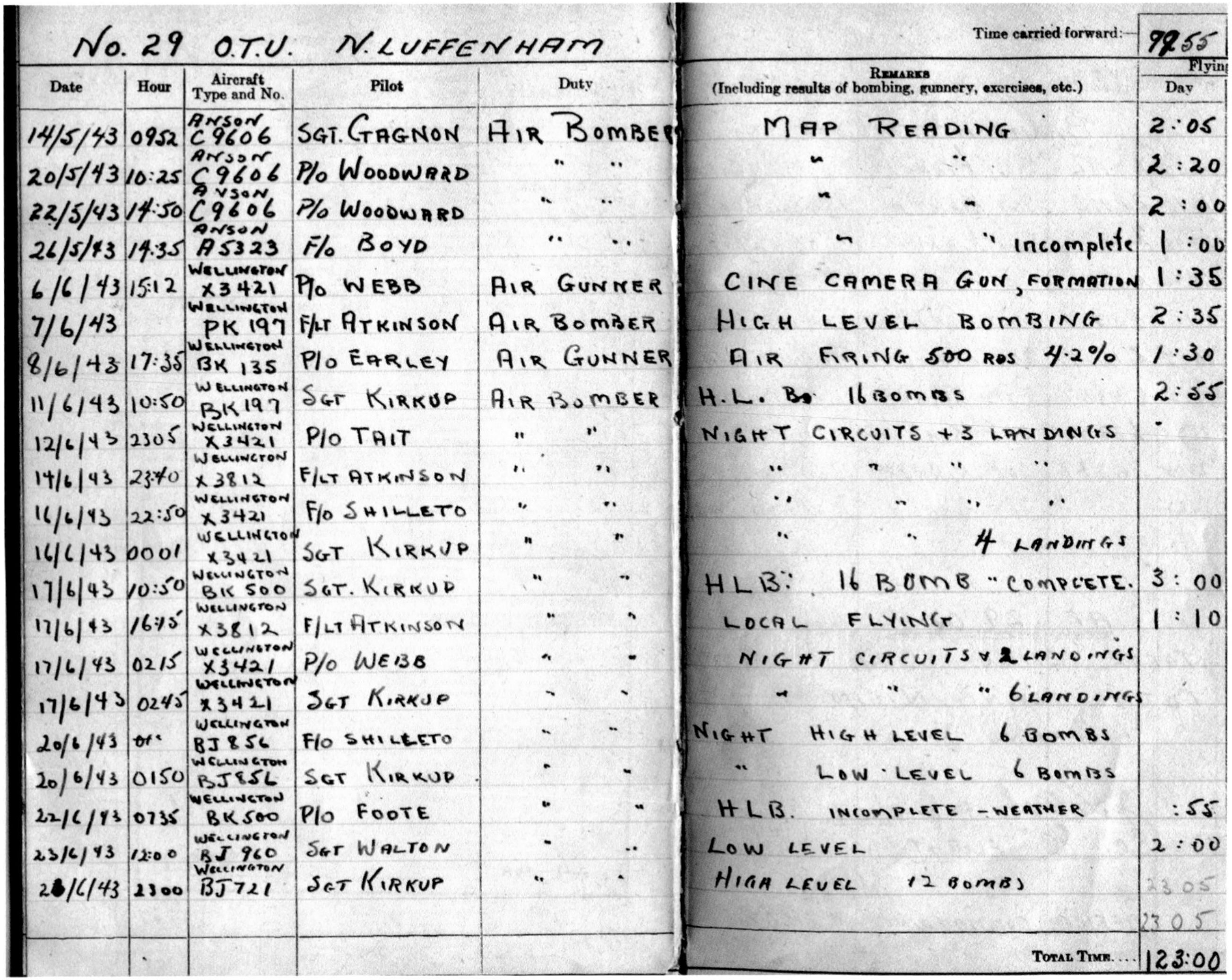

No. 29 O.T.U.   N. LUFFENHAM

Time carried forward: — **99 55**

Date	Hour	Aircraft Type and No.	Pilot	Duty	REMARKS (Including results of bombing, gunnery, exercises, etc.)	Flying Day
14/5/43	0952	ANSON C 9606	SGT. GAGNON	AIR BOMBER	MAP READING	2:05
20/5/43	10:25	ANSON C 9606	P/O WOODWARD	" "	" "	2:20
22/5/43	14:50	ANSON C 9606	P/O WOODWARD	" "	" "	2:00
26/5/43	14:35	ANSON A 5323	F/O BOYD	" "	" " incomplete	1:00
6/6/43	15:12	WELLINGTON X 3421	P/O WEBB	AIR GUNNER	CINE CAMERA GUN, FORMATION	1:35
7/6/43		WELLINGTON PK 197	F/LT ATKINSON	AIR BOMBER	HIGH LEVEL BOMBING	2:35
8/6/43	17:35	WELLINGTON BK 135	P/O EARLEY	AIR GUNNER	AIR FIRING 500 ROS 4.2%	1:30
11/6/43	10:50	WELLINGTON BK 197	SGT KIRKUP	AIR BOMBER	H.L. B. 16 BOMBS	2:55
12/6/43	2305	WELLINGTON X 3421	P/O TAIT	" "	NIGHT CIRCUITS + 3 LANDINGS	-
14/6/43	2340	WELLINGTON X 3812	F/LT ATKINSON	" "	" " " "	
16/6/43	22:50	WELLINGTON X 3421	F/O SHILLETO	" "	" " " "	
16/6/43	0001	WELLINGTON X 3421	SGT KIRKUP	" "	" " 4 LANDINGS	
17/6/43	10:50	WELLINGTON BK 500	SGT. KIRKUP	" "	HLB: 16 BOMB "COMPLETE.	3:00
17/6/43	1645	WELLINGTON X 3812	F/LT ATKINSON	" "	LOCAL FLYING	1:10
17/6/43	0215	WELLINGTON X 3421	P/O WEBB	" "	NIGHT CIRCUITS & 2 LANDINGS	
17/6/43	0245	WELLINGTON X 3421	SGT KIRKUP	" "	" " " 6 LANDINGS	
20/6/43	01	WELLINGTON BJ 856	F/O SHILLETO	" "	NIGHT HIGH LEVEL 6 BOMBS	
20/6/43	0150	WELLINGTON BJ 856	SGT KIRKUP	" "	" LOW LEVEL 6 BOMBS	
22/6/43	0735	WELLINGTON BK 500	P/O FOOTE	" "	HLB. INCOMPLETE – WEATHER	:55
23/6/43	12:00	WELLINGTON BJ 960	SGT WALTON	" "	LOW LEVEL	2:00
28/6/43	2300	WELLINGTON BJ 721	SGT KIRKUP	" "	HIGH LEVEL 12 BOMBS	23 05
						23 0 5

TOTAL TIME.... **123:00**

83 Sqdn.   (P.F.F.)   RAF CONINGSBY

Time carried forward:— 234.05 | 332.2

Date	Hour	Aircraft Type and No.	Pilot	Duty	REMARKS (Including results of bombing, gunnery, exercises, etc.)	Day	Night
Aug 21	11.20	Lancaster T	P/o Duncan	Air Bomber	Local Flying	.50	
21	22.30	Lancaster K	P/o Duncan	Air Bomber	Cross Country + Y Runs		3.20
23	15.35	Lancaster T	P/o Duncan	Air Bomber	Cross Country + Y Runs	1.95	
24	11.15	Lancaster T	P/o Duncan	Air Bomber	High Level Bombing SABS 37ᵡ	2.25	
25	13.00	Lancaster Q	P/o Duncan	Air Bomber	Y Runs	1.55	
25	21.00	Lancaster S	P/o Duncan	Air Bomber	OPS — DARMSTADT (36)		7.5
27	11.45	Lancaster H	P/o Duncan	Air Bomber	Y Runs	1.25	
27	18.00	Lancaster T	P/o Duncan	Air Bomber	S.A.B.S + Y Runs	3.30	
28	16.00	Lancaster N	P/o Duncan	Air Bomber	Y Runs + Gee Bombing	1.55	
29	11.40	Lancaster W	P/o Duncan	Air Bomber	Acceptance Test + Y Runs	2.50	
29	18.00?	Lancaster C	S/Ldr. Sparks	Air Bomber	OPS — KOENIGSBERG (37)		6:0
					SHOT DOWN. P.O.W. STALAG LUFT I		

9 SQUADRON.

| | | | | | | Time carried forward:— | 169:40 | 95:40 |
| Date | Hour | Aircraft Type and No. | Pilot | Duty | Remarks (Including results of bombing, gunnery, exercises, etc.) | | Flying Times | |
							Day	Night
2-12-43	1635	LANCASTER JA690	F/O PEARCE.	AIR BOMBER	OPS. BERLIN. (2)		—	7:15
3/4-12-43	0029	LANCASTER JA 690	F/O PEARCE.	AIR BOMBER	OPS. LEIPZIG (3) —MID UPPER WOUNDED, A/c DAMAGED			6:45
4-12-43	1745	LANCASTER DV396	F/O COMANS	AIR BOMBER.	WOODBRIDGE — BASE.		:40	
12-12-43	1240	LANCASTER J5010	F/O PEARCE.	AIR BOMBER	BOMBING D.N.CO.		:45	
12-12-43	1730	LANCASTER W4964	F/O PEARCE.	AIR BOMBER.	BOMBING & CIRCUITS			1:40
13-12-43	1835	LANCASTER W4964	F/O PEARCE.	AIR BOMBER.	CIRCUITS & BUMPS.			1:15
27-12-43	1150	LANCASTER LL745	F/O PEARCE.	AIR. BOMBER	AIR TEST - LANDED WITTERING		1:15	
27-12-43	1540	LANCASTER LL745	F/O PEARCE.	AIR BOMBER	WITTERING — BASE		:30	
29-12-43	1050	LANCASTER W5010L	F/O PEARCE.	" "	N.F.T. LEVELING BOMBSIGHT		1:00	
29-12-43	1700	LANCASTER W5010L	F/O PEARCE	AIR BOMBER	OPS. BERLIN (4)			7:15
				DECEMBER.	TOTAL FLYING DAY. — 4:10 TOTAL FLYING NTE. — 24:10 28:20 OC "A" FLIGHT.		4:10	24:10
								TOTAL TIME....

Date	Hour	Aircraft Type and No.	Pilot	Duty	Remarks (including results of bombing, gunnery, exercises, etc.)	Day	Night
					Time carried forward:—	185·15	243·35
26.3.43	1945	Lancaster F ...285	F/Lt Pearce	Air Bomber	OPS. ESSEN (20)		5:10
29.3.44	Noon	Lancaster C ...883	F/L Pearce	Air Bomber	Bombing - DNCO	1:20	
30.3.44	2205	Lancaster F ...285	F/Lt Pearce	Air Bomber	OPS NUREMBURG (21)		8:20
					MARCH 1944		
					TOTAL DAY --- 6:50		
					TOTAL NITE---- 55:35		
					TOTAL FLYING 62:25		
					OC "A" FLIGHT.		
					TOTAL TIME..	186·45	256·55

Right: Flt Lt W. (Bill) E. Pearson's service certificate. (Gordon Wilson)

Royal Canadian Air Force

This is to certify that

Flight Lieutenant   Canada J.21611
RANK   NUMBER

PEARSON, William Edgar
NAME IN FULL

Served on Active Service with the

Royal Canadian Air Force

From 28 January, 1942 and was retired under K.R. (Air) 151(1) (: having completed a term of voluntary service during an emergency and transferred to the RCAF (Reserve), General Section, Class "E"

on the 21st day of Sept 19 45

Particulars of Active Service

Service in theatre of war YES   Number of occasions wounded None

Orders, Decorations, Medals, Mentions and commendations awarded during above service

Air Bomber Badge, Canadian Volunteer Service Medal and clasp, Operational Wing + BAR

Sept 21st, 1945
DATE

FOR CHIEF OF AIR STAFF

Night Vision Test B'Mch.   15/22 (F/Lt)
13-4-44 R Holt Sgt

R.C.A.F. Form R.95
(R.A.F. 414)
20M-12-41 (1371)
H.Q. 1062-3-78

CERTIFICATES OF QUALIFICATION AS FIRST PILOT

Name BLACKMAN, W. J.   Rank LAC Sgt F/Sgt WO2 P/o WO1 P/o F/L

(i)   Certified that the above named has qualified as a first pilot (day)
on Lancaster I & III landplanes w.e.f. 13/2/45
Unit 1668 H.C.U.   Signature [signature] W/CDR C.I.
Date 15/2/45   Rank

(ii) Certified that the above named has qualified as a first pilot (night)
on _____ landplanes w.e.f. _____
Unit _____   Signature _____
Date _____   Rank _____

(iii) Certified that the above named has qualified as a first pilot (day)
on _____ seaplanes w.e.f. _____
Unit _____   Signature _____
Date _____   Rank _____

(iv) Certified that the above named has qualified as a first pilot (night)
on _____ seaplanes w.e.f. _____
Unit _____   Signature _____
Date _____   Rank _____

Above: Bomber Command veteran Bill Blackman. (Gordon Wilson)

Left: Flying Officer Bill Blackman's flying qualifications. (Gordon Wilson)

F/O Bill Blackman's
medals, awarded for
service over Europe.
(Gordon Wilson)

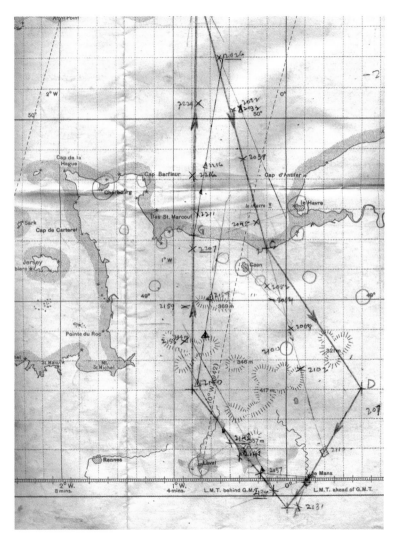

Above: Flt Lt David Walsh in the cockpit of Lancaster B.X KB843 NA-D *Dolly*. The nose art, comprising thirty-two bombs, is noteworthy as the average Lancaster only had a life expectancy of forty hours. (Anthony Walsh)

Left: Map of route to Le Mans for the Bomber Command raid on rail system targets, 7/8 March 1944. (Jerry Vernon)

Right: Flt Lt David Walsh in the cockpit of KB843. (Anthony Walsh)

Left: The crew of KB843 NA-D. Left to right are Mid-Upper Gunner Flt Sgt Ted Taylor, Tail Gunner Flt Sgt Norman Pratt, Bomb Aimer F/O Arnold Lindsay, Pilot Flt Lt David Walsh, Navigator F/O Officer Jim Harris, Flight Engineer Sgt Jim Hope and Wireless Operator P/O Ken Daley. (Anthony Walsh)

Left: Flt Sgt Ken W. Brown, pilot of No. 617 Squadron Lancaster ED918/G AJ-F, meets King George VI at RAF Scampton on 27 May 1943. (Via Gordon Wilson)

Opposite: Sgt John H. Crammond and crew. (Kevin Scotland)

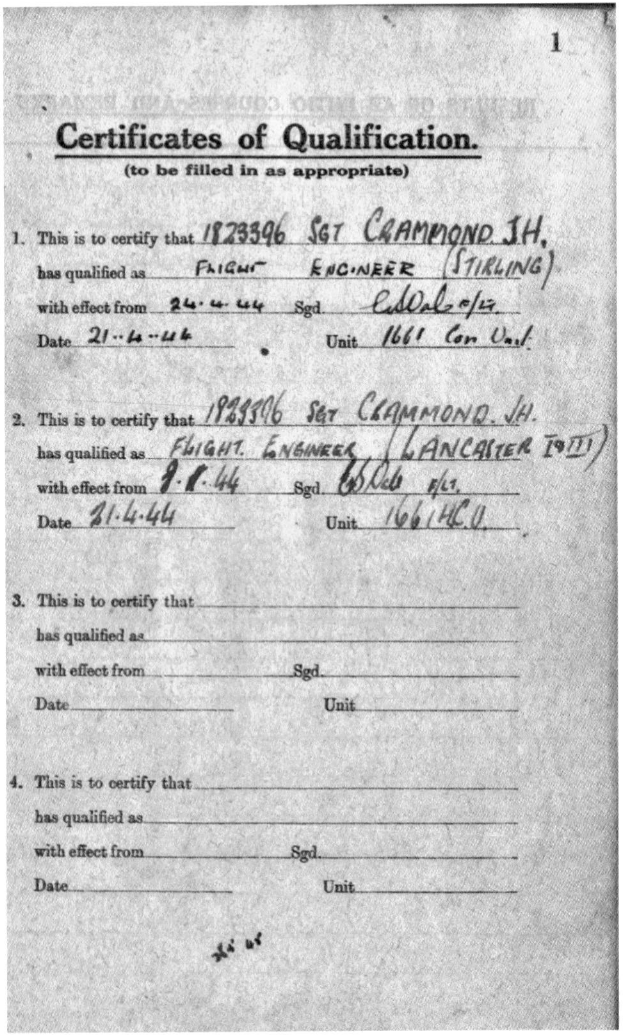

1

Certificates of Qualification.
(to be filled in as appropriate)

1. This is to certify that 1823396 SGT CRAMMOND. JH.
   has qualified as FLIGHT ENGINEER (STIRLING)
   with effect from 24·4·44   Sgd. C.S.Dale O/C
   Date 21··4··44   Unit 1661 Con Unit.

2. This is to certify that 1823396 SGT CRAMMOND. JH.
   has qualified as FLIGHT ENGINEER (LANCASTER I&III)
   with effect from 9·1·44   Sgd. C.S.Deb O/C
   Date 21·4·44   Unit 1661 H.C.U.

3. This is to certify that _____
   has qualified as _____
   with effect from _____ Sgd. _____
   Date _____   Unit _____

4. This is to certify that _____
   has qualified as _____
   with effect from _____ Sgd. _____
   Date _____   Unit _____

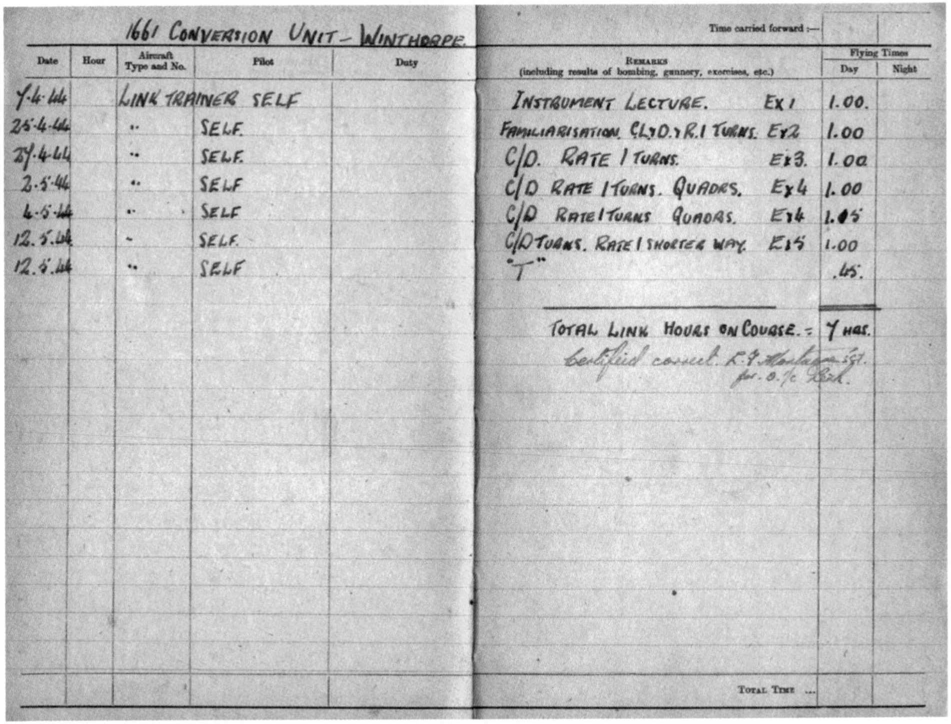

1661 CONVERSION UNIT - WINTHORPE

Time carried forward :—

Date	Hour	Aircraft Type and No.	Pilot	Duty	REMARKS (including results of bombing, gunnery, exercises, etc.)		Flying Times Day	Night
7·4·44		LINK TRAINER	SELF		INSTRUMENT LECTURE.	Ex1	1.00.	
25·4·44		"	SELF.		FAMILIARISATION. C/D. & R.1 TURNS	Ex2	1.00	
27·4·44		"	SELF.		C/D. RATE 1 TURNS.	Ex3.	1.00	
2·5·44		"	SELF		C/D RATE 1 TURNS. QUADRS.	Ex4	1.00	
4·5·44		"	SELF		C/D RATE 1 TURNS. QUADRS.	Ex14	1.05	
12·5·44		"	SELF.		C/D TURNS. RATE 1 SHORTER WAY.	Ex15	1.00	
12·5·44		"	SELF		"T"		.45	

TOTAL LINK HOURS ON COURSE. = 7 HRS.

certified correct. E.I. Maslan Sgt.
for O/C Ldr.

TOTAL TIME ...

Above and next six pages: Sgt John H. Crammond logbook. (Kevin Scotland)

Left: Sgt John H. Crammond's certificate of qualification. (Kevin Scotland)

1661 Conversion Unit. — Winthorpe.

Time carried forward: 3 HRS

Hour	Aircraft Type and No.	Pilot	Duty	Remarks (including results of bombing, gunnery, exercises, etc.)	Day	Night
	Stirling 'G'	F/S Burness	2nd Engineer	Ex.1	2.25	
	'O'	F/S Burness	2nd Engineer	Ex2	.40	
	'Y'	F/S Burness	2nd Engineer	Ex2	1.55	
	'W'	F/S Burness	Engineer	Ex2	2.15	
	'W'	F/O Slade	Engineer	Ex3	1.10	
	'W'	F/S Burness	Engineer	Ex4	2.25	
	'U'	F/S Slade	Engineer	Ex5	2.25	
	'O'	F/S Slade	Engineer	From Swinderby	.30	
	'N'	F/S Slade	Engineer	Ex6 H.L.B.	3.35	
	'S'	F/S Slade	Engineer	Ex10	3.05	
	'A'	F/S Burness	Engineer	Ex11	1.25	
	'A'	F/S Burness	Engineer	Ex7		1.10
	'N'	F/S Burness	Engineer	Ex8		2.00
	'N'	F/S Slade	Engineer	Ex9		1.30
	'H'	F/S Slade	Engineer	Ex18 H.L.B.		2.25
	'U'	F/S Slade	Engineer	Ex13		3.40
	'R'	F/S Burness	Engineer	Ex14		3.20
	'A'	F/S Slade	Engineer	Ex16		6.20

Total for 1661 Con. Unit Winthorpe
Day 23.40
Nite 20.25
Total 44.05
Date 15-5-44
Signed
O.C. "B" Flight

Total Time 23.40 20.25

No 5 L.F.S. Syreston — Lancaster Finishing School.

Time carried forward: 23.40 20.25

Date	Hour	Aircraft Type and No.	Pilot	Duty	Remarks (including results of bombing, gunnery, exercises, etc.)	Day	Night
24-5-44		Lancaster 'R'	F/Sgt. Slade	Engineer	Ex 17.2	2.20	
25-5-44		'T'	F/Sgt. Slade	Engineer	Ex 3	0.55	
26-5-44		'S'	F/Sgt. Slade	Engineer	Ex 7		2.00
28-5-44		'V'	F/Sgt. Slade	Engineer	Ex 4	3.10	3.50
28-5-44		'B'	F/Sgt Slade	Engineer	Ex 5		.50
26-5-44		'N'	F/Sgt. Slade	Engineer	Ex 2	1.05	
28-5-44		'B'	F/Sgt. Slade	Engineer	Ex 6		.25
6-6-44		'C'	F/Sgt. Slade	Engineer	Ex 7		2.55

Summary for Course. Type. Lancaster I & III
Unit 5 L.F.S.
Date 7-6-44
Signature
Total Day Hrs. 7.30
Total Night Hrs 6.10
Total at 5 L.F.S. 13.40
Grand Total Day 31.10
Night 26.40

Total Time 31:10 26.40

First logbook page

44 SQUADRON. DUNHOLME LODGE

Time carried forward :— 69.55 | 46.40

Date	Hour	Aircraft Type and No.	Pilot	Duty	Remarks (including results of bombing, gunnery, exercises, etc.)	Flying Times Day	Night
					"A" FLIGHT.		
			JULY. 1944.				
11.7.44		H	F/SGT SLADE	F/E	H2S X-COUNTRY. H.L.B.	2.45	
12.7.44		M.	F/SGT SLADE	F/E	H.L.B.	1.40	
12.7.44		H	F/SGT SLADE	F/E	OPERATIONS CULMONT CHALINDREY RAILWAYS		8.25
14.7.44		B	F/SGT SLADE	F/E	H.L.B.	1.05	
14.7.44		H	F/SGT SLADE	F/E	OPERATIONS — VILLNEUV-ST-GEORGE RAILWAYS		7.00
15.7.44		H	F/SGT SLADE	F/E.	AIR TEST	.15	
15.7.44		H	F/O SLADE	F/E	OPERATIONS — NEVERS RAILWAYS		7.20
18.7.44		H	F/O SLADE	F/E	OPERATIONS CAEN GERMAN ARMY. MUST HELPED OF WAR	3.30	
19.7.44		H	F/O SLADE	F/E	F/A	1.30	
19.7.44		H	F/O SLADE	F/E	OPERATIONS — LEUDESSEC ANT RAILWAYS SHUTTLE STOS	4.05	
20.7.44		4	F/O SLADE	F/E	OPERATIONS — COURTRAI FLYING BOMB SITE		3.45
31.7.44		H	F/O SLADE	F/E.	H2S.	1.05	
31.7.44		H	F/O SLADE	F/E	OPERATIONS — JOIGNY LAROCHE. RAILWAY YARDS	5.25	
					TOTAL DAY HOURS.	22.25	
					TOTAL TRAINING HRS.	6.50	
					OPS. (NIGHT.)		26.30
					GRAND TOTAL. DAY.	66.20	
					NIGHT.		73.10
			W/CMDR				
		o/c 44. SQUADRON.					
					O.C "A" FLIGHT.		

Total Time :— 6620 | 73 10

Second logbook page

44. SQUADN.   DUNHOLME LODGE

Time carried forward :— 6620

Date	Hour	Aircraft Type and No.	Pilot	Duty	Remarks (including results of bombing, gunnery, exercises, etc.)	Flying Times Day
					FLYING BOMB SITE	
1.8.44		Q	F/O SLADE	F/E	OPERATIONS — BRETEQUE.	3.2
2.8.44		H	F/O SLADE	F/E	OPERATIONS - TROSSY. V-1 LAUNCHING SITE	4.1
4.8.44		J	F/O SLADE	F/E.	F/A	.45
5.8.44		H	F/O SLADE	F/E	OPERATIONS - ST LEUDESSENT. V-1 V-2 STORAGE SITE	4.5
7.8.44		H	F/O SLADE	F/E	FORMATION	.55
7.8.44		H	F/O SLADE	F/E	OPERATIONS- SEQUEVILLE. TROOP CONCENTRATIONS	
18.8.44		E	F/O SLADE	F/E	LOCAL FLYING.	01.00
26.8.44		H	F/O SLADE	F/E	OPERATIONS — KONIGSBERG. (LANC & WYTON) SUPPLY PILOT IN LITHUANIA FOR RUSSIAN FRONT	
27.8.44		H	F/O SLADE	F/E	WYTON — BASE	0030
28.8.44		H	F/O SLADE	F/E	H2S.	.50
29.8.44		H	F/O SLADE	F/E	FORMATION.	1.00
29.8.44		H	F/O SLADE	F/E	OPERATIONS — KONIGSBERG. DOCK AREA AGAIN. LARGEST RAF RAID	
31.8.44		H	F/O SLADE	F/E	OPERATIONS— AUCHY- LES- HESDIN. V-2 ROCKET STORES	4.0
					OPERATIONAL TIME:- DAY. 16.30	
					NIGHT. 25.50	
					TRAINING TIME :- DAY:- 5.00	
					TOTAL TIME FOR AUGUST. :- 47.20	
					OC 'A' FLIGHT	
					W/C 44 SQDN	
		√ ONE OF THIS MOST SUCCESSFUL RAIDS OF THE WAR AND ALSO LONGEST				
	X	TO HAVE LANDED IN RUSSIA & REFUELLED ETC				

Total Time :—

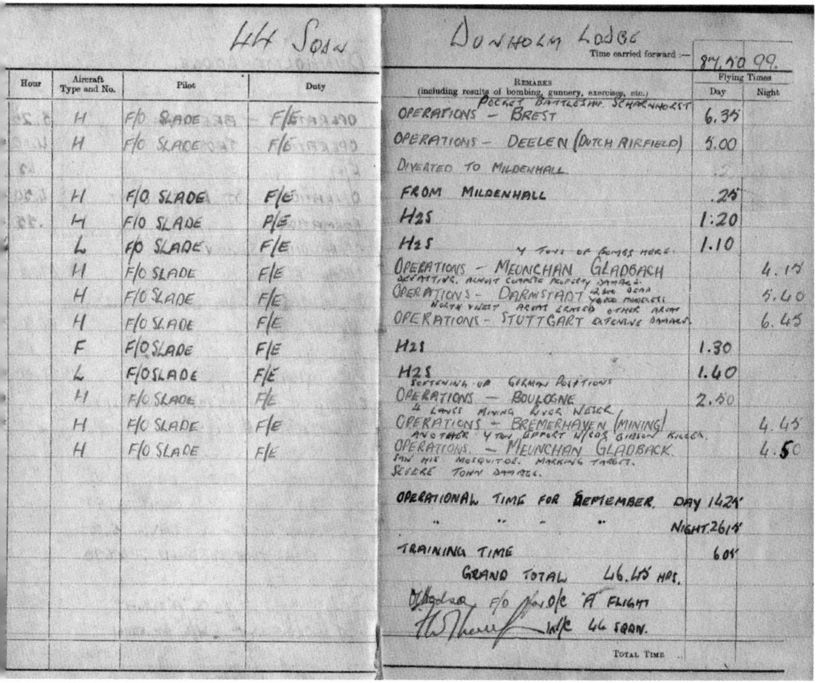

44 Sqdn — Dunholm Lodge

Time carried forward :— 84.50 99.

Hour	Aircraft Type and No.	Pilot	Duty	Remarks (including results of bombing, gunnery, exercises, etc.)	Day	Night
	H	F/O SLADE	F/E	Pocket Battleship Scharnhorst. OPERATIONS – BREST	6.35	
	H	F/O SLADE	F/E	OPERATIONS – DEELEN (DUTCH AIRFIELD)	5.00	
				DIVERTED TO MILDENHALL		
	H	F/O SLADE	F/E	FROM MILDENHALL	.25	
	H	F/O SLADE	F/E	H2S	1:20	
	L	F/O SLADE	F/E	H2S	1.10	
	H	F/O SLADE	F/E	4 tons of bombs here. OPERATIONS – MEUNCHAN GLADBACH		4.15
	H	F/O SLADE	F/E	OPERATIONS – DARMSTADT		5.40
	H	F/O SLADE	F/E	OPERATIONS – STUTTGART extensive damage		6.45
	F	F/O SLADE	F/E	H2S	1.30	
	L	F/O SLADE	F/E	H2S	1.40	
	H	F/O SLADE	F/E	Softening up German positions. OPERATIONS – BOULOGNE	2.50	
	H	F/O SLADE	F/E	OPERATIONS – BREMERHAVEN (MINING)		4.45
	H	F/O SLADE	F/E	OPERATIONS – MEUNCHAN GLADBACK. Saw his Mosquito marking target. Severe town damage.		4.50

OPERATIONAL TIME FOR SEPTEMBER DAY 14.25
" " " " NIGHT 26.15
TRAINING TIME 6.05
GRAND TOTAL 46.45 HRS.

F/O O/C 'A' FLIGHT
W/C 44 SQDN.

Total Time

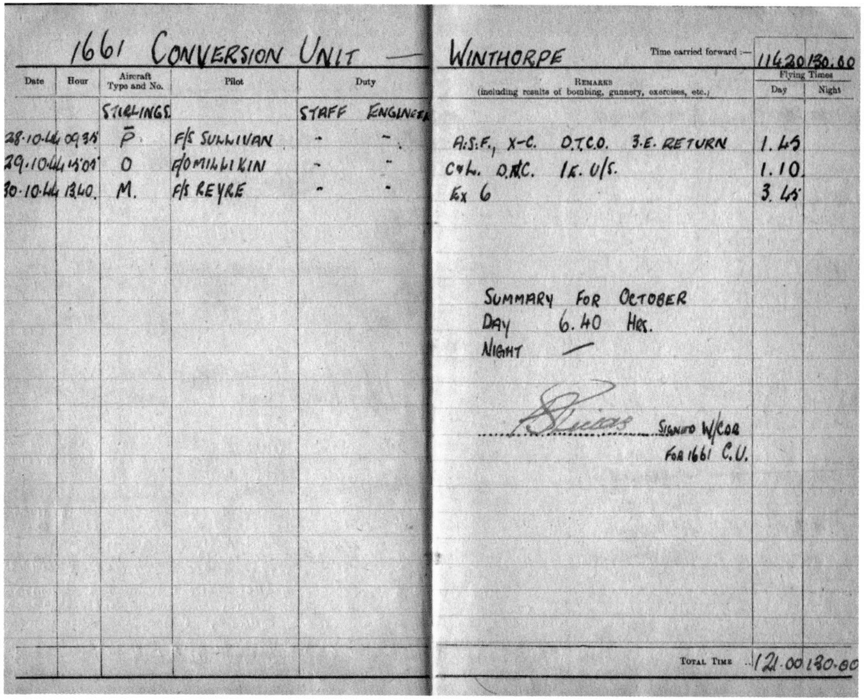

1661 CONVERSION UNIT — WINTHORPE

Time carried forward :— 114.20 130.00

Date	Hour	Aircraft Type and No.	Pilot	Duty	Remarks (including results of bombing, gunnery, exercises, etc.)	Day	Night
		STIRLINGS		STAFF ENGINEER			
28.10.44	09.35	P	F/S SULLIVAN	– –	A.S.F., X-C. O.T.C.O. 3.E. RETURN	1.45	
29.10.44	15.01	O	F/O MILLIKIN	– –	C+L. D.N.C. 1E. U/S.	1.10	
30.10.44	13.40	M.	F/S REYRE	– –	Ex 6	3.45	

SUMMARY FOR OCTOBER
DAY 6.40 HRS.
NIGHT —

SIGNED W/CDR
FOR 1661 C.U.

TOTAL TIME 121.00 130.00

Logbook pages — 1661 H.C.U. Heavy Conversion Unit, November 1944.

Date	Hour	Aircraft Type and No.	Pilots	Duty	Remarks (including results of bombing, gunnery, exercise, etc.)	Day	Night
					Time carried forward :—	121.00	130.00
2.11.44	1430	Stirling 'A'	F/O Milliken				
			F/O King	Staff Eng.	Ex 2 & 3 DNC.	1.45	
9.11.44	1800	G	F/O King	—	" 13	4.00	4.00
10.11.44	0100	L	F/O King	—	H.L.B.		2.00
11.11.44	1410	B	F/L Spriggs	—	Ex 2.	1.30	
			F/L Simons	—	Ex 10	4.00	
14.11.44	11.45	L	P/O Roper	—			
14.11.44	0840	O	F/O Browne				
			F/Sgt Donaldson				
			Sgt Hayes	—	Ex 1 (Double Detail)	2.30	
15.11.44	1805	V	F/O Browne				
			F/Sgt Standring				
			F/Sgt Berr	— —	Ex 1 (Double Detail)	1.45	
16.11.44	1120	B	P/O Cameron	— —	Ex 10 H.L.B. & R.S.F. Not carried out.	2.15	
18.11.44	1000	A	F/O Browne				
			F/Sgt Hayes		Ex 2.	1.45	
18.11.44	1800	E	F/O Browne				
			F/Sgt Standring	—	Ex 2	.45	
19.11.44	19.15	A	F/Lt Hancock				
			P/O Cameron	— —	Ex 8		1.45
21.11.44	11.40	M	F/Lt Spriggs				
			F/O Andrews	— —	Ex 2 & 3	Total Time 2.15/34.45	

Date	Hour	Aircraft Type and No.	Pilot	Duty	Remarks	Day
					Time carried forward :—	139.20
21.11.44		N.	P/O Walton	Staff Engineer	Ex 13 DNC.	

SUMMARY FOR NOVEMBER.

DAY 18.20
NIGHT 10.00.
TOTAL 28.20

Signed W/Cdr.

Total Time 138.20

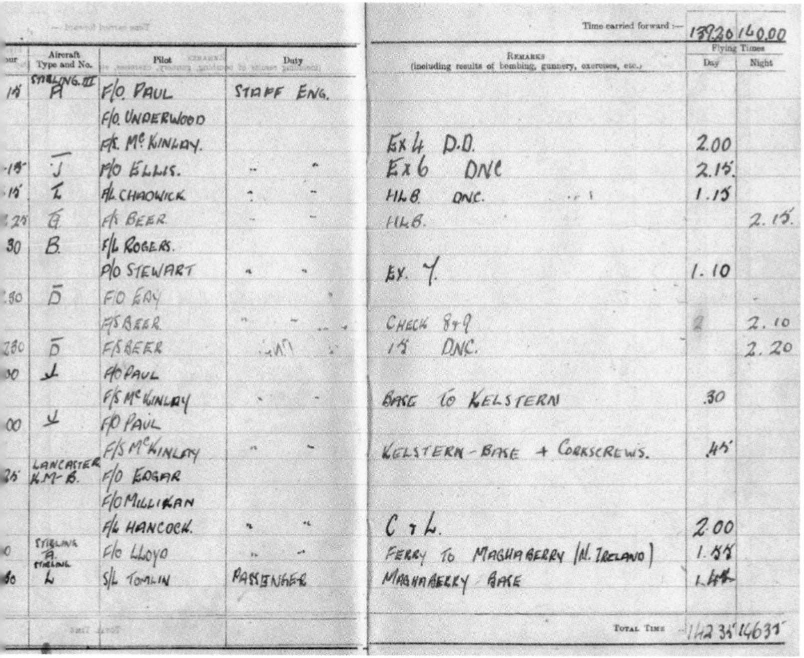

Left logbook page:

	Aircraft Type and No.	Pilot	Duty	Remarks (including results of bombing, gunnery, exercises, etc.)	Day	Night
				Time carried forward :—	13926	1600.00
.15	STIRLING III A	F/O PAUL F/O UNDERWOOD FL. McKINLEY.	STAFF ENG.			
.15	J	P/O ELLIS.	" "	Ex 4 D.D.	2.00	
.15	I	A/C CHADWICK	" "	Ex 6 DNC	2.15	
.25	G	F/S BEER		HLB. DNC.	1.15	
30	B	F/L ROGERS.		HLB.		2.15
		P/O STEWART	" "	Ex. 7.	1.10	
.30	D	F/O FRY	" "			
		F/S BEER	" "	CHECK 8 & 9		2.10
.30	D	F/S BEER		18 DNC.		2.20
.00	J	F/O PAUL				
		F/S McKINLEY	" "	BASE To KELSTERN	.30	
.00	J	F/O PAUL				
		F/S McKINLEY		KELSTERN- BASE + CORKSCREWS.	.45	
.25	LANCASTER K.M.B.	F/O EDGAR F/O MILLIGAN A/C HANCOCK	" "	C & L.	2.00	
.30	STIRLING A STIRLING	F/O LLOYD	" "	FERRY TO MAGHABERRY (N. IRELAND)	1.55	
.30	L	S/L TOMLIN	PASSENGER	MAGHABERRY BASE	1.44	
				Total Time	14235	14635

Right logbook page:

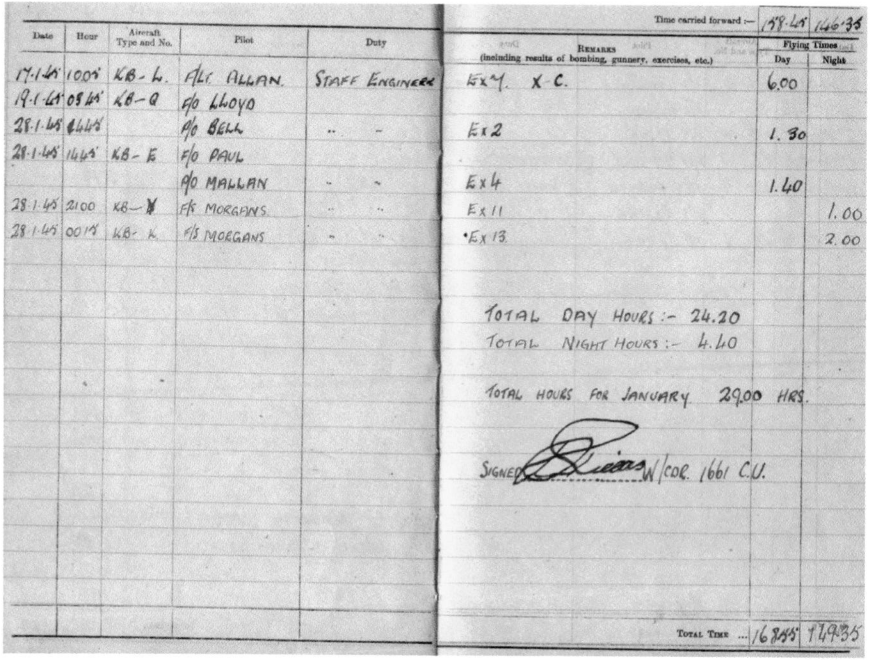

Date	Hour	Aircraft Type and No.	Pilot	Duty	Remarks (including results of bombing, gunnery, exercises, etc.)	Day	Night
					Time carried forward :—	158.45	146.35
17.1.45	1005	KB-L	FLT ALLAN	STAFF ENGINEER	Ex 4. X-C.	6.00	
19.1.45	0945	KB-Q	F/O LLOYD	" "			
28.1.45	1445		P/O BELL	" "	Ex 2	1.30	
28.1.45	1645	KB-E	F/O PAUL	" "	Ex 4	1.40	
			P/O MALLAN	" "			
28.1.45	2100	KB-	F/S MORGANS	" "	Ex 11		1.00
28.1.45	0015	KB-L	F/S MORGANS	" "	Ex 13		2.00
					TOTAL DAY HOURS :- 24.20		
					TOTAL NIGHT HOURS :- 4.40		
					TOTAL HOURS FOR JANUARY 29.00 HRS.		
					SIGNED W/CDR. 1661 C.U.		
					Total Time	16845	149.35

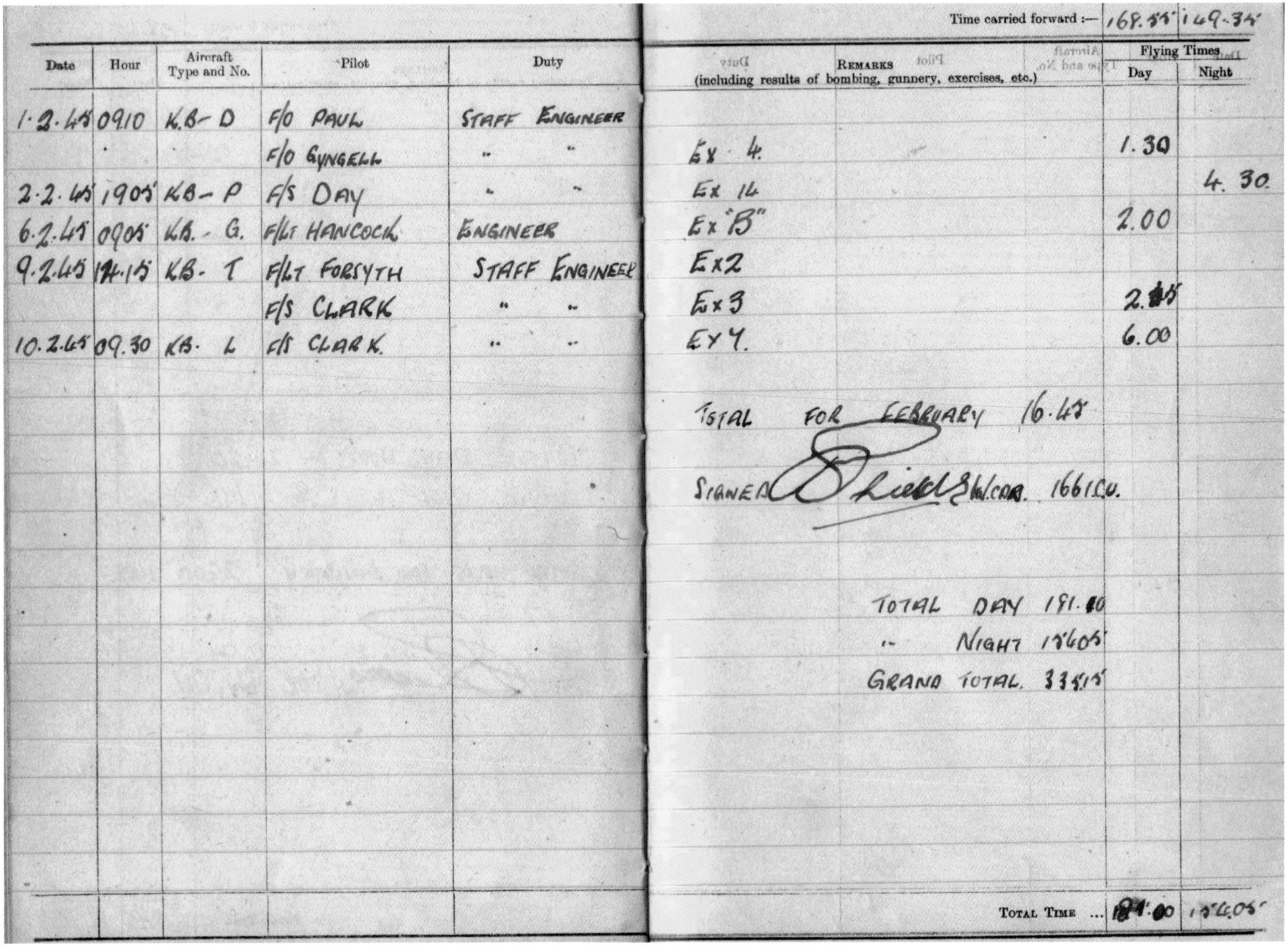

Time carried forward :— 168.55 149.34

Date	Hour	Aircraft Type and No.	Pilot	Duty	Duty (including results of bombing, gunnery, exercises, etc.)	Remarks	Aircraft Type and No.	Flying Times Day	Night
1.2.45	0910	KB-D	F/O PAUL	STAFF ENGINEER					
			F/O GYNGELL	" "	Ex 4.			1.30	
2.2.45	1905	KB-P	F/S DAY	" "	Ex 14				4.30
6.2.45	0905	KB-G	F/LT HANCOCK	ENGINEER	Ex "B"			2.00	
9.2.45	14.15	KB-T	F/LT FORSYTH	STAFF ENGINEER	Ex 2				
			F/S CLARK	" "	Ex 3			2.15	
10.2.45	09.30	KB-L	F/S CLARK	" "	Ex 4.			6.00	

TOTAL FOR FEBRUARY 16.45

SIGNED .... W/CDR. 1661 C.U.

TOTAL DAY 191.40
" NIGHT 18605
GRAND TOTAL 33515

TOTAL TIME ... 191.00 154.05

Above: Sgt Art C. Sewel (middle). (Art Sewel)

Right: P/O Jack W. Shelson. (Ann Allen (*née* Shelson))

Above: Flt Sgt Joseph R. Laportre, rear gunner on No. 425 (Alouette) Squadron RCAF. Flt Sgt Laporte had previously bailed out of Halifax PN172 KW-G when it was hit by flak near Gosselies on the night of 15/16 March 1945. (Canadian Museum of Flight)

Left: The Victoria Cross: For Valour. The Victoria Cross (VC) is the highest military decoration awarded for valour to members of the armed forces of the UK and Commonwealth countries. (Via Martin Keen)

Above: Group Captain Leonard Cheshire VC, OM, DSO & Two Bars, DFC and Warrant Officer Norman Jackson at Buckingham Palace after they had both been invested with the Victoria Cross. (Via Martin Keen)

Right: Squadron Leader Ian Willoughby Bazalgette VC, DFC. (Via Martin Keen)

ETA's & TIMING.

Always split flight plan at English & Enemy coast.

Give ETA's for entering and leaving defended areas. (aids Gunners)

Give ETA's as being ahead of or behind ETA. schedule.

If off track and no good for or w/s give approx ETA of any defended area just off track –

Plotters & set ops ETA's must agree. (within 6 min)

3 min/hr allowed for evasive action etc –

60° method is the only method used to waste time. after 60° for 1/4 time. then 120° for 1/2 time then 60° for 1/4 time – this keeps you closer to track

Always check posn of any defended Areas before wasting time. and then a/c allowing for this

Dont ORBIT as you cut across the bomber stream.

Exceptions Orbit if you are too near △ and wont be able to get onto correct heading in time

Orbit at turning point near △ – not recommended

Waste time at the last safe opportunity.

Keep sufficient time in hand to allow for wind shifts etc –

Best place to waste time is over the sea. Alter waste time course just before crossing enemy coast to confuse enemy plotters – if over enemy territory waste time over open country – always keep 1 min in hand for bombing run – i.e. if TOT 0130 your last ETA should be 0129.

Always keep 3 min hour in hand to △

If late on △ ry to pilot as to whether you drop TI's provided bombing run is good.

Pathfinder Navigator P/O Donald Currie's notes. (Bomber Command Museum of Canada)

5

THE FLYING LANCASTERS

There are presently (May 2015) two organisations that have a flying Lancaster in their collection, the only two flying examples left in the world from the 7,374 built. In Britain there is the RAF Battle of Britain Memorial Flight (BBMF), and in Canada there is the Canadian Warplane Heritage Museum (CWHM). The two aircraft flew the same skies in the summer of 2014 when the CWHM Lancaster crossed the Atlantic to do a series of appearances, described in chapter 7, with the BBMF Lancaster.

Battle of Britain Memorial Flight

One man is credited with saving the historic Second World War aircraft and establishing a display flight in Britain for special occasions and air shows. His legacy continues today as the BBMF. His name was Wing Commander Peter D. Thompson DFC. Thompson joined the Royal Air Force Volunteer Reserve in January 1939 and was called to full-time service on the outbreak of war. He completed the Hawker Hurricane OTU and saw action with Nos 32 and 605 squadrons.

Thompson was among a group of pilots who flew Hurricanes off the aircraft carrier *Ark Royal* to land at Hal Far in the defence of Malta. Upon his return to England he was awarded the DFC. Subsequent service saw action in the Western Desert, Sicily and Italy. He returned to England and commanded No. 129 Squadron flying the North American Mustang. He remained in the RAF after the war, retiring in 1975 as a wing commander, but retaining the rank of group captain (G/C).

The height, and turning point, of the Battle of Britain was generally agreed to be 15 September 1940. The bombing campaign of the Luftwaffe was turned back by young men – very young men – as the last line of defence prior to invasion. Over 500 fighter aircrew lost their lives in the valiant effort to attack the bombers and escorting fighters and so gain the upper hand in the air battle. The origins of the BBMF started five years later, on 15 September 1945, with the first celebratory fly-past of the Battle of Britain over the City of London led by the famous G/C Douglas Bader DSO DFC in a Spitfire.

It became a traditional celebration led by the two fighters, Hurricane and Spitfire, but as the 1950s progressed it became harder and harder to find serviceable aircraft. The RAF had phased out the old fighters and the only Spitfires available were three civilian versions. It was felt that such an important time in Britain's history should be celebrated correctly, and fittingly, with fighter versions of the aircraft leading the fly-past.

This is where Thompson became involved with the BBMF story. He was station commander at Biggin Hill, Kent, during the 1950s. A Hawker Hurricane Mk IIc LF363 based at Biggin Hill had been restored and returned to the station in 1956. It should be mentioned that Biggin Hill always had its own large commemorative air show. Thompson had bigger visions than one remaining aircraft and pushed for a Battle of Britain flight. The RAF gave Thompson the authority to form a special flight, but said that no public funds could be used for fuel, maintenance or personnel to operate it – some authority!

He obtained the three previously mentioned Spitfires, the photo reconnaissance versions, and, amid great fanfare, press and television, flew them to Biggin Hill escorted by Hawker Hunters and Gloster Javelins – the old and the new. Thompson used the power of advertising to his advantage. At the 1957 royal tournament, which that year had a Malta exhibition, he ground taxied a Spitfire Mk XVI, associated in the public's mind with the defence of Malta, which received great acclaim. The particular aircraft, TE330, was refurbished and flew together with a Hurricane over Westminster Abbey on 15 September 1957 as part of the newly named Historic Aircraft Flight.

In 1958 Thompson was posted away, and that was not the only change, good or bad, that was in the flight's future. The flight had a name change to Battle of Britain Flight and moved to North Weald in Essex, followed by another move to Martlesham Heath in Suffolk. Donations of aircraft for display at RAF station gates, and of the Spitfire TE330 to the USAF Academy, thinned the ranks of available aircraft.

A series of incidents in 1959 ended the career of the Spitfire XVIs. They were originally preserved on gate display at Neatished, Norfolk, and Bentley Priory, Stanmore, headquarters of Fighter Command in the Second World War. It is believed that Spitfire SL574 was later removed from the pedestal at Bentley Priory, sold and replaced with a replica.

1961 saw another move to Horsham St Faith, Norfolk, followed by another move in 1963 to Coltishall, Norfolk. In these years the flight consisted of a Hurricane LF363 and a Spitfire PM631. The addition of Spitfire PS853 in 1964 signalled the changing fortunes of the flight, which had come dangerously close to not existing at all. Another Spitfire donation by Vickers-Armstrongs brought the strength up to four aircraft.

The flight was involved in the classic 1969 film *Battle of Britain*, and when completed a Spitfire Mk IIa, P7350, was donated to the flight. The flight changed its name to Battle of Britain Memorial Flight in 1969. November 1973 saw the transfer of a new, exciting and poignant aircraft to the BBMF – the Avro Lancaster PA474 from Waddington, Lincolnshire. By 1976 the flight was once again on the move, this time to Coningsby, Lincolnshire, where it remains today. Public tours were initiated in 1986 and continue to this day.

Restorations and donations continued to build the fleet of aircraft, Spitfires and Hurricanes, and in 1993 another new type was introduced to the BBMF – a Douglas Dakota III, ZA947. This aircraft was ideally suited to training crews on tailwheel aircraft prior to assignment on the Lancaster.

The BBMF recalls the past, links to the present by being visible to millions and inspires the youth to join the RAF of the future. Schedules and routes are created to get the highest number of appearances in the least amount of flying time, the idea being to keep operating costs low both in the amount of fuel used and the amount of flying hours going on the aircraft; engine overhauls are extremely expensive, so many considerations, such as using a reduced engine boost and lining up many appearances for the one flight, become very important. The normal display season is from late April to late September, with serious preparations beginning in March of each year after the winter maintenance program.

A selection of fly-pasts in recent years: 15 September 1990, fiftieth anniversary of Battle of Britain Day; 6 May 1995, sixtieth anniversary of VE Day; 19 August 1995, sixtieth anniversary of VJ Day (poppy drop); 9 April 2002, queen mother's funeral cortege as it moved down The Mall; 17 May 2003, sixtieth anniversary of the Dambusters Raid; 5 June 2004, sixtieth anniversary of D-Day landings (million-poppy drop); 6 June 2004, Normandy beaches in France; 17 June 2006, queen's eightieth birthday; 28 June 2012, RAF Bomber Command Memorial unveiled (poppy drop); August–September 2014, flights with Canadian Warplane Heritage

Museum's Lancaster.

The flight has been very successful over the years in maintaining aviation history and reminding the public of the role of the RAF in Britain's past. The BBMF is indeed a living museum to remember those who gave up everything to preserve Britain and a way of life. Approximately 135,000 aircrew served in Bomber Command during the Second World War; nearly 74,000 of them became casualties. Some were wounded or captured, but 55,573 were killed.

PA474

PA474's history began on 31 May 1945 at Hawarden, Flintshire, north Wales. The B.I Lancaster was built by Vickers-Armstrongs for the Tiger Force in the Far East to combat the Japanese. Two nuclear bombs, dropped on Hiroshima and Nagasaki in August 1945 by the USAAF, ended the war and the need for RAF bombers to proceed overseas. PA474 was redundant.

In August 1945, PA474 was flown to 38 Maintenance Unit (MU) in Llandow, south Wales, for storage. In 1946 it was converted to a Lancaster PR (photographic reconnaissance). This included modifications such as removal of the gun turrets and installation of a second pilot's position, a radar and two cameras in the floor of the rear fuselage. Once again it was returned to storage at Llandow. More time passed before it was assigned, in 1948, to No. 82 Squadron, which had reformed at Benson, south Oxfordshire. No 82 Squadron was initially assigned survey work in Nigeria, the Gold Coast, Sierra Leone and The Gambia. PA474 joined No. 82 Squadron after it had moved to Kenya. The squadron returned to Benson in 1952 and a year later was re-equipped with English Electric Canberra jets. The end of the 'piston era' was in sight, and PA474's active squadron service came to an end.

The aircraft was loaned to Flight Refuelling Ltd at Tarrant Rushton, Dorset, the developer of the 'probe-and-drogue' type of mid-air refuelling for drone research work. The company was founded by Sir Alan Cobham in the 1930s and exists today as Cobham PLC. Two years later it was obtained by the College of Aeronautics at Cranfield for further study and evaluation of aerofoil sections. The college evolved into a university, and along with its association with the United Kingdom Defence Academy it has become an important centre in applied research, development and design.

The long-term destination was thought to be the RAF Museum at Hendon, but in the meantime it went to No. 15 Maintenance Unit at Wroughton, Wiltshire, in 1964. In the summer of 1964 PA474 appeared in two major films: *The Guns of Navarone*, the story of an Allied commando team sent to destroy a seemingly impregnable fortress overlooking the Aegean Sea, and *Operation Crossbow*, the story of the Allied operations against the V-1 flying bomb and the V-2 rocket.

The autumn of 1964 saw the Lancaster on its way – still serviceable, so it flew there – to RAF Henlow, Bedfordshire, for final preparation and delivery to the planned RAF Museum. This is where the history of PA474 takes the strange and fortuitous twist that kicks off its new life, still flying in the twenty-first century. In 1965, Wing Commander M. A. D'arcy was the CO of No. 44 Squadron, by then flying another Avro product, the Vulcan. Aware of the squadron's history as the first squadron to be re-equipped with the Lancaster, he requested that PA474 be transferred to RAF Waddington, Lincolnshire, for restoration work with a view to later museum display.

The markings decided upon were KM-B and aircraft R5868. These were the markings of Squadron Leader John D. Nettleton VC, who led a low-level raid by six aircraft on Augsburg on 17 April 1942. He persevered against all odds. His formation lost four aircraft en route and one over the target, and with his rear guns out of action he bombed the diesel engine factory and piloted the only aircraft to return home, albeit one riddled with holes.

It took two years for PA474 to be approved for regular display flights as the restoration progressed with the addition of two gun turrets that had previously been removed. A move in 1973 to join the Battle of Britain Memorial Flight at Coltishall, Norfolk, and finally Coningsby, Lincolnshire, resulted in the addition of the mid-upper gun turret and the 'City of Lincoln' coat of arms being displayed.

Many colour schemes have been used over the years to commemorate certain special events or people. The photographers really appreciate the different markings, as they get a 'new' aircraft every so often. The year 1979 saw a change to AJ-G, No. 617 Squadron's ED932, the aircraft flown by Wing Commander Guy Gibson VC, DSO*, DFC* on the famous Dambusters Raid of 16/17 May 1943. In 1984 it was SR-D, a No. 101 Squadron aircraft. This squadron provided electronic countermeasures through ABC (Airborne Cigar) and Window. SR-D, ME592, based in Ludford Magna, Lincolnshire, crashed in Sweden after a raid on Stettin on 29/30 August 1944. The pilot, F/O Gordon Piprell RCAF, was twenty-two years old; the average age of the crew, and I repeat the average age, was twenty years young.

By 1988 it was PM-M2, ED888, of No. 103 Squadron. It flew and survived the most sorties of any Lancaster: 140. Five years later it was WS-J, W4964, a No. 9 Squadron aircraft with the distinctive nose art of 'Johnnie Walker: Still Going Strong', a definite favourite among photographers. In 1995 it was time for a major wing-spar overhaul. The Lancaster was constructed quickly, with a short lifespan in mind. The assumption was quite correct, with the life of a wartime Lancaster ranging from one sortie to 140 sorties due to enemy action or accidents. In 1996 the aircraft was painted to represent QR-M, EE176, a No. 61 Squadron aircraft which also achieved 100-plus sorties. The nose art was the Walt Disney character Mickey Mouse pulling a bomb trolley, with the slogan 'Mickey Moocher'. In 2006, PA474 appeared as EE139, named the *Phantom of the Ruhr*. It was uniquely marked HR-W of No. 100 Squadron, Waltham, Lincolnshire, on her port side and BQ-B of No. 550 Squadron, North Killingholme, Lincolnshire, on her starboard side to denote time

spent with both squadrons. In September 2012 the aircraft was marked to represent KC-A, DV385, another No. 617 Squadron aircraft, with the distinctive nose art featuring the Walt Disney character Thumper the rabbit, from the film *Bambi*, drinking a foaming mug of beer.

Canadian Warplane Heritage Museum

Perhaps Mount Hope, Ontario, was a most unlikely location for an aviation museum, or perhaps it was not. Tucked away near (though not too near) the metropolis of Toronto, not only does it have a large collection of aircraft on display, but some of the aircraft are actually airworthy and take part in air shows. The Canadian Warplane Heritage Museum (CWHM) also allows its members, for a tax-deductible donation, to enjoy a flight in one of these rare 'warbird' aircraft. What an opportunity in the twenty-first century, to experience flight in an historic aircraft of the last century.

One of the restored flying aircraft is the CWHM's Lancaster, one of only two Lancasters flying in the world today. It is the only Lancaster in existence in which the general public can actually enjoy a flight. The very essence of a museum is to collect and preserve history and make it available so that the general population might learn about the past; the museum's Lancaster certainly does that, and it is a tribute to those involved, both volunteers and staff, that such an opportunity exists.

The museum is housed in an imposing set of buildings at the John C. Munro Hamilton International Airport, a former RCAF station. A dramatic piece of aviation sculpture captures your attention as you approach the museum – a Canadair CF-104 Starfighter mounted so that its needle nose is pointed towards the sky. The museum was not always as modern as it is now, and it suffered setbacks on its way to becoming the living aviation museum it is today.

It all started with some aviation enthusiasts who needed a place to store and operate their newly purchased Second World War aircraft. Originally seeking a Supermarine Spitfire or North American Mustang, they settled on a Fairey Firefly. This unique aircraft was a purpose-designed fighter/reconnaissance aircraft for aircraft carriers and saw service against the German battleship *Tirpitz* and in the Far East against the Japanese forces. The aircraft was ferried back to Toronto from Georgia, USA, and underwent restoration in the early 1970s.

The four enthusiasts, Dennis Bradley, Alan Ness, John Weir and Peter Matthews, intended to fly the Firefly at air shows. It was flight tested by Ormond Haydon-Baillie and acquired a Royal Navy paintjob. The author was lucky enough to see an impromptu air show by Haydon-Baillie in a CAF Canadair CF-5 at Canadian Forces Base (CFB) Gimli, Manitoba, and another impromptu air show in a Hawker Sea Fury at CFB Moose Jaw, Saskatchewan, days prior to the planned air show. In both cases, the author has never seen an aircraft do a pass so low to the ground. Unfortunately, Haydon-Baillie was killed in a flying accident on 3 July 1977 in Germany, while performing in a North American Mustang. You certainly would never forget him or his flying ability. Haydon-Baillie was a larger-than-life figure, born to fly.

In the summer of 1972, Canadian Warplane Heritage (CWH) was formed as a non-profit corporation which allowed the four founders to obtain insurance and fly the Firefly at air shows. The aircraft was then moved to Condor Aviation at Mount Hope. Not content with just the Firefly, a de Havilland Chipmunk was added to the collection after the CWH was recognised as a registered charity. Shortly thereafter, a North American Harvard was obtained by CWH and joined two other privately owned Harvards to make up a three-plane display team.

A Supermarine Seafire, a de Havilland Tiger Moth and the Goodyear FG-1D Corsair (another carrier-based aircraft) were added, bringing the collection to six aircraft by the end of 1973. The year 1974 saw expansion with the purchase of hangar no. 4 and growing public demand to be part of the CWH. This resulted in a member-oriented organisation being formed. A North American B-25 Mitchell was added from Deleware, USA.

The first CWH International Air Show was held in June 1975 and featured forty warbird aircraft. The event attracted 30,000 people and was an overwhelming success. By the end of the year the collection had grown with the addition of a Cessna Crane and a Westland Lysander. Not all aircraft were operational, and restoration projects kept pace with the flying activities. CWH aircraft won two awards at Oshkosh, the home of the annual fly-in of the Experimental Aircraft Association, in 1976. The first award went to the B-25 Mitchell for being the Most Improved Warbird, and the second to the Firefly for being the Best Rare Warbird.

By the end of 1976, a Fairchild Cornell and Grumman TBM-3E Avenger were added to the fleet. The year 1977 saw the third annual air show, with the US Navy Blue Angels and the CAF Snowbirds demonstration teams attending. Gliders, helicopters and aerobatics displays rounded off the very successful day. The CWH was on a growth momentum, and next came the organisation's greatest ambitious move, the purchase of an Avro Lancaster X, FM213, from the Royal Canadian Legion. It should be noted that the aircraft was on a pedestal at the time.

Unfortunately, the year was to have highs *and* lows in the history of CWH. Alan Ness, one of the original founders, was killed flying the Fairey Firefly at the Canadian National Exhibition (CNE) air show.

The year ended with the first publication of *Flightlines*, the CWH magazine. By 1978 a replacement Firefly was found in Australia and the fourth successful air show was flown. The revenue from the air show proved to be the greatest source of funds. The fifth air show in 1979 was also a financial success, allowing the CWH to fly eight aircraft at the CNE air show and three aircraft, the Mitchell, Avenger and Corsair, at the Confederate Air Force's air show in Harlingen, Texas. The Canadian Warbird fraternity were represented well, and the CWH gained invaluable publicity.

An attempt was made to lift the Lancaster's fuselage by helicopter in June, but the attempt failed as the load was too heavy. Finally, in November the wings arrived by road and the fuselage arrived slung beneath a CAF Chinook helicopter. A swinging load threatened to destabilise the helicopter, but the expertise of the crew won through and the fuselage was delivered to CWH. The Lancaster restoration could begin.

The year 1980 brought another North American B-25, albeit one based in Vancouver. An Avro Anson, Bristol Bolingbroke airframes and Fleet Fawn biplane became part of the collection. The annual air show was televised for the first time by CTV. The next year saw the North American Harvards in a CBC television series and also heralded a name change: it was now called the Canadian Warplane Heritage Museum (CWHM). A Douglas DC-3, Auster AOP, Beech Expeditor and Dennis Bradley's personal airplane, a North American P-51D Mustang, joined the museum's aircraft. A Fleet Fort and North American Yale completed the inventory.

Airplanes left the collection also. The CWHM Avro CF-100 Canuck was donated to RCAF Association 447 Wing at Mount Hope. The wing mounted it on a pedestal outside their building. The year 1982 saw restoration begin on the Lancaster and tourists to the museum indicated the potential revenue of catering to visitors. The yearly June air show by this time is a fixture, with new acts and aircraft each year, both civilian and military. The Douglas DC-3 Dakota flew again and won the People's Choice award at the Oshkosh annual fly-in. A private Beechcraft T-34 Mentor took up residence in the hangar.

The year 1983 saw a Stinson HW75 Voyager, Fairchild Argus and a North American T-6 Texan included in the museum. Hangar no. 3 was purchased to house the growing number of aircraft and allow room for restoration. A government grant was obtained and the Lancaster restoration started to gather momentum. Four Packard Merlin engines were acquired from the Oshawa Lancaster, KB889.

Certainly national and perhaps some international publicity occurred in the publication of a special edition of the Canadian Aviation Historical Society's magazine on the CWHM and the Lancaster in 1984. The year also saw the edition of a Hawker Hurricane Mk XII from the Strathallan Collection in Scotland and the loss of the North American Mustang due to an engine failure.

In June 1984 the Lancaster was officially dedicated to the memory of Pilot Officer Andrew C. Mynarski VC and was painted to reflect his aircraft, KB726 VR-A. Many of his crew were present – Art de Breyne, Pat Brophy, Jack Friday, Jim Kelly and Mynarski's sister Stephanie Holowaty.

The 1984 air show demonstrated the highs and lows and risks of the air show business. The first day was a great success, with an exciting 'Tora Tora Tora' aerial display, but unfortunately the second day was cancelled due to bad weather. The CWHM suffered a large financial loss. It was decided to hand over running of the 1985 air show to a City of Hamilton committee. A worldwide reunion of Second World War Allied airmen in Toronto visited in 1985 to see the progress of the Lancaster restoration. A Lancaster Support Club (LSC) was formed to gather funds for the ongoing work. Its mandate was threefold – to promote interest in the restoration of FM213, to get members in the club and, most importantly, to raise funds to support the restoration.

By 1986 the LSC had raised $20,000 for the Lancaster restoration, which was donated to the CWHM. The Hawker Hurricane that year was a great air show success, with former fighter pilots in the VIP enclosure. Sprinklers were added to the hangars and the Beech Expeditor won the Best Transport award at Oshkosh.

Spring 1987 saw the creation of the Lancaster Flight Operations Committee to draft operating manuals and crew instructions. The long restoration project was coming to an end and the exciting next stage, the actual aircraft flying, was becoming a reality. The third Rolls-Royce

Merlin engine was under rebuild, an 800-hour process, and arrived in September to be installed in the no. 4 engine position. The Lancaster was now 80 per cent complete, which represented 30,000 hours' work. Every nut, bolt and screw had to be installed and inspected by licensed maintenance personnel to satisfy Transport Canada.

The Bristol Bolingbroke components arrived from the Western Canada Aviation Museum, Winnipeg, in April. A Fleet Finch was donated in September. The year 1988 started with the addition of a Douglas A-26 Invader.

A major milestone occurred in the timeline of the Lancaster's renovation: the fourth Merlin engine arrived and was installed in the no. 1 engine position. The installation of all the engine controls and accessories began. A more suitable undercarriage was obtained from the Lancaster's successor, the Avro Lincoln. Lancaster tyres were no longer available, so Dunlop tyres for the Avro Shackleton were ordered. In April, CWHM President Dennis Bradley announced that the Lancaster's first public flight was scheduled for Saturday 24 September 1988 at the Hamilton Airport. In July the aircraft received its post-restoration paintjob, and in August all four Merlin engines were run up.

On 9 September the Canadian Department of Transport did an inspection and found some minor snags which had to be corrected. The first test flight of the *Mynarski Memorial Lancaster* took place on Sunday 11 September 1988. Pilot-in-command was Squadron Leader Tony Banfield, RAF, co-pilot was Bob Hill and engineers were Norm Etheridge and Tim Mols. The second test flight required that the landing gear be lowered using the emergency compressed air-system followed by a successful landing.

The original crew of KB726 and Mynarski's sister were present for the first public flight. A 'typical' Second World War Lancaster crew were introduced in their original uniforms. The president, Dennis Bradley, introduced the crew for this inaugural flight, Pilot Stu Brickendam, co-pilot Bob Hill and engineers Norm Etheridge and George Sobering, DFC. The commanding officer of No. 419 Moose Squadron presented the fire axe used by Mynarski to try and free Brophy from the rear turret, to be flown on the inaugural flight. Several solo passes in front of the crowd were followed by a pass with the CWHM Hawker Hurricane and a Supermarine Spitfire.

The year 1989 began with requests from many Canadian cities to have the Lancaster visit. During the summer and autumn the aircraft flew across Canada with visits to Oshkosh and Minneapolis in the USA. It is estimated that over 2 million people witnessed the Mynarski Lancaster in flight. The series of flights were not without problems – a broken piston required an on-the-road fix in CFB Greenwood, Nova Scotia.

The 1990 air show, now called the Hamilton International Air Show, celebrated the fiftieth anniversary of the Battle of Britain before a record crowd of 40,000. Dame Vera Lynn, the Commonwealth's 'Forces Sweetheart', sang her 1940s hit 'We'll Meet Again'. This was followed by a formation pass led by the Lancaster with the Mosquito, Hurricane and Spitfire.

The next year was a sad one for the original crew of the Mynarski Lancaster, with both the pilot, Art de Breyne, and the rear gunner, Pat Brophy, passing away.

The year 1992 was another year of gain and loss. CWHM purchased a Spitfire Mk IX and flew the Yale for the first time, but the Firefly was damaged during an emergency landing. This was nothing compared to the loss which occurred in 1993. Hangar no. 3 was destroyed by fire, with the loss of the Spitfire, Hurricane (S377 from BBMF), Avenger, Auster, Stinson and the president's Aero Commander. The office complex and engineering and maintenance area were also destroyed. The only thing that saved the Lancaster and Fleet Finch was a concrete dividing wall. A 'Flames to Flight' fund was started to raise funds for the museum rebuild.

24 September 1994 saw the groundbreaking ceremony for the new museum on Airport Road, Hamilton Airport. In March 1995 the last of the roof trusses were in place. The year 1995 could also be called the 'year of the jets'. The CWHM took possession of a de Havilland Vampire, Hawker Hunter, Canadair T-33 and a Canadair CF-104D Starfighter.

In March 1996 the museum opened its doors to the public again. The official opening in April was presided over by HRH the Prince of Wales, who is the museum's patron. In the autumn a single-seat Canadair CF-104 and an Avro CF-100 Canuck, on loan from the Canadian Aviation & Space Museum in Ottawa, Ontario, arrived.

By coincidence, the author had spent many hours in the cockpit of that particular CF-100, 100785, with No. 414 (Electronic Warfare) Squadron at North Bay, Ontario, during the Cold War of the early 1970s. The first Remembrance Day service was held at the CWHM's new facilities on 11 November.

The year 1997 saw the addition of an Antonov AN-2, which was later exchanged for a Grumman Tracker, a Spitfire and a Canadair CF-5 jet fighter. A Canadair F-86 Sabre arrived in the autumn of 1998 and a tenth-anniversary celebration was held to remember the success of the Lancaster's first flight. In 1999, an education director was appointed and the CWHM started a new path of educating young people in aviation-related subjects.

Spring 2000 saw a second airplane, a Canadian Vickers PBY-5A Canso, painted to remember Canadian VC winner Flight Lieutenant David Hornell of No. 162 Squadron RCAF (Bomber Reconnaissance Squadron). Hornell was the aircraft captain of a Canso that attacked the U-boat U-1225 in the North Atlantic. Hornell's aircraft was badly damaged during the attack and on fire when he ditched in the sea. There was one serviceable dingy, which was shared among the crew, who took it in turns in the frigid water. They were rescued after twenty-one hours, but Flight Lieutenant Hornell died shortly after being picked up.

A Sigorsky S-51 Dragonfly helicopter was received in the collection. Over 6,000 students attended the youth programs. A display of flags of nations that participated in the British Commonwealth Air Training Plan was erected outside the CWHM in 2001. CWH director Carey Moore was killed when his Hawker Sea Fury crashed at the Sarnia, Ontario air show.

2002 was the inaugural year for the Father's Day Air Show, 'Soar with Legends', as the Hamilton International Air Show had been cancelled in 2001. October saw the Dakota and Lancaster put on a 'Command Performance' for Her Majesty the Queen over the capital city, Ottawa, during her visit to Canada in 2002.

A de Havilland DHC-5 Buffalo arrived for preparation as a static exhibit in 2003 and some history was discovered on the CWHM Lancaster. The aircraft had a landing accident in 1952 and the centre wing section had to be replaced by one from a retired Lancaster, KB895. That particular Lancaster flew five missions over Germany in 1945 with No. 434 Squadron RCAF. A fifteenth-anniversary celebration was held of the first flight of the *Mynarski Memorial Lancaster* with a two-day Allied air forces reunion.

A McDonnell CF-101 Voodoo was retrieved from a pedestal at Ottawa International Airport, Ontario – the former location of CFB Uplands – in 2004. It was displayed as a static exhibit in October. The CWHM received an enquiry from the British Ministry of Defence in 2005 about flying the Lancaster to Britain for the sixtieth-anniversary celebrations of VE-Day. The invite was declined at that time. In September a Canadair CT-114 Tutor jet trainer arrived. It was a well-known aircraft that received its publicity through the CAF/RCAF 'Snowbird' demonstration team.

In the summer of 2006 the CWHM returned to the Oshkosh air show after an eighteen-year absence. The Lancaster was accompanied by the Mitchell and Expeditor. The June 2007 'Flyfest' saw the Lancaster fly in formation with a Spitfire and Hurricane. The twentieth year for the Lancaster's first flight, 2008, was celebrated with a 'Flyfest' flyby in June, including a Spitfire, Hurricane and Messerschmitt 109E, and a gala and dinner in September.

Two further airplanes joined the CWHM in 2008, a Boeing Stearman and a North American Harvard. February 2009 saw the historic 'Silver Dart' replica come to CWHM in preparation for its first flight. It was then shipped to Baddeck, Nova Scotia, to re-enact the first powered flight in Canada, which took place on 23 February 1909. In June the Westland Lysander flew again after sixty-three years.

In August 2009 the Lancaster went on tour of western Canada, visiting Thunder Bay, Ontario, Calgary, Alberta, and culminating at the air show in Abbotsford, British Columbia. This last flight included flying over, through and around the Canadian Rockies. On board was 'crewman' Ms Lisa Sharp, a volunteer with CWHM. The author was fortunate enough to see the Lancaster fly at the Abbotsford air show and was thrilled by the sound of the four Merlins along with thousands of other aviation enthusiasts.

The end of the year saw a donation of a Nanchang CJ-6A and Grumman Avenger that replaced the aircraft lost in the 1993 hangar fire. In the summer of 2010 the Lancaster made another western Canada tour, stopping at Thunder Bay, Ontario, Winnipeg, Manitoba, Calgary, Alberta, Edmonton, Alberta and Windsor, Ontario. Thousands lined up at each stop to go through the aircraft.

In July 2011 the CWHM created its own flag, which was paraded at the Remembrance Day ceremony in November. A large bronze statue of fighter ace George 'Buzz' Beurling, the hero of Malta, was unveiled. In eleven years the education program had grown from 6,000 students to 18,000 – a tribute to the CWHM and its staff. The next generation of primary piston trainers, the Chipmunk, arrived at the museum in the spring of 2012. The Beechcraft CT-134 Musketeer had served with No. 3 Flying Training School at Portage La Prairie, Manitoba.

In 2013, the CWHM Lancaster, known as *VeRA*, had completed twenty-five years' service since her inaugural flight and Norm Etheridge, the original engineer leader, was on board for a commemorative flight. The Lancaster Engine Overhaul Appeal was also launched to get funds for the upcoming necessary overhauls. *VeRA* landed on the grass at the Geneseo air show in New York, billed as 'The Greatest Show on Turf'. It also appeared in an episode of *Air Aces* on the History Channel.

The world's only flying de Havilland Mosquito, at Jerry Yagen's Military Aviation Museum, Virginia Beach, USA, appeared at Hamilton Airshow. In 2014 the Grumman Avenger neared its restoration completion and there was a visit from a Boeing B-17 Flying Fortress at the Hamilton Airshow.

VeRA was painted in 'Ropey Shark Teeth' markings, Lanc KB772 VR-R, for the Hamilton Airshow. The greatest Lancaster announcement of its CWHM life was that it would take part in the Thwaites Lancaster Bomber United Kingdom Tour, flying alongside the BBMF Lancaster in September 2014. See chapter 7 for an account of the tour.

FM213

During the war, Britain saw the need to increase their aircraft production and turned to the Commonwealth for the answer. Production had to take place far enough away to avoid disruption by the Luftwaffe and close enough that a reasonably safe supply line could be set up: Canada was the answer. The National Steel Car Corporation (NSCC) had established a production facility at Malton, Ontario, the present site of Toronto Pearson International Airport, just prior to the war for their new aircraft division. An agreement was reached by NSCC to manufacture the Lancaster under licence and the engineering specifications arrived early in 1942. It was not until late summer that the first example of the Lancaster, R5727, was flown to Canada for examination and to establish standard production settings.

The NSCC Lancasters were the Canadian version of the Mk B.III and were called the Mk B.X. The later models, including FM213, had the American Packard Merlin 224 engines and, most importantly, all sub-assemblies were totally interchangeable with the British versions in the event of battle damage. By the end of 1942, NSCC had become a Crown Corporation and was renamed Victory Aircraft Ltd. The first Lancaster prototype (KB700) came off the assembly line in August 1943 and was named the *Ruhr Express*. It was the first of 430 aircraft produced by Victory Aircraft. The National Film Board of Canada was extremely interested in the aircraft and set out to record all its movements, much to the discomfort, operational interference and chagrin of the RAF and RCAF.

KB700 eventually completed forty-nine missions with No. 419 'Moose' Squadron RCAF at Middleton St George and was destroyed in a landing accident in January 1945. This was also the same RAF station and squadron that KB726 belonged to when it was shot down in June 1944 and Mynarski was awarded the VC. KB726 had a very short life of forty-six operational hours before being shot down. This was not a totally unusual event and contributed to the superstitious habits of some crews.

The CWHM Lancaster FM213 was built by Victory Aircraft at Malton in July 1945, at that time producing an aircraft a day. It was finally air tested and accepted after hostilities ceased and was put in storage. Although it was accepted by the RCAF the next year, it would be 1951 before conversion was completed to a Mark 10MR/MP (maritime reconnaissance/maritime patrol) aircraft.

En route to its first assignment, No. 405 Squadron RCAF at Greenwood, Nova Scotia, it suffered a heavy landing accident at RCAF Station Trenton, Ontario. It was dismantled and returned to its conversion site, de Havilland. A replacement centre section was found in Alberta, from KB895, and by 1953 had been modified to MP standards. After duty with No. 405 Squadron in Greenwood, FM213 was assigned to No. 107 Rescue Unit,

Torbay, Newfoundland, as CX213. In addition to normal search-and-rescue duties, CX213 took part in Operation Duck-Butt sorties. This was to provide both an airborne search-and-rescue aircraft and homing beacon for RCAF aircraft, including single-engine jet fighters, transiting the North Atlantic en route to Europe to fulfil NATO requirements.

In November 1963, FM213 was flown to Trenton with over 4,000 hours of flying logged and placed in storage awaiting sale for scrap metal. Rescued by the Goderich, Ontario chapter of the Royal Canadian Legion, in particular Bill Clancy, the aircraft was flown from Trenton to Goderich Airport. En route it performed some impromptu air shows at former wartime bases. It sat for a few years before being mounted by its jacking points on pylons – a very important decision if FM213 was ever to fly again. Extensive negotiations took place before the aircraft became a part of the CWHM. Dismantled, it was made ready for the largest piece, the stripped fuselage, to make the flight of its lifetime – suspended from a Canadian Armed Forces Boeing CH-147 Chinook helicopter.

Two tries were necessary to get the fuselage airborne, slung from a No. 450 Squadron RCAF Chinook helicopter. Short slings and rotor downwash were blamed for the failure of the first try. The fuselage arrived at Hamilton on 5 November 1979 – now the real work was to begin, getting FM213 airborne again. Had CWHM bitten off more than it could chew? It was a charitable foundation of volunteer members with lots of sentimental heart, but could that be translated into sustained and committed effort? Four years passed with some work being done before the outlook changed for FM213. A government grant and a temporarily unemployed maintenance engineer came together to bring the project to life. Norm Etheridge was the engineer in charge of the trainees and volunteers who were tasked not to restore, but to completely rebuild FM213.

It needed professional leadership – that of Etheridge – to guide the work, which at times was dirty, monotonous and boring. The volunteers perhaps thought of the glamour of installing engines and not the laborious scrubbing to remove decay from the wing and other surfaces. But the results eventually showed and the beautiful finished fuselage was a case in point. The H2S dome was removed to represent the KB726 configuration.

Some pieces had to be remade or recast to exacting standards stipulated by Transport Canada. No company was safe from approach by Etheridge, from the bottom of the organisation to the very top! The Dowty hydraulic system was a perfect example, working both locally with Dowty Canada and the Dowty head office in England! It is worthy of note that even a heavy bomber built seventy years ago had some wooden pieces to fulfil its construction needs. All the trades were indeed needed to get the Lancaster back in the air.

The major sections of the aircraft – outer wings, flaps, control surfaces, tailplane –required long, painstaking work under close supervision to rebuild. The gun turrets, Frazer-Nash models, were rebuilt with the restriction that they were not operable in flight. In 1985, the engineless aircraft was displayed at the Hamilton Airshow and attracted a lot of attention. The Lancaster Support Club was in attendance to get further members, support and donations.

The original engines were beyond repair and four were found in Ottawa on aircraft KB889, which was being exported to England. Restored to working order in Minneapolis, the first one arrived in May 1986 in time to be hung in the inboard starboard position for the Hamilton Airshow. It should be mentioned that various departments in Air Canada offered their facilities to assist in the restoration work. A June 1988 photo shows all four engines and propellers in place.

The main landing gear, due to no available Lancaster tyres, was replaced with a set from the Avro Lincoln. The Lincoln tyres were available as the Lincoln landing gear was used on the Avro Shackleton, the RAF long-range maritime patrol, which remained in service until 1990. The decision was made to have the Mynarski Lancaster airborne in front of the public on 24 September 1988, a brave decision of commitment to facilitate the advertising and power of the world press and television. Six weeks before the big day, all four engines ran together for the first time.

Finally, on 11 September 1988, twenty-four years since her last flight to Goderich, FM213, now known and painted as KB726 VR-A, the *Mynarski Memorial Lancaster*, civilian registration C-GVRA, lifted off and completed her first flight. The pilot on the historic flight was RAF Squadron Leader Tony Banfield, former commanding officer of the BBMF, with Bob Hill as co-pilot, and engineers Norm Etheridge and Tim Mols. The aircraft flew as planned on 24 September 1988, with members of the original 13 June 1944 Cambrai raid crew in attendance, plus Mynarski's sister, Stephanie Holowaty. The attendees included Art de Breyne, pilot; Jim Kelly, wireless operator; Roy Vigars, flight engineer; Bob Brodie, navigator; and Pat Brophy, rear gunner.

'What a lot of people do not realize is it is a civilian airplane and has to be operated according to Transport Canada regulations,' said Don Schofield, the present Lancaster chief pilot. The registration is under the tailplane on the side of the fuselage. The military camouflage does not meet civilian aircraft colour restrictions, and as such it has to always travel with a special Transport Canada exemption. The museum is very much aware of its legal liability and works very hard to make sure it does not expose itself to any legal challenges.

The Lancaster flying season is from early spring to late September depending on the weather and crew availability. Weather permitting, a fly-by of the Cenotaph in November is also scheduled. There is a one-day annual recurrent training prior to flying operations commencing for the year. Each pilot must do a one-hour review flight plus normal, abnormal and emergency procedures with the training captain, Don Schofield, prior to flying as pilot in command for the season. Three landings are required to finish the review trip due to the pilot not having flown the Lancaster for the last ninety days while it was undergoing annual maintenance.

Schofield mentioned that he has been 'incredibly privileged' to fly the Lancaster for so many years.

The Lancaster takes an enormous amount of effort to keep it flying. The winter maintenance program sees extensive non-destructive testing, dye testing and sonograms. The science of metallurgy and stress analysis as it exists today did not exist in the 1940s. Schofield said, 'How long we can go on, we do not know. However, unless something happens that we do not see coming we should be able to keep operating. We spend huge sums of money every year to keep the Lancaster in the air.' In the past there have been some very critical pieces of the aircraft requiring replacement. There were no spares available anywhere in the world and the pieces have had to be replicated and of course pass rigorous inspection. Schofield commented, 'As long as you are prepared to fire unlimited amounts of money at it you could keep going forever.'

The CWHM Lancaster crew consists of a minimum of four: the two pilots, the flight engineer and a crewperson. Air shows only have the minimum number on board. The aircraft was designed as a single-pilot airplane and everything critical is within reach of the left-seat pilot. Transport Canada requires that a multi-engine airplane of that size have full dual controls. The second pilot sits on a fold-up seat known as the 'Dickey Seat', which was used by the flight engineer in wartime operations. Immediately behind the pilots is the flight engineer facing the starboard side of the fuselage. A lot of the system controls, such as fuel, are mounted on a panel located on the fuselage behind the second pilot.

'Some of the things on that airplane are absolutely genius level and others are somewhere between Rube Goldberg and Heath Robinson, such as the master switch for the electrics are eighteen feet behind the pilots.' CWHM has a fourth crewperson, seated halfway back in the fuselage, to turn this switch off in event of an emergency and perform any other duties as required off the headset. It is very noisy inside the aircraft and

to communicate the pilots and flight engineer must remain on headsets throughout the flight. Transport Canada regulations state that any equipment on board *VeRA* must be serviceable so CWHM took out all the wireless, navigator and air-sea rescue equipment and installed four seats to be able to take members on a revenue-generating flight. In transit, flights can have up to eight persons on board.

The requests for the demonstration season are received at the CWHM up to February. A calendar map is then set up for the year, including all the annual 'must-do' appearances, and sent to Schofield for consideration. Based on crew availability and financial considerations – the CWHM is a private, self-supporting charitable organisation – the Lancaster schedule is created. There are presently five Lancaster pilots, soon to be six, and four of those pilots are qualified as pilot-in-command.

When asked about the serviceability of the Merlin engines with so many moving parts, Schofield said, tongue in cheek, that 'as long as there are people with money flying Mustangs there will be no insurmountable problem with engine parts'. There is a lot of after-market remanufacturing, refurbishing, rebuilding and exchange of parts to keep them flying. All the CWHM museum aircraft are overly maintained because of the age and nature of the aircraft, and the Lancaster, in spite of its size, is no exception.

The Merlin engine has a relatively short life compared to the engines of today, with 400 operating hours to a major overhaul. A minor top overhaul costs £67,000–83,000 and the supercharger failure in the 2014 UK tour could eventually cost approximately £138,000 or so, as the debris had ended up in the crankcase. The Merlin is fine if you are established in cruise and droning along – that is what it was designed for – but if you have a lot of condition changes, that is when the problems start to arise. A series of touch-and-go landings with many power changes is a good example of this.

I asked Schofield to describe a typical member's trip and he recounted the following information that I have turned into my narrative with occasional direct quotes. Away from base, the transport to the airport is arranged for a set time for the entire crew. Arrival at the airport is a well-rehearsed scenario after doing it so many times. If the aircraft is on static display, the air show organisers are instructed to remove the spectators from the aircraft forty-five minutes prior to the flight and refuelling if necessary. The flight crew drop off their flight bags and take off for the air show or a crew briefing. The pilots and flight engineer attend this briefing, which covers such items as abnormal, emergency and alternate operations as necessary due to aircraft, air traffic control and weather.

Returning to the aircraft, the crew talk with spectators outside and inside the aircraft if it is open for tours. This can sometimes lead to long days for the crew. The daily inspection is performed by the ground crew and any discrepancies, as well as quantities added, are entered in the logbook. Reaching the engines does require the use of ladders or stands, which must now be removed. The pilots and the engineer(s) walk around the aircraft and do an external visual inspection together, starting at the right rear-entrance door. Schofield said that for spectator purposes 'the pilot takes the logbook from the engineer, which is then inspected … for all checks and quantities added'. The pilot-in-command, outside the aircraft, signs the bottom, shakes hands and passes the logbook back before boarding the aircraft. Almost a mirror of what happened in the Second World War.

Entering the aircraft, the pilot is constrained by the 'first prop[eller] turning' (FPT). The Lancaster is allocated a taxi or show time and using this the time is worked backwards to the FPT. An airline-style document called the Quick Reference Handbook is used for all sequential checklists, such as an on-entering-aircraft check, flight engineer's check, pilot's check, before-start check, after-start check, before-take-off check, after-take-off check, in-range check, before-landing check, after-landing check and shutdown check. It is a challenge-and-response checklist with the right-seat pilot reading the checklist and the pilot-in-command, always in the left seat, answering with the correct responses.

Once the four engines are started and the after start check is complete, it is time to taxi to the runway – keeping in mind that, because of the nose-high attitude, you cannot see straight ahead to taxi. Taxiing is done by remaining the same distance from the edge of the taxiway. The Lancaster's brake system is activated by a hand grip on the control column. The more you move the lever, the more braking you get. The tailwheel is fully castoring and allows the tail to swing with differential braking. Power is increased to get the aircraft rolling and then differential braking and the use of the outboard engines, no. 1 or no. 4 as required, will initiate and stop a turn. The brakes are pneumatic and a light aircraft at idle power uses the brake pneumatic pressure faster than the air pumps can replenish. The only way to recharge the brake bottles is to stop the aircraft and bring up the power on no. 3 and no. 4 engines, the ones with the air compressors, and let them roar away to build up pressure again – quite confusing for some onlookers, but now you know!

Talking about hydraulics, Schofield said, 'That is what really killed Pilot Officer Mynarski – the Second World War hydraulic [system] was high-volume and low-pressure. Huge pipes, some up to an inch in diameter, that used something called Girling fluid. This fluid was vegetable-based, highly toxic and, most importantly, very highly flammable fluid.' The designers did not use hydraulics if at all possible and hence the pneumatic brakes. The high-volume hydraulic users were the landing gear and bomb-bay doors.

The brakes, which are actually quite small, are all pneumatic. When you release the brake lever the air is vented overboard, and Schofield mentioned that 'if you are in the airplane or close by outside you will hear the hissing, puffing and wheezing of the air going overboard. When the brakes get really hot the air also smells really bad.'

The main tyres have old-fashioned inner tubes on the Lancaster and are a huge sixty-four inches in diameter. They are inflated to fifty-four psi and designed to work off grass. The museum has recently spent approximately £42,000 on ten new tyres. To save the tyres, the museum has a landing preference – grass, asphalt, normal concrete and, to be totally avoided if possible, high-traction concrete.

Prior to departure all the critical emergencies are rehearsed, such as rejected take-off and engine fire in the air. In my airline flying days it was referred to with tongue in cheek as the 'I will you will' procedure. Lining up on the runway, Schofield commented, 'You will notice that the airplane just doesn't stop – it rolls forward a few feet. This is to straighten the tailwheel. The brakes are held on by your hand and the inboard engines, no. 2 and no. 3, are run up to thirty inches, zero boost for the CWHM Lancaster. All the Lancaster engines rotate in the same direction and if the power is applied to all engines simultaneously you would not be able to control the aircraft from turning sharply and departing the runway.'

Schofield then explained that 'you take your thumb [right hand] and push up the no. 1 throttle and as it passes no. 2 and no. 3 [throttles] you catch them with the palm of your hand and then you extend your pinky and grab no. 4 so they are all going up [power] in unison. No. 1 is leading and nos 2 and 3 are following, followed by no. 4.' This counteracts the asymmetric power due to the direction of propeller rotation until the rudder becomes effective around forty knots. The pilot in the right seat will then put his left hand behind the throttles to make sure they do not retard due to vibration. When take-off power is set, the right-seat pilot taps the pilot-in-command's hand and takes over setting the throttles. The pilot-in-command can now put both hands on the control wheel. Any tendency to swing at this airspeed will take full application of rudder immediately to stop the swing.

Approaching fifty knots, the tail starts to feel light and the control column is eased forward. This brings the airplane into a level attitude on its main wheels and the cockpit actually goes down four feet because the airplane is no longer in its tail-down ground position. The airplane takes off at 100 knots. Schofield mentioned that once the plane is properly airborne 'you put the brakes on. Those wheels weigh 780 lbs each and they are spinning, they have a torque factor all of their own.' When the wheels stop rotating, the pilot-in-command signals for gear up; the right-seat pilot from now on gets very busy.

The inertia and the control forces are so high that the only practical way to fly is with two hands. The pilot-in-command steers the airplane and calls or signals for all actions, such as gear up, climb power and after-take-off checklist, all being actioned by the right-seat pilot. Schofield said that 'the guy in the right seat is a very busy person. The pilot-in-command asks for power changes by signalling with the number of his fingers, either up or down, for the right-seat pilot to move the throttles to adjust the manifold boost pressure the indicated number of pounds.'

Final approach is flown at 120 knots, reducing to 105 knots and 100 knots at touchdown. The right-seat pilot maintains that speed with the throttles. After touchdown, the Lancaster uses a lot of runway to slow down as the crew are trying to save as much wear on the brakes as possible. For the same reason, Schofield does not like tailwinds and avoids them at all costs. Schofield said, 'If I have a choice of runway I will choose the runway with the wind from the right as this cancels the normal tendency for the aircraft to turn to the left.' The CWHM has a nominal limit of a 10-knot crosswind. The ability to handle the crosswind is a combination of experience and currency. Schofield, as chief pilot, flies fifty hours a year on training, air shows and members' flights. It takes a skilled man to handle that job; the CWHM are lucky to have Captain Don Schofield.

Lancaster B.I PA474 of the
BBMF, based at RAF Coningsby.
(UK Open Government Licence)

This page and opposite: PA474 is currently the only airworthy Lancaster in Europe. (Martin Keen)

Side view of PA474 clearly showing the positions of the three gunners, as well as the main cockpit. (Martin Keen)

Right: Front view of PA474 showing the vertigo-inducing position of the bomb aimer/front gunner. (Martin Keen)

Left: Rear view of PA474 in flight. This photograph demonstrates the rear gunner's vulnerability to fire from pursuing fighters. (Martin Keen)

Above and right: The BBMF Lancaster is often accompanied by examples of the flight's Spitfires and Hurricanes during fly-pasts and air show appearances. (Martin Keen)

PA474 accompanied by a Supermarine Spitfire, perhaps the war's most iconic fighter, and a Hawker Hurricane, the plane responsible for the majority of RAF victories during the Battle of Britain. (Martin Keen)

Starboard side of PA474. In this excellent view can be seen the observer's window blister and drift sight/recorder. (Liz Dodds)

City of Lincoln

Right: The Mynarski dedication carried on CWHM's FM213. (Martin Keen)

Left: Despite the nose art and squadron codes changing periodically on PA474, the name *City of Lincoln* is permanently applied. The five poppy symbols commemorate ceremonial poppy drops over London. (Liz Dodds)

The Canadian Warplane
Heritage Museum's
superb Lancaster B.X,
FM213/C-GVRA, *The
Mynarski Memorial
Lancaster*. (Martin Keen)

Above and right: FM213 wears the markings of KB726 VR-A, the No. 419 Squadron RCAF aircraft in which Andrew Mynarski won the Victoria Cross. (Martin Keen)

Right: KB726 as it touches down on the runway after another successful flight. (Martin Keen)

Left and opposite: KB726 in flight. (Martin Keen)

The sturdiness of the Lancaster meant that despite its weight and size the pilot could perform aggressive evasive manoeuvres to avoid fire from anti-aircraft batteries or pursuing fighters. (Martin Keen)

A fantastic shot of the Lancaster's hard-working propellers, powered by four twelve-cylinder Rolls-Royce Merlin piston engines. (Martin Keen)

This page, opposite and overleaf: The undoubted highlight of the 2014 UK air show season was the opportunity to see two airworthy Lancasters together for the first time in many decades. (Martin Keen)

Two Lancasters, airborne and flanked by fighters – a sight rarely seen since the end of the war. (Martin Keen)

6

THE MUSEUM LANCASTERS

There are two very special Lancaster museums that exist in the world. One is in England and the other is in Canada. They both are trying to preserve the history of the Lancaster in a unique way. At the present time, they have each restored a Lancaster to ground-running condition and made them accessible to the general public as a living exhibit instead of the usual silent, dormant, pristinely painted aircraft sitting in a hangar or on a pedestal. Bomber Command Museum of Canada (BCMC) is in Nanton, Alberta, and the Lincolnshire Aviation Heritage Centre (LAHC) is in East Kirkby, Lincolnshire.

In June 2015 it was announced that another museum is attempting to join the group of ground-running Lancasters. The Alberta Aviation Museum in Edmonton, Alberta, has obtained KB882 Lancaster B.X (arctic reconnaissance), which had been on display outside at Madawaska Airport, Edmundston, New Brunswick, for fifty years and was now decaying rapidly in spite of the effort of local volunteers. KB882 was built at the Victory Aircraft Ltd factory in Malton, Ontario, and ferried to England on 4 March 1945. It flew its first operational trip to Dortmund with No. 428 (RCAF) 'Ghost' Squadron at RAF Middleton St George. We hope they succeed in bringing another Lancaster to life.

The fact that aviation aficionados and the public alike can still stand nearby and listen to four twelve-cylinder Rolls-Royce Merlin piston engines more than seventy years after they were developed is truly unique. One can only imagine, in the 1940s, the sound of hundreds of Lancasters as they droned away during the night on their assigned routes to targets deep in enemy territory. The four Lancaster Merlins were still heard in the 1960s, prior to the Lancaster being withdrawn from service. Then, in the 1970s for the BBMF and the 1980s for the CWHM, the sounds of Lancaster Merlins were heard once again in the skies of Britain and Canada respectively – perhaps a reminder to the citizens of Britain that, against all odds, these brave bomber crews, night after night, set out to do their part in defending the British Isles and world freedom.

The BCMC Lancaster, in the summer of 2014, taxied under its own power for the first time since restoration. The LAHC has been taxiing its Lancaster for years and offers taxi rides to help defray the cost of running the Lancaster and the museum. The author believes that there are now only two flying and two taxiing Lancasters remaining in the world from over 7,000 built. The other Lancasters, less than twenty displayed worldwide, are mounted on pedestals or on static display only. It is indeed a privilege to feature the four Lancasters in this book, with individual aircraft history and photographs, and to encourage the reader to visit one of these venues to support the effort to keep these four remaining Lancasters active.

The BCMC sits on the edge of the town of Nanton, right beside the highway. The apron is so small that traffic on the highway has to be diverted to one lane to allow the aircraft to be towed into position for the run-up displays. A temporary wire barrier is put in place to keep spectators back from the aircraft. Needless to say, not many people drive by without stopping to look at the Lancaster, especially when it has its engines running. There are ambitious plans underway to enlarge the active display area by relocating it to beside the hangar.

Nanton is forty-six miles from the major city of Calgary, Alberta, and in a predominantly agricultural area. During the Second World War it was surrounded by active stations of the British Commonwealth Air Training Plan due to its terrain and good flying weather. Some seventeen miles north of Nanton, at High River, Elementary Flying Training School No. 5 operated for virtually the entire duration of the war. At the Vulcan station, seventeen miles east of Nanton, the BCATP operated Service Flying Training School No. 19 and, during the early years of the war, Flying Instructor School No. 2. Another Service Flying Training School, No. 15, was located at Claresholm, twenty-five miles south of Nanton.

The LAHC is located on the former East Kirkby RAF station close to the A155. The storage hangar has a large apron area which leads to a grass runway. This allows the Lancaster plenty of manoeuvring room and an accessible active display area. East Kirkby is twenty-four miles from Lincoln. It is in the heart of 'bomber county', so called because of the large number of Second World War stations that were situated in the county of Lincolnshire. East Kirkby is surrounded by historic former bomber stations with familiar names such as Coningsby, Spilsby, Woodhall Spa, Bardney and Metheringham.

The museums were founded for completely different reasons, but both have achieved the distinction of preserving a ground-operational Lancaster to allow post-war generations to remember, experience and admire the accomplishments of the past, while enjoying the freedom of the present. They truly are a living monument to Bomber Command, with all its triumphs, tragedies and contributions to ultimate victory. Through the museums, we, the public, 'will remember them'. It really is all about the crews of the Lancaster, with the larger-than-life ground-operational aircraft keeping alive the memory of those who are gone.

The BCMC

While East Kirkby has some reason to have an aviation museum, being a Second World War airfield, the small prairie town of Nanton has none. Once again, it was started by some people who had the foresight to draw attention to their community and at the same time preserve some of the surrounding aviation heritage. Three citizens were the driving force behind what eventually turned into the BCMC. They were George White, Howie Armstrong and Panton Garratt.

White was a local farmer and rancher who lived on his family land, which they had homesteaded in the late nineteenth century. There were flying training stations in the vicinity and he was used to seeing training aircraft in the skies above his family's ranch during the war years. He did in fact obtain his own flying licence, but never had the chance to take it further; there was not much time left in the day after the farm chores were done. White had the initial idea to take a surplus aircraft from the war and put it on display as a memorial and as a tourist attraction to get the highway traffic to stop and perhaps put some badly needed money into the local economy.

Talking with friends, he had instant support. Armstrong was a Nanton entrepreneur who owned Armstrong's Department and Variety store. He championed the small town in any way he could and one of his achievements was to label the piped-in town water as 'Canada's Finest Drinking Water' and provide a tap for passing travellers. Nanton Water Ltd later became one of the first companies in Canada to bottle and sell drinking water. Garratt operated the McKeague and Garratt Hardware store, an invaluable source of material that would be used to display and, more importantly, preserve an aircraft exposed to the harsh prairie weather.

In 1960 a number of surplus B-25 Mitchell bombers were being flown to the relatively close Claresholm, Alberta airfield for disposal. White wrote to Crown Assets and enquired as to the cost of one of these aircraft. The selling price of $2,500 was too much for the group, so they enquired if there was anything else available. They were told that some Lancasters would be put up for tender at a nearby airfield, a long-term storage facility near Vulcan, Alberta. An offer of $513 (£286) was accepted and the group now owned a Lancaster, albeit in a rural airfield – as it turned out, this was a blessing in disguise.

On 12 February 1959, FM159 had been flown by a civilian crew from Calgary to Vulcan. It was an ex-RCAF No. 407 Squadron aircraft. By March the engines and propellers had been taken off and, along with the fuselage, had been put in storage. The Nanton group acquired the aircraft on 11 August 1959. Now the transit problems arose. The main landing gear was too wide for the rural gravel roads, and then there was the matter of the numerous telephone poles. The eventual answer was to tow the aircraft by the shortest route across the fields for a distance of seventeen miles.

Permission was obtained from all the farmers involved, with the proviso that the aircraft move would have to wait until after the crops were off the fields. Volunteers and equipment were readied for the big day. Archie Clark, who had experience with towing large equipment, was chosen to do the towing. The tailwheel was secured on the truck flatbed and two logging chains were attached to the main landing gear for security. The aircraft was then towed backwards across the prairie fields.

Ditches were filled and excavated, wire fences removed and rebuilt, as the armada of volunteers moved along with the Lancaster. The route included towing through a ford in the Little Bow River and crossing a railway line before getting to the highway for the final route into Nanton. The telephone lines required that someone rode on top of the aircraft and helped ease the fuselage underneath the wires. The strange procession came to a halt for the night at the Canadian Pacific Railway's tracks just two miles from Nanton. Permission to cross the tracks was not given until the next morning. A guard was set up to protect the aircraft! The next morning the tow was completed, processing down the highway for the triumphant entry into town on the 28 September 1960. The Lancaster was parked by Highway No. 2 and immediately proved itself to be an eye-opener for the passing traffic.

The fuselage was totally complete, just as it had been when put in storage. Unfortunately, sitting on the ground at the edge of town exposed it to passing souvenir hunters and vandals. By the autumn of 1961, in spite of the best efforts of the volunteers, FM159 was a gutted shell of its former self. Broken Perspex, stolen cockpit instruments, damaged turrets and torn fabric control surfaces turned the once proud Lancaster into a sorry sight of dereliction; had the effort of attracting attention to the town been all for naught?

The year 1962 saw a change of fortune for the aircraft. The original 'three preservers' mounted a campaign to save the aircraft from total destruction. Engines and propellers had been purchased earlier and in December the work began to mount them to the fuselage to form a complete-looking aircraft. In 1963 the aircraft was secured onto on steel mounts. The tailwheel was raised to put the aircraft in a horizontal position and prevent easy access to the insides of the aircraft. Aluminium windows were added later to prevent further damage from bird droppings, and the aircraft was painted in wartime colours.

Nose art was added in the form of naming the aircraft 'B' for Bull Moose. Bomb tally was added, showing fifty missions flown and three enemy fighters shot down. A sign was constructed to indicate the part that the Lancaster bomber had played in the defeat of the Nazis. A chain-link fence surrounded the aircraft and prevented easy access. Volunteers, under the guidance of Ray McMahon, continued to maintain FM159 as it sat beside the highway for the next twenty years.

In 1985 an article in the *Nanton News* by Herb Johnson drew attention to the plight of Lancaster FM159. Vandalism and the prairie climate were continuing to take their toll on what had become a very unique and desirable historic aircraft to interested persons and organisations outside the Nanton community. The town council decided to ask White, an instigator of the Lancaster purchase, to see if enough local interest existed to form a society to look after the old aircraft. They were overwhelmed by the response. The assessing began to see where to get the expertise to look after the aircraft and how to fund further preservation by housing the aircraft in a permanent building. The following is an excerpt from the executive summary of the proposal to create a museum: 'The most important aircraft in the museum will be the well-known Nanton Lancaster Bomber, which will be restored to its wartime configuration and to a "taxiable" status.'

The Nanton Lancaster Society (NLS) was subsequently formed and became the key carers of the Lancaster. In spring 1986, the members began an inspection of the aircraft. The first hurdle was to get the padlock open on the crew door! Access was then gained by a fifteen-foot ladder to the horizontally mounted aircraft. By design, the steel mounting of FM159 on its landing gear preserved the fuselage intact as opposed to the cutting and welding of a pedestal-mounted aircraft. Although stripped of its interior equipment and instruments, the aircraft had remained clean thanks to Harry Dwelle sealing the broken Plexiglas with metal sheeting.

The year 1987 saw the beginning of letting the general public access the aircraft, which has continued to the present day. An event was scheduled called 'Open Bomber Days', with stairs built to the crew door and a ladder to the escape hatch in the bomb aimer's compartment in the nose of the aircraft. Some of the tin in the cockpit area was removed to let daylight in.

More than 700 people toured the aircraft over the weekend. The connection between the Lancaster and the visitors surprised the members of the society. Everything from 'Uncle Harry flew these in the war', 'My Mum worked on these in Malton, Ontario', to 'I have a few hours in the Lancaster'.

Visitors volunteered to help the NLS in many ways. They included Jon Spinks, an aviation aficionado who was an expert on finding parts for the Lancaster. In 1987 he fully restored the vandalised pilot's instrument panel. Spinks also encouraged the society to expand their horizons and start collecting other aircraft of the BCATP before they were all gone for scrap or other collections. Perhaps the most important advancement of the NLS at this time was the decision to honour the men and women associated with Bomber Command who contributed to its success during the Second World War. The people who built the aircraft and those who maintained it, the people who trained the pilots to fly the aircraft and those who flew it in active service would all be honoured – quite a commitment from a farming community of 2,000 people on the eastern slopes of the Canadian Rocky Mountains.

Over the years millions of visitors from far and wide, and especially Alberta residents, came to see the 'Nanton Bomber' and it featured in many a family photograph. It had achieved what White, Armstrong and Garratt hoped it would: publicity for their small prairie town. Nanton became the little town that put itself on the tourist map with one old aircraft towed across some fields. FM159 would have further exciting transitions in its future, but what of its past? Careful research and the stories of veterans who had flown in the Lancaster would provide answers to questions about whether it crossed the Atlantic and saw action, and about its life after hostilities ceased.

Exact records are not available, but FM159, construction no. 3360, was built at Victory Aircraft, Malton, probably in the latter half of May 1945. It was the 360th Lancaster of the 430 built in Canada. The momentum of the war effort – Canada and Japan were still at war – caused FM159 to be flown to England after VE (Victory in Europe) Day between 29 and 31 May 1945. The aircraft was saved from being scrapped due to its lack of flying time and the possibility of joining the Tiger Force for operations in the continuing war in the Far East. Two months at No. 20 Ashton Down and No. 32 St Athan maintenance units and the aircraft was flight tested and flown back to Canada on 30 August 1945, to RCAF Scoudouc, New Brunswick.

Subsequently, FM159 was flown to Yarmouth, Nova Scotia, for storage, as after VJ Day on 14/15 August there was no longer a Tiger Force requirement. Fear of salt-air corrosion prompted aircraft to be moved in the autumn to former BCATP airfields in the drier climate of Alberta. FM159 was flown to the former No. 2 Flying Instructor School at RCAF Pearce, which is north-east of Fort Macleod. A companion aircraft was KB732 VR-X, *X-Terminator*, a veteran of eighty-four missions. The aircraft were either properly stored in the hangars or purchased for parts and pieces that could be used with ingenuity by the local farmers.

FM159 once again was saved from this indignity and flown to Fort Macleod in March 1946. It remained there for five years until 1951. In August of that year it was flown back east to No. 6 Repair Depot at RCAF Trenton, Ontario. Finally, in March 1953, FM159 came back to life again. It was flown to Malton, Ontario, for overhaul and conversion by de Havilland to a maritime reconnaissance (MR) version. About 100 of the returned Lancasters continued on to serve the RCAF, while nearly 200 were scrapped. The conversion included the installation of a co-pilot position and radar, plus sonobuoy capability, additional fuel capacity and blister windows for observation. Seven months later, in October 1953, FM159 began flying duties with No. 103 Search and Rescue Unit, based at Greenwood, Nova Scotia.

By January 1955 it was scheduled for radar system upgrades by Fairey Aircraft at Dartmouth, Nova Scotia. By June of 1955 the aircraft had been assigned to No. 407 (MR) Squadron at RCAF Comox, British Columbia. The aircraft had left the Atlantic Ocean and now would serve the RCAF on the Pacific Ocean. Shortly thereafter, FM159 left on an Arctic reconnaissance patrol, an annual tasking called 'Nanook'. It was part of the ongoing survey of sea routes to document when the routes were available for Distant Early Warning Line resupply ships. The winter resupply of the North American Air Defence Command radar sites in the Arctic by aircraft was expensive, so the sooner the ships could get through the ice the better. For further reading on this subject and NORAD intercepts, see *NORAD and the Soviet Nuclear Threat* by the author.

During this deployment, FM159 nearly became a victim of the notorious Arctic weather. While on patrol out of Resolute Bay, Cornwallis Island, Nunavut, low ceilings and fog moved in over the whole area. Despite proceeding to Thule in Greenland and examining every possibility of a landing airfield, the only open landing area was at Alert, Ellesmere Island, Nunavut – the northernmost point in Canada. It is just 508 miles from the North Pole. FM159 eventually landed there, nearly out of fuel and with nowhere to go, after a flight of twelve hours and twenty-five minutes. The no. 4 engine failed on the runway after landing; the fuel tank was empty. That is how close FM159 came to being a statistic.

The aircraft continued to serve with No. 407 (MR) Squadron and was even tasked with NORAD penetration exercises in April 1956. Intercepted by RCAF Avro CF-100s, it continued on for training purposes and did a simulated bomb run on Spokane, Washington, USA. It succeeded its mission prior to interception by USAF F-86 Sabres, and so earned the right to paint a small 'bomb' on the side of the fuselage: mission accomplished. Squadron service continued until December 1958 when it was flown to Calgary, Alberta, and once again parked, destined for an unknown future.

Two months later FM159, along with other No. 407 Squadron Lancasters, was flown to RCAF Vulcan, Alberta. The Lancaster contribution to No. 407 Squadron was completed in May 1959, to be replaced by the

Lockheed P2V-7 Neptune. This is where White, Armstrong and Garratt became involved with FM159, and the rest, as they say, is history.

So what happened after the 'Open Bomber Days' in 1987 to get FM159 to the ground-running example it is today? The public showed that they were interested in the project by their attendance, and the NLS was gathering strength both in caring for FM159 and educating future generations about the Lancaster and Bomber Command.

A blizzard in 1989 tore the port elevator off and left it dangling from the horizontal stabiliser. This really drew attention to the fact that the forty-five-year-old aircraft would not last much longer if left exposed to the prairie climate. A museum building was required to house the aircraft and provide space for educational displays. The Town of Nanton provided an interest-free loan, and together with numerous individual donors made it possible for the aircraft to be removed from its supports and towed by tractor in 1991 into the newly built but unfinished hangar. Calling it a hangar stretched the imagination; it was a cover for the Lancaster that sat on a donated gravel floor.

Prior to the Lancaster getting a roof over its head, it had been decided by the NLS in 1990 to dedicate the Lancaster to a local unknown hero who had served with the RAF Bomber Command. This was done as a way to publicise and recognise all who had served in Bomber Command during the Second World War, lest their courage and heroism be forgotten – not to mention the ultimate sacrifice that was made by so many. This provided a focus for the museum volunteers, as the Lancaster now had a name and a personal story behind it. What a great way to perpetuate the story of one brave pilot, with the most important aircraft in a vibrant, growing museum dedicated to Bomber Command. Heroic deeds can fade with time and memory. Everything the museum stands for is centred on the 'Bazalgette' Lancaster.

The Nanton Lancaster was dedicated in a ceremony on Friday 27 July 1990 to the memory of S/L Ian Willoughby Bazalgette VC, DFC, RAF VR, a local 'Alberta boy'. Those in attendance included his sister Mrs Ethel Broderick (née Bazalgette) and two of his former crew: Charles 'Chuck' Godfrey DFC, Bazalgette's wireless operator; and George Turner, Bazalgette's flight engineer. Hamish Mahaddie DSO, DFC, AFC and Bar had selected Bazalgette among others for the Pathfinders, and during his evening banquet speech it was obvious that he felt very deeply for those crew who had paid the ultimate sacrifice doing the very important but dangerous job of marking the target. A dedication plaque was unveiled by Mrs Broderick to officially name the Nanton Lancaster Society's FM159 Lancaster as the *Ian Bazalgette Memorial Lancaster*.

Bazalgette (Baz) was born in Calgary, Alberta, to English/Irish parents, and in his youth moved back to England. Initially serving in the Royal Artillery, he soon volunteered as a pilot in the RAF Volunteer Force. After completing flying training and a Vickers Wellington OTU he was posted to No. 115 Squadron at RAF Marham, Norfolk. The squadron subsequently moved to RAF Mildenhall, Suffolk, and RAF East Wretham, Norfolk. He was awarded the DFC on 1 July 1943. The citation read,

> This officer has at all times displayed the greatest keenness for operational flying. He has taken part in many sorties and attacked heavily defended targets such as Duisberg, Berlin, Essen and Turin. His gallantry and devotion to duty have at all times been exceptional and his record commands the respect of all in his squadron.

He completed his tour of operations after converting to the Lancaster Mk II with the Bristol Hercules VI radial engines. Posted as an OTU flight commander to RAF Lossiemouth and RAF Milltown in Scotland, he continually pestered the recruitment officer, Group Captain T. G. 'Hamish' Mahaddie DSO, DFC, AFC, to let him do a tour in the Pathfinder Force.

His wish finally came true, and on 27 April 1944 he commenced training at RAF Warboys, Huntingdonshire (now Cambridgeshire). Experienced on the Lancaster, Baz was now flying the Mk III Lancaster in the PFF. Upon completion of training he was assigned to No. 635 PFF Squadron at Downham Market, Norfolk, on 5 May 1944. Forty Lancasters were lost from this station during wartime, part of a total station loss of 107 aircraft. The focus of bombing began to change prior to D-Day, with the requirement for pinpoint targets in France prior to the Allied invasion rather than the previous area-bombing technique.

The PFF were now required to mark smaller targets, with the emphasis being on more accurate bombing runs. Baz and his crew were gaining more experience and performed the supporter, illuminator and sky/visual marker roles – operations that required greater time over target and sometimes at a lower, more vulnerable altitude. On D-Day, Baz was on supporter operations to mark the Longues coastal batteries. The next day he was supporting the Army advance by bombing the surrounding area of Caen. This raid was followed by an attack on the Luftwaffe airfield at Rennes. An interesting coincidence is that Baz was on the Cambrai railyard raid of 12/13 June as deputy master bomber. This was the same raid that saw P/O Andrew Mynarski earn his VC.

The end of June saw Baz as deputy master bomber at the Lens marshalling yards, beginning operations against the 'V' weapons at Coubronne and Le Grand Rossignol. Nearly two weeks' leave was followed by another attack on Caen, a month after his first trip there. The remainder of July saw raids on L'Hey, Nucourt (V1 storage), Wesseling (synthetic oil factory), Kiel, Stuttgart, Hamburg and StLo (Army support). After this, Baz was due to go on leave again and was not on the battle order. His own aircraft, ND950 F2-M, had not returned to Downham Market due to fog.

However, an opportunity arose to get one more trip on 4 August, his fifty-eighth, and he was assigned ND811 F2-T for the raid on Trossy St Maximin, which is twenty-five miles north of Paris. It was a daylight trip to bomb the V1 installation. It had been bombed over the previous two days, so the defences were ready for another attack. Both the master bomber and deputy master bomber had been put out of action, so it was up to Baz to mark the target as the primary visual marker. Baz faced a wall of flak to get the marking done for the main bomber force.

The following is the citation accompanying the awarding of the Victoria Cross to S/L Ian Bazalgette, as published by the *London Gazette* on 17 August 1945:

On August 4, 1944, Squadron Leader Bazalgette was master bomber of a Pathfinder squadron detailed to mark an important target at Trossy St Maximin for the main bomber force. When nearing the target his Lancaster came under heavy anti-aircraft fire. Both starboard engines were put out of action and serious fires broke out in the fuselage and starboard mainplane. The bomb aimer was badly wounded. As the deputy master bomber had already been shot down the success of the attack depended on Squadron Leader Bazalgette, and this he knew. Despite the appalling conditions in his burning aircraft he pressed on gallantly to the target, marking and bombing it accurately. That the attack was successful was due to his magnificent effort. After the bombs had been dropped the Lancaster dived practically out of control. By expert airmanship and great exertion Squadron Leader Bazalgette regained control, but the port inner engine then failed and the whole of the starboard mainplane became a mass of flames. Squadron Leader Bazalgette fought bravely to bring his aircraft and crew to safety. The mid-upper gunner was overcome by fumes. Squadron Leader Bazalgette ordered those of his crew who were able to leave by parachute to do so. He remained at the controls and attempted the almost hopeless task of landing the crippled and blazing aircraft in a last effort to save the wounded bomb aimer and helpless air gunner. With superb skill and taking great care to avoid a small French village nearby, he brought the aircraft down safely. Unfortunately it then exploded and this gallant officer and his two comrades perished. His heroic sacrifice marked the climax of a long career of operations against the enemy. He always chose the more dangerous and exacting roles. His courage and devotion to duty were beyond praise.

Dave Birrell, the BCMC archivist and librarian, pointed out that there were two errors in the citation: Baz was not the master bomber on that raid, and fires did not break out in the fuselage. Perhaps a case of the finer details lost due to the confusion of war. The following day, 5 August 1944, S/L I. W. Bazalgette was permanently awarded his Pathfinder Force badge. How ironic, and what a tragedy. Baz's parents donated his medals to the RAF Museum at Hendon, where they are on display today.

By coincidence, his sister Ethel was in the area which had been liberated by Allied troops. She worked for the US 9th Air Force Command and was able to visit Senantes and hear her brother's story from the local schoolteacher. The two aircrew that died in the crash, F/L Hibbert and F/Sgt Leeder, were removed from the wreckage and buried by the Germans. The local villagers then searched the wreckage more thoroughly and discovered the ashes of S/L Bazalgette, which they placed in a casket. With his sister in attendance, a church service was held on 8 October 1944 and S/L Bazalgette was permanently laid to rest in the village of Senantes, a connection to the villagers of Senantes firmly established by the Bazalgette family.

By 1991, with the Lancaster now dedicated to S/L Bazalgette, the focus of the NLS slowly shifted to Bomber Command itself. Related aircraft and displays were under development. The basic hangar was expanded to house a library, archives, storage area and office. Emphasis was placed on artefacts, aviation art and interpretive information displays. In 2003, big doors were added to the hangar to enable the Lancaster to be pulled out on to the apron. It is difficult at times to realise that this endeavour was all performed with volunteer labour: a community rallying behind a concept to honour the heroes of another time, for they indeed were all heroes and we should never forget what they gave us – freedom.

One of the original founding directors of the NLS was Dave Birrell. A former geophysicist in the oil and gas industry, he changed career to become a schoolteacher and assumed a job at the local school in Nanton. He joined the NLS in 1986 as part of his becoming involved in the local community, anticipating 'cutting grass underneath the Lancaster in summer time'. He was initially responsible for treasurer duties such as collecting memberships and accepting donations. Birrell has now been involved with the museum for nearly thirty years, and he played his part in preserving the *Ian Bazalgette Memorial Lancaster* and the memory of Bomber Command. He remarked, 'My time with the museum has been multi-faceted, which has held my attention and prevented me from losing interest.' Birrell was awarded the Queen's Jubilee Medal in 2011 for his service to the museum.

In 2000 a suitable room became available in the lean-to portion of the hangar, which included the front entrance. Shelves were erected, filing cabinets filled and computers installed, and Birrell had thus created a library and archives area for reference and research. This was of great assistance to the author during research for the book *The Lancaster Manual*, and I was able to look at Art Sewel's logbook (see chapter 4), which he had donated to the museum. A summer student was hired later to catalogue photographs and put them on a database. Birrell is looking forward to playing his part in the further planned expansion of the living museum to make the public aware of the part that Bomber Command played in the victory of the Second World War.

In 2002 John Phillips was made a director, and shortly thereafter ('railroaded' in his words!) was given the mandate to oversee the refurbishing of the Lancaster. He previously had spent years helping out in the shop on projects as varied as cleaning displays and working on the Bolingbroke. In 2004 work started on the no. 3 engine, called starboard inner in Britain, and it ran from 2005 for three years until joined by no. 4 (starboard outer) engine in 2008. In 2011 Phillips was awarded the Queen's Jubilee Medal for his work with the museum. It would not be until 2012 that no. 2 engine, port inner, would run without a propeller. In July 2013 a completed no. 2 engine ran, to be joined shortly afterwards by no. 1 engine, port outer, on the truly memorable date of 24 August 2013. On that day, the sound of four Merlin engines running in unison was heard throughout Nanton.

The engine restoration years were full of propeller overhauls, seal, gasket and O-ring replacements, debris removal, internal engine timing of crankshaft and camshaft, carburettor diaphragm replacement, enriching adapters, flow tests, valve-gear sludge removal, piston ring renewal, cylinder blocks being hot tanked, cylinders honed, and blade cuffs repaired. The job was made easier by the fact that from time to time the cowlings had been opened and the engine rotated, with preserving oil added to help the general preservation. The original museum engine crew had expanded to seven, and every member who had worked on the engine got a chance to run it – a nice reward for all the volunteer labour.

The starting of no. 3 engine coincided with Canada's Bomber Command Memorial being built during the summer of 2005. It was dedicated at a ceremony on 20 August 2005. The forty-one-foot memorial is made of five panels of polished black granite. Four of these each have about 1,600 names engraved per side. The central panel includes the name and purpose of the memorial (on both sides), as well as the Bomber Command crest and a photo of a Canadian bomber crew. It is located on the front lawn of the Bomber Command Museum. The memorial's 10,659 engraved names include Canadians that served in Bomber Command and were killed in the line of duty.

The year 2007 saw a theatre and meeting rooms added to the museum.

In 2010, the NLS decided that the name of the museum would be changed to Bomber Command Museum of Canada to better reflect the scope and objectives of the museum in its present state. Two major expansion projects in 1997 and 2007 resulted in space for thirteen aircraft in a 37,000-square-foot hangar. The museum has evolved into a facility that restores aircraft to runnable status. The future plans include a 33,600-square-foot hangar with a run-up display area of 56,700 square feet.

A Lancaster with four running engines sitting chocked on a ramp – what could be next? Phillips had been assisted in the restoration by Greg Morrison, an aircraft maintenance engineer and former instructor at the Southern Alberta Institute of Technology aviation program. Morrison had started his association with the BCMC on a summer job and he has volunteered ever since. The no. 3 engine was chosen to be restored first because it had a DC generator and an air compressor for the brakes. Nearly fifty years since the engine last ran, Morrison did the first start on no. 3 engine, which would be the first milestone to the eventual taxiing of FM159.

Morrison mentioned that 'after getting the no. 4 engine going I spent over a year fixing leaks and broken lines on the pneumatic system'. The aircraft now had reliable brakes. Previously the aircraft main wheels had been chocked and the tractor and tow bar were left connected to the tailwheel during engine runs. The work progressed, and Morrison turned his attention 'to the hydraulic system, fixing the reservoir, filter and hand pump'. Another volunteer got the engine-driven pump working and the aircraft now had working bomb-bay doors and flaps.

By August 2013 the four engines were running, and now standard operating procedures had to be put in place for every run-up. Morrison said, 'The engines sounded better when they were idled between 700 to 850 rpm. We also decided that 1,600 rpm should be the maximum during the run-up because we noticed that higher than that the crowd started to cover their ears; it was a pretty good roar!' Morrison created a special checklist – not all systems were operating and some had been altered to non-standard configurations – and a training Powerpoint for the run-up crew.

On the night run-up of 25 April 2014, the author was invited on-board. Morrison drove the tractor to position the aircraft on the small apron. The wingspan of a Lancaster is 102 feet and the distance from the hangar to the white line at the edge of the highway is seventy-five feet! FM159 is positioned at an angle for the run-up and, with the propeller blast over the road, volunteers are positioned to warn unwary visitors. That night was the first public run-up after the winter. Morrison was the flight engineer on-board and I witnessed the checklist responses for the engine start and night run-up sessions. Unbeknownst to me at the time, FM159 had seen its first taxi after fifty-five years on the previous Tuesday.

Phillips and Morrison discussed the procedure to be followed and then mentioned the taxi scheduled for August. Morrison said, 'Nobody is here so let's just do it and go ten, maybe twenty feet. If there is a problem we have until August to fix it. I said to John [Phillips] that I will release the brake handle and just let it creep and then pull full hard brakes on to make sure it will stop going straight. Release the brake again and go maybe ten feet.' So FM159 became the fourth Lancaster in the twenty-first century to taxi under its own power. On 4 August 2014, the public saw FM159 taxi with four Merlin engines running for the first time. What an accomplishment for the BCMC and its volunteers.

The LAHC

The LAHC could not have had a more different beginning. A father's overwhelming grief, followed by his long time coming to accept it and finally his curiosity to see where his son was buried in Germany led eventually to the son's remembrance in the form of a museum. The museum was founded not only to honour a fallen son and brother, but also all those who had served or who had given their lives with Bomber Command. It was the Panton family, under the leadership of the two surviving brothers, who created the museum that has one of the only two ground-running Lancasters in the world, the other one being the aforementioned BCMC.

The story begins with Edward S. Panton, a First World War survivor who was a farm labourer, shepherd, wagoner and gamekeeper variously employed by farmers in Lincolnshire and the surrounding counties. In 1942 the family was living on a hill at Old Bolingbroke, near Spilsby, Lincolnshire. They had a view of the new airfield being built at East Kirkby and in 1943 witnessed the arrival of No. 57 Squadron Lancasters from Scampton, followed shortly thereafter by the Lancasters of No. 630 Squadron.

Edward's second-youngest son, the twelve-year-old Fred Panton, was fascinated by the aircraft. The word would spread among his pals – 'The Lancs are going to take off!' – and bicycles would be furiously pedalled to the end of the runway. Standing in the fields, and at times on the road, the boys would witness the Lancasters depart. Panton later told his granddaughter Kate that 'the ground vibrated and shook' as the heavily laden aircraft passed over their heads. He mentioned that 'on a clear night you could see the other Lancasters climb away from Coningsby and Spilsby'. The friends would watch the crew buses arrive at the dispersal area and the crews enter the aircraft. The Lancasters were then taxied around the perimeter track to the end of the runway to depart alternately from each side.

Panton recalled that there were six to eight men that looked after each aircraft parked at dispersal. Except for major overhaul or repair, the aircraft spent their life outside in the elements. This continued all year and was especially harsh in the winter months of wind, rain and snow, as the ground crew repaired and serviced the aircraft for the next trip. Panton said, 'In my opinion, the aircrew were the cream of the country and the ground crew were the salt of the earth.'

Panton's next-oldest brother, Christopher, had previously joined the Air Training Corp at Worksop, and in 1943 he completed his training to be a flight engineer. He was assigned to the Handley Page Halifax bomber. A contemporary of the Lancaster, it was one of the four-engine bombers employed by the RAF and Allied bomber squadrons. Sgt Chris Panton started his tour with Nos 405 and 409 squadrons, No. 6 (RCAF) Group, at Middleton St George. He subsequently moved to No. 433 (Porcupine) Squadron at Skipton-on-Swale, North Yorkshire, to complete his operational tour of thirty trips.

The raid on Nuremberg of 30/31 March 1944 was part of the Battle of Berlin, which ended on this very costly raid to the Allies. The German defences correctly identified Nuremberg as the main target and were ready for the main bomber stream of 572 Lancasters, 214 Halifaxes and 9 Mosquitos – 795 aircraft in total. The main bomber stream was attacked by night fighters before reaching the Belgian border, and during the next hour eighty-two bombers were lost before reaching the target. Thirteen bombers were shot down on the return trip, making it, at 11.9 per cent, the costliest raid of the whole war in Bomber Command. Over 500 airmen died that night, and the Battle of Berlin ended.

Speaking with P/O Bill Pearson about his trip that night (his twenty-first) as part of the PFF, I asked him how he survived the terrible odds. He replied, 'Lucky. Just lucky.' This should have been Chris Panton's final flight (his thirtieth), completing his tour of operations. Unfortunately, Panton's luck ran out that night, along with that of five of his crew. Three survived to tell the story. Just forty miles from Nuremberg they were attacked by a night fighter from below – they never saw it – and the starboard inner engine caught fire. The pilot, Christian Nielsen, dived the aircraft steeply from 20,000 feet to 15,000 feet to try and extinguish the flames. Nielsen ordered the crew to bail out. The rear gunner bailed out and the wireless operator and pilot were blown out of the fuselage by an explosion, possibly caused by a partially empty fuel tank. Five aircrew never made it out, including Chris Panton.

Fred Panton remembers the day when a local lad delivered a telegram to say that Sgt Chris Patton had not returned from a mission and was classified as missing until further information became available. His dad had him go to the post office every morning before school to see if there was any news. Four months later, the Red Cross confirmed the five crew members who had lost their lives. Fred did not have to go the post office anymore. He said that 'it was a very, very sad time' and that his father 'took the news very, very badly'.

Fred Panton left school, nearly fourteen, and went catching rabbits until 1949. His father had bought a small farm at Stickford, Lincolnshire, and Panton was able to realise his dream of starting poultry farming. His younger brother Harold joined him in 1953 and they have been partners ever since. Second World War buildings were being disposed of, and Panton was dealing with the Ministry of Works (MOW) to purchase them for the poultry business. At the same time, the MOW was disposing of surplus aircraft such as the Halifax bomber. Panton thought it would be a good idea to purchase a Halifax bomber, the same aircraft that his brother Chris flew on, for the farm at Stickford. His father would not hear of it. Panton also suggested going to Germany to see where Chris was buried, but his father did not want him to go. The years passed, Panton stopped asking and the war years faded from his memory – but not totally.

In 1971, his father turned seventy-five and had a change of heart, or maybe came to terms with a very painful time in his life, and suddenly asked his son Fred to go to Germany now and photograph Chris's grave. Panton said that he had been 'wanting to do it for thirty years'. But where and how was he to start looking for the information? This was before the internet. As luck would have it, he was put in touch with a local poultry farmer turned author who was writing a book on the Nuremberg raid. His name was Martin Middlebrook and he lived nearby, so they were able to meet easily. Middlebrook gave Panton all the details regarding the crash site, the initial burial ground and subsequent reinterment to the War Cemetery.

Panton set off with his friend Derek Hipkin to find the crash site in a range of hills near the village of Friesen. By chance they established contact with the burgomaster, who took them by tractor to the crash site. Panton was able to gather a few small pieces of his brother's aircraft to bring home. They visited Chris's initial burial spot at Butenheim cemetery, a small, beautiful and well-kept country cemetery. Next was the visit to his final resting place in 1948 at Durnbach War Cemetery, near Munich. All five crew members are buried with their own individual headstones. Panton recalls that touching his brother's stone brought all the memories of Chris and of the war flooding back. In a way, the visit renewed an interest in the Second World War that had been dormant for many years.

The next week, after returning from Germany, a lady named Madge Bailey, who worked for the Pantons, handed him an advertisement from the Sunday newspaper and Fred Panton's life changed forever. It said, 'Lancaster bomber for sale. Squires Gate, Blackpool.' Unfortunately the aircraft was withdrawn at the auction as it did not meet its reserve price, and subsequently a private buyer, the Rt Hon. Lord Lilford, managed to purchase it. Disappointments rarely come alone. Three weeks after returning from Germany, Panton's father Edward passed away. He had seen the photographs of his son's crash site and burial plot prior to his death.

Lord Lilford subsequently loaned the aircraft to the RAF, where it served as a 'Gate Guardian' at RAF Scampton. After ten years there, in 1983, he offered the aircraft, NX611, to Fred Panton, who jumped at the chance to buy it. The rest, as they say, is history. But where did the aircraft come from, and how did it end up at RAF Scampton? What of its first thirty years in aviation? Did it have any provenance, as they say in the world of antiquities?

Avro Lancaster Mk VII NX611 started its aviation life on 16 April 1945 at the Austin Motors Longbridge plant near Birmingham, England. Austin had contributed to the Royal Flying Corps in 1914 by building biplanes. In the 1930s it manufactured Fairey Battles, which were exported to Canada for training purposes, and later Hawker Hurricanes, Short Stirlings and Avro Lancasters. The Stirlings and Lancasters were transported by road in sections to a large assembly building at Birmingham Airport.

Too late for the war in Europe, NX611 was prepared for the Tiger Force in the Pacific to oppose Japan. Also too late for the war in the Pacific, it was put in long-term storage at No. 38 Maintenance Unit at RAF Llandow near Cardiff, Wales. It remained there until it went to France as part of a fifty-nine-aircraft deal in 1952. Some engines had been replaced, overhauled or uprated and some items, such as radar, navigation equipment and fuel tanks, had been added to bring it up to maritime reconnaissance status. Mid-upper gun turrets were removed and a ventral radome installed.

NX611 was flight tested by S/L J. Wales and F/E D. Wilson on 8 May 1952 at RAF Langar, near Nottingham. NX611, now called WU15 and painted navy blue, began its Aeronavale career on 30 May 1952; it had sat idle for seven years, but managed to avoid the scrapheap. Flown to France by a Navy crew, it was introduced to its maritime reconnaissance role at Unit 10F (Flottille) Reception and Training Centre near Lorient. It was given the new identification of 10F4. For four years it was mainly involved with trials and experimental work, before being assigned to Flottille 25 as 25F7 in 1956. Flottille 25 was tasked with 'show-the-flag' long-distance flights. In October 1956 it was 25F7's turn.

The exercise, called 'Coelacanth' after a rediscovered fish off the coast of Madagascar, was assigned to Lancasters numbered 25F5, 25F7 and 25F8. The Lancasters carried a crew of twelve, which included two co-pilots. The route followed was directly out to the Atlantic and then southwards, stopping at the naval bases of Agadir and Dakar. Stops at Abidjan,

Brazzaville and Elisabethville preceded the long flight across the Indian Ocean to Diego Suarez on the northern tip of Madagascar. Three days of crew rest and then 25F7 flew to Tananarive and Durban, fuelling stops en route to the 'CAPEX' exercise in Cape Town, South Africa. By now the Suez Crisis had started, and the trio of Lancasters started home, carefully avoiding the conflict area in Egypt and arriving back in November 1956.

The other side of the world also needed a military presence to protect the French colonies from communism without and independence within. The 1954 memory of the loss of Indochina still lingered. The flag would have to be shown in New Caledonia. The Lockheed Neptune was assuming maritime reconnaissance duties from the Lancasters, freeing them up for other duties. In 1957, three overhauled and tropics-suited Lancasters were sent to the South Pacific for shipping lane patrols, nuclear test site surveys and air-sea rescue flights. The new unit was 9S, and all the personnel, crew of eleven per aircraft, were taken from units 22F, 24F and 25F – all experienced Lancaster crews for the long flights, which required careful navigation procedures. It took approximately sixty flying hours to position the aircraft at Tontouta; this was the naval base close to Noumea, the capital of New Caledonia.

This was the start of a seven-year commitment to patrol the vast area of French Polynesia. It stretched for 4,500 miles in length across the Pacific Ocean. Long flights with few navigation aids were the standard operation, with DR skills honed to perfection.

In 1958, after overhaul at Le Bourget by UTA, WU15 (NX611) was on its way to Morocco to serve with 55S and 52S. The S denoted a training unit, and it was probably involved with multi-engine heavy conversions. By November 1962 it had been overhauled again, painted Pacific white, and was destined for 9S assignment in the South Pacific, routed by way of Malta, Turkey, Persia (now Iran), Pakistan, India, Cambodia, Singapore, Indonesia and Australia to New Caledonia. Due to the loss of the third

Lancaster, WU21, WU15 and WU13 were very busy; however, their time was coming to an end. WU13 was donated to the New Zealand Museum of Transport and Technology in April 1964. WU16 had been donated to the Royal Australian Air Force (RAAF) in Perth, Australia, in 1962, and subsequently had been moved to the Aviation Heritage Museum at Bull Creek. What would become of WU15, so far from home?

Thanks to the persistence and dedication of an organisation calling itself the Historic Aircraft Preservation Society (HAPS) of Biggin Hill, England, the aircraft was flown to Sydney, Australia, on 13 August 1964 by 9S and that ended its twelve years of service with L'Aeronavale. HAPS had previously enquired about the French Lancasters but had not received any reply, let alone encouragement, from France to preserve any of their redundant Lancasters. It came as a great surprise in July 1964 when WU15/NX111 was offered, with delivery to Australia in August. Things had to move very fast in order to pull this repatriation and preservation off.

Under the leadership of Bill Fisher in England and Bruce Miles, who became the flight manager, in Sydney, the aircraft was prepared for departure to England the following April. Support poured in from all quarters to make it happen; not least was the support of the original manufacturer, Sir Roy Dobson and the Hawker/Avro Group. The volunteer crew, led by Wing Commander John Hampshire DFC, were all present or former RAAF or airline crew. The other personnel on board were all interested members of the public who had paid for the privilege of experiencing the delivery flight.

The delivery flight departed from Sydney Mascot Airport on Anzac Day, 25 April 1965. Although still carrying the roundels and colour of L'Aeronavale, it now had the new British registration G-ASXX displayed – it truly was returning to its roots in England. It would fly a slightly different route home than its flight from England to New Caledonia. Leaving Australia, it flew through Singapore, Malaya, India, Pakistan,

Bahrain, Cyprus and France to Biggin Hill, England. G-ASXX touched down at 15.33 on 13 May 1965, three minutes late, after sixty-nine hours and 12,000 miles of flight. Shortly thereafter the Lancaster was grounded due to time expiry on an engine and propeller; being grounded on a Battle of Britain fighter base definitely had limited public appeal. Was it to become synonymous with FM159, the BCMC Lancaster in Nanton that was vandalised as it sat neglected and available to souvenir hunters?

Once again it was volunteers to the rescue, painting the aircraft in Bomber Command night livery. The target was to get the aircraft flying again by the anniversary date of the Dams Raid in May. Finally, on 17 May 1967, after four hair-raising test flights, NX611/G-ASXX was given its permit to fly. The previous weekend it had been christened 'Guy Gibson' and had the code HA-P painted on. On 19 May, NX611/G-ASXX proceeded to RAF Scampton for the twenty-fourth reunion of the Dams Raids, to be met by Sir Barnes Wallis, inventor of the 'bouncing bomb'. In September it went to Blackbushe, Hampshire, and then spent the winter grounded again. Due to its geographical proximity to Farnborough Royal Aircraft Establishment, Blackbushe was used to develop the Fog Investigation and Dispersal Operation (FIDO) system to enable aircraft operations in heavy fog. Ironically, it was the appearance of NX611 that prompted the personnel at RAF Waddington to get PA474 airborne again (see chapter 5). The cost of £300 per hour to keep NX611 flying was prohibitive for some air show organisers; the dream was becoming too expensive.

Nine months later, in June 1968, NX611 flew to Bristol Filton Airport and returned for the annual Bristol Aeroplane Company air show, and also commemorated the fiftieth anniversary of the RAF. By March 1969 the aircraft was moved to Lavenham near Bury St Edmunds, Suffolk, an old USAAF airfield now owned by a local farmer. This move had been orchestrated by the new Reflectaire Preservation Group, which had taken over NX611 from the former HAPS Group. At the same time, the other aircraft in the collection were gradually moved to Lavenham. NX611, similar to what is happening at the BCMC and the LAHC today, conducted four-engine run-ups from time to time – much to the delight of dignitaries and the general public.

The initial wave of interest and revenue soon faded and the rent issue again forced another move. The scramble was on again to get the necessary permit to fly. Hawker Siddeley engineers from Woodford started their assessment of NX611's condition. Meanwhile, the hunt was on for another location for the collection. This turned out to be RAF Hullavington, Wiltshire, which had a large hangar available and was then being used as a Parachute Training School. The flight move was completed in February 1970, with Mrs Eve Gibson, the widow of the late Wing Commander Guy Gibson VC, DSO, DFC of Dambuster fame, welcoming the Lancaster to Hullavington.

A dramatic, disappointing blow occurred the same month. The Ministry of Defence would not allow any visitors to the aircraft or any notices to be displayed. Furthermore, electrical power would not be available in the hangar. This meant that there was no way of getting revenue and that restoration work on the collection could not take place. Any future location would have to be accessible to visitors, preferably in large numbers, to finance the museum and keep the Lancaster in the air. This turned out to be Squire's Gate Airport, Blackpool. The flight was delayed by an engine problem and further maintenance requirements necessary for the permit to fly.

Finally, on 26 June 1970, the twenty-five-year-old aircraft departed Hullavington for Blackpool. En route it did a low-level pass down Lake Bala training lake for Ron Valentine, a former bomb aimer with No. 617 Dambuster Squadron, who was riding in his old position in the aircraft. Would the Blackpool venue be kind to John Roast, the chairman of Reflectaire Ltd, and the loyal group of museum volunteers? The summer brought a fair share of visitors as the collection was set up for display. The collection also included military vehicles and equipment, which added to the general interest. The intended area for the museum was close to the original wartime assembly sheds, which gave the area a sense of historic importance.

However, the financial decline continued and two original salaried employees departed with wages owing; not a good omen for the future of NX611. A brief respite with some filming work in February 1971, the Granada series *Family at War*, was not enough, and by November 1971 the company was asked to dispose of assets to cover outstanding financial commitments; this included NX611. The last time that it would move under its own power for nearly twenty-five years was during the filming of a high-speed taxi down the runway.

This disposal of assets by Reflectaire Ltd would be the first face-to-face meeting of Fred Panton and NX611. On 29 April 1972, Lot 63 was the Lancaster and an assortment of spares. John Roast, in an attempt to impress the possible buyers, started an engine. It did not meet its reserve price, and was withdrawn from auction. Subsequently, as mentioned previously, Lord Lilford negotiated a price acceptable to the liquidators and NX611 slipped out of Panton's reach. He kept abreast of all possibilities and, always the dealmaker, suggested that NX611 could be the 'Gate Guardian' at RAF Scampton to replace Lancaster R5868, which had gone to the RAF Museum at Hendon. Lord Lilford handed over the aircraft on a ten-year loan to the RAF to be used at Scampton as a reminder of No. 617 Squadron's former wartime presence. NX611 had found a permanent home at last, under the care of the RAF's Engineering Wing.

The task of dismantling the aircraft in Blackpool fell to eleven volunteer Scampton airmen working on their own 'leave' and within a strict budget. The fact that the aircraft was built in sections aided the careful dismantling and transportation of the pieces. Six 'Queen Mary' (a special large trailer) loads completed the road trip to Scampton. Once again the preservation, restoration and reassembly had to be done in spare time with volunteer labour. This was August 1973, and a target date of April 1974 was set for the gate installation. The Blackpool salt air had contributed to the corrosion of the engines and propellers.

Weathering trials were completed in March, with a few leaks appearing in the cockpit area. Then NX611 was painted in its wartime scheme and readied for the move to the main gate. The outer wings and engines were removed, in addition to the inner propellers, mainplanes and tailplane. Other obstacles were temporarily removed as the aircraft was towed, pushed, pulled and manoeuvred into position at the main gate. It was on 25 April 1974 that NX611 was attached to the steel-and-concrete supports for the three axles. It was now secure in its new home. It was given the code YF-C. Three bombs designed by Sir Barnes Wallis were positioned in front of the aircraft. They were the Grand Slam, the Tallboy and the Bouncing Bomb. It became a major attraction with former Lancaster aircrew and ground crew, aircraft aficionados, historians and present RAF personnel, as well as the general public.

Shortly after the NX611 handover ceremony from Lord Lilford to the commanding officer of RAF Scampton on 17 May 1974, Fred Panton left for Canada. He wanted to meet the surviving members of his brother's crew, albeit thirty years later. He had been too young to appreciate the visit his brother's pilot had made to his parents in 1945 to explain what happened that night. He managed to meet up with Harry Cooper, the wireless operator, in Vancouver and Jack McClaughan, the rear gunner, in Winnipeg. On this trip he was not able to trace pilot Christian Nielsen, who had moved to the USA and indeed passed away just six months before Panton was able to trace him to Illinois, USA. Stories were shared and Panton learnt more about his brother Chris. I think this visit to Canada, along with the previous visit to Germany, made Panton more determined than ever to do something for his brother's memory.

The extremely successful poultry farming business continued with his brother Harold, and then, in 1981, another phone call would start the adventure of a lifetime. A friend called to say the airfield at East Kirkby was up for private sale. This was the same airfield that Panton had watched being built, where he had watched the arrival of the Lancaster squadrons and their nightly departures on bombing raids. It now had poultry houses on it, as well as the original control tower. This would turn out to be a combination that the Pantons could not resist! This would allow them to have the Lancaster on a former wartime base where Lancasters had actually been based. The purchase was completed and, notwithstanding the changing of the poultry sheds to turkey sheds, the first thing done was to fix up the control tower. This was the same control tower that had guided the Lancasters he had watched as a boy; Panton could now stand on the balcony and remember those days, or imagine the days to come.

Two years later, in 1983, the concern was over what would happen to NX611 at the end of the loan period. The Panton brothers had been in touch with Lord Lilford's representatives and had come to an agreement that they would have a chance to purchase the aircraft if it ever came up for sale. For thirty years Fred Panton had wanted to have a bomber aircraft in memory of his brother; he now had a location, and all he needed was an aircraft. He finally realised his dream on 1 September 1983 with the purchase of NX611. Now the Pantons had most of the puzzle – the aircraft and the location.

The pieces of the puzzle still missing included how to move it from Scampton and how to store it at East Kirkby: the original T2 hangar had been dismantled, but the concrete base was still there. The plan was to leave the Lancaster at Scampton until a hangar was built at East Kirkby to keep it undercover. This would take four years, and involved a considerable financial investment in the new building. The dismantling,

moving and reassembly by a crew from RAF Abingdon would take just over three months. The original idea was that the Pantons would be able to look at the aircraft and the control tower whenever they wished, a private memorial to their brother Chris.

How did it change from a private memorial to the living museum it is today? The commanding officer of RAF Scampton had commented to the Pantons that they should make it available to the public to see what an important part the Lancaster had played in Britain's wartime history and not keep it locked up in a hangar. Fred and Harold discussed it at length and decided that a museum was the right choice. The next two years were spent collecting memorabilia and period pieces of a wartime station and making the artefacts ready for suitable display, both in the hangar surrounding the NX611 and the control tower, which was often referred to as the 'Watch Office'. The Lincolnshire Aviation Heritage Centre began life in July 1988, and in August 1989 the Marshal of the Royal Air Force, Sir Michael Beetham, officially opened the museum.

The Lincolnshire Aircraft Recovery Group (LARG) had been given space in the main hangar in 1987 to erect displays of their work. The serious activity of aircraft recovery, a part of aviation archaeology, started in 1973 for the LARG and its aim was to remind people of the sacrifice of Bomber Command aircrew by either recovering the aircraft and/or erecting memorial plaques at crash sites. The recovery of an aircraft is the high point of months, sometimes years, of meticulous research. Many regulations and constraints govern the dig, so great care has to be taken to get it right the first time. The wreckage is then cleaned extensively prior to display at East Kirkby.

Dave Stubley is an original member and has worked with the LAHC since it opened. Originally based in the control tower, the group now has a workshop in a Nissen hut in addition to its displays. An example of one display is the recovered wreckage of a No. 97 Squadron Lancaster, ME625, which was involved in a mid-air collision with Lancaster ND981 on 23 June 1944 and crashed in a drainage dyke near Crowland, Lincolnshire. Five years' work by hand, aided by two JCBs, yielded about 60 per cent of the aircraft. The first engine was discovered about one foot below ground level at the bottom of the dyke and the last engine was found at twenty-five feet below the surface. The wings had been recovered during wartime. A memorial plaque was erected close to the crash site on 23 June 2014, seventy years after the accident.

Prior to the Ministry of Defence (MoD) Protection of Military Remains Act of 1986, a recovery dig was fairly straightforward. Dave mentioned that you now 'have to apply for a MoD licence, create a project design for the County Archaeologist and submit a post-dig report. The licence will only be approved if there are no human remains or bombs on board and your application agrees with the MoD records.' Locations of aircraft come from many sources, including newspapers, the stories of farmers and the donated notes of schoolboy Fred Robinson, who cycled around the countryside noting crash sites. Dave said, 'There are thousands of sites in Lincolnshire, nearly all from training and night-flying accidents.' Most of the farmers are cooperative with LARG after the crop has been removed from their land.

The visitors started to arrive, and they have never stopped in the twenty-five years since the museum opened. Year over year the numbers steadily increased, which met the Pantons' requirement that the museum must stand on its own two feet financially. During this time, NX611 continued to be restored through the addition of a mid-upper gun turret plus a refurbished hydraulic system to allow the flaps and large bomb doors to be operated. In 1991 the Roy Chadwick Memorial was unveiled to remember the designer of the Lancaster. One of the regular visitors to the museum would always pass the remark to Fred Panton, 'Wouldn't it be lovely to start one of the engines on the Lancaster?' This continued for many years until 1994, when Panton wondered if it was possible; after all, the engines had not run since 1971, twenty-three years before.

About this time, Ian Hickling, a former engineer with the RAF BBMF, spoke to Panton about the possibility of starting an engine and was subsequently hired to attempt it. Another new part of the Pantons' adventure had begun. Hickling examined the engines and found that they all rotated freely; with that as an indication of condition, the decision was made to attempt to start engine no. 3. This engine had a hydraulic pump on it. Hickling, and engineering associate Roy Jarman, started by removing the propeller, which allowed them to remove, inspect, clean and refurbish accessible parts of the engine, followed by the electrical and fuel systems. Four months and 1,200 man hours later, the no. 3 engine was ready to start.

The local fire department was on hand as Hickling cranked the engine over. A second attempt was made after some adjustments in April 1994, and six revolutions later there were a few coughs of blue smoke and the engine came to life. Over the weeks the revs (revolutions per minute) of the engine were gradually increased to 2,500, and that gave a very satisfactory sound from the exhaust of the Merlin's twelve cylinders. Success breeds confidence. No. 2 engine went through the same process, and four months later it too burst into life. Both inner engines were now running. No. 4 was followed by no. 1 engine, and sixteen months later, in July 1995, NX611 looked like and sounded like an operational Lancaster.

Plans were also underway to taxi the aircraft under its own power. Six weeks of checking the brakes and hydraulic system and the Lancaster was ready to go. Its first private taxi was in April 1995, on three engines, and then came the first public taxi in August with all four turning. It was a very emotional time for the Pantons after all the disappointments, delays and successes that they had been through to get to this day. A museum with a ground-taxi Lancaster on an old wartime station in memory of their brother Chris – this was some achievement for poultry farmers.

Initially the taxi runs were performed by ex-RAF, specifically BBMF, personnel familiar with the Lancaster. However, the museum was a family-run business and training began to get a family member 'checked out' on taxiing the Lancaster. Andrew Panton is Fred Panton's grandson, and after completing school he started his training immediately to taxi the legendary aircraft; some challenge, some achievement. A training scheme was set up to satisfy the museum's insurance company, and Andrew completed the required training between 2007 and 2011. Observing, taxiing with pilot supervision and finally taxiing solo was the culmination of 500 hours of training.

The museum continued to grow, with school tours, squadron reunions, 1940s-style dances and engine/taxi runs. Corporate days included a run in the Lancaster and a meal at the museum. The staff increased but their cost was always less than the revenue generated, with the result that the museum maintained a healthy financial state. In the 1990s it was decided to name NX611 *Just Jane* after the wartime cartoon character in the *Daily Mirror* newspaper. The real Jane, Chrystabel Leighton-Porter, christened the aircraft in 1997, which now had the *Just Jane* nose art suitably placed.

Then an American visitor in October 1999 turned out to be a link with Christian Nielsen, Chris Panton's pilot. He was a family friend. Further enquiries revealed that Nielsen's uniform, medals and logbook and had been given to a youth in the town, name and address unknown. A couple of years later, Panton received a letter from a collector in Wales to enquire if he was related to Chris Panton as he had bought the aforementioned items in America and the logbook had listed the crew members. Panton arranged for them to meet, and in what turned out to be another pinnacle in his quest for memorabilia associated with his brother he acquired the uniform, medals and logbook of his brother's pilot. Once a year, at the 1940s dance, his grandsons wear the uniform carefully.

A second starring role in a movie occurred in 2001. The BBC TV drama *Night Flight* featured *Just Jane* doing 'tail-up' fast-taxi runs. This was made possible by neighbouring farmer Graham Larnyman, who owned the well-kept main runway. The weather cooperated and the scenes looked very authentic, with the actors wearing the wartime gear of heavy bombers. In 2003 Fred Panton received an MBE from Prince Charles at Buckingham Palace. The former resident squadrons of East Kirkby, No. 57 and No. 630, still have an annual reunion and wreath-laying ceremony at East Kirkby.

In 2010 the Pantons firmly declared that it is their intention to prepare NX611 to take to the air again. Some key components and parts had been obtained from the Bomber Command Museum of Canada in Nanton – aviation museums cooperating for the sake of world aviation history. When all the pieces have been collected and refurbished, work could begin on having NX611 join FM159 and PA474 in the air again, where they all truly belong. Some visitor comments:

> If you haven't been along to see *Just Jane* at the LAHC you don't know what you're missing, a warm welcome, great people and a fantastic educational experience and location full of history. See you all again soon!

> If you've never been to visit Jane, you need to. Something very special has been created at East Kirkby.

What a story, what perseverance from the Pantons, what a living museum to the memory of their brother Christopher Whitton Panton.

Some of the photographs of *Just Jane* at the museum look like they are actual wartime scenes. This is because the aircraft was carefully positioned against authentic buildings or grassy areas, and the personnel working with the aircraft were dressed in period uniform using authentic wartime equipment. Gary Bainbridge is one of those personnel and pursues his hobby as a collector with an emphasis on education, for himself and the public, which he refers to as 'living history'. He collected all the necessary period pieces to fully outfit himself as a wartime Lancaster wireless air gunner and then studied the role of the radio operator so that he could educate the public on the special occasions when he played the role in the museum's Lancaster.

He belongs to a group of collectors known as the Summer of 1944 Group. They meet in a restored RAF billet hut, which also functions as a reproduction-building facility to make items for their own use or donate to a museum, such as aircrew oxygen bottles. The group does events for the National Trust and English Heritage as their expertise is not restricted to the RAF. Gary believes that 'by dressing in authentic uniforms and having, and using, authentic equipment you can talk about what it was like to wear the wartime uniforms and operate the particular equipment'. Educational re-enactment is the aim of the group.

The members of the group come from all walks of life, with their emphasis on education. A 'Kit Talk' meeting is held prior to any event to ensure that all members are correctly attired and know their assigned role. There are experts in many disciplines who will lead the briefing to ensure maximum authenticity. Each member/collector has their own interest within the greater interests of the group. The Summer of 1944 Group often combines with other groups at events throughout the summer months. A well-known photograph of their work at the LAHC is the group portraying ground crew surrounding the David Brown bomb tractor and trailers in front of *Just Jane* and the aircrew, who are about to board the aircraft.

Two very different beginnings – a family's remembrance and a small town's effort to get attention – have resulted in the world, in 2015, having two famous Lancaster aircraft that the historians, aficionados and general public alike can tour, feel and observe. All can now listen to the sound of the famous Merlin engines. In addition, the accompanying displays in both museums remind us that freedom did not just happen; it was earned by those young men, some of whom gave their all for us.

'We Will Remember Them'

Left: Ethel Bazalgette unveiling FM159 dedication to her brother S/L Ian Bazalgette VC DFC. (Bomber Command Museum of Canada)

Below: FM159 being towed across-the Little Bow River as it travels cross-country from RCAF Vulcan to Nanton. (Bomber Command Museum of Canada)

Opposite left: NX611/G-ASXX, Lancaster B.VII *Just Jane*, at the Lincolnshire Aviation Heritage Centre, East Kirkby. (Martin Keen)

Opposite right: FM159, the *Ian Bazalgette Memorial Lancaster*, at the Bomber Command Museum of Canada, Nanton. (Gordon Wilson)

Above: FM159's vandalised cockpit, 1986. (Bomber Command Museum of Canada)

Above left: FM159 as it looked before restoration, with sheets of aluminium over its window to protect it from vandalism. (Bomber Command Museum of Canada)

Left: FM159 now wears the codes F2-T in remembrance of Bazalgette's No. 635 Squadron Lancaster, ND811. (Gordon Wilson)

The *Ian Bazalgette Memorial Lancaster* performing engine runs at one of BCMC's regular public open days. (Doug Bowman)

Left: Canada's Bomber Command Memorial at BCMC, Nanton, with FM159 serving as a most suitable backdrop. The memorial lists the names of 10,659 RCAF personnel lost during the Second World War. (Carl Orde)

Right: Fraser Nash FN20 rear turret, as fitted to FM159. (Gordon Wilson)

Left: A beautifully restored Fraser Nash FN50 Lancaster mid-upper turret on display alongside FM159 at Nanton. (Gordon Wilson)

FM159 parked outside her hangar at
BCMC. (Gordon Wilson)

A Lancaster night run is a spectacular sight and sound, especially so when close access is possible, such as here at Nanton. (Doug Bowman)

More pictures from the fantastic night run at Nanton. (Doug Bowman)

Right: David Stubley of the Lincolnshire Aircraft Recovery Group. (A. & K. Markham Photographers)

Left: The late Fred Panton, with brother Harold and their Lancaster *Just Jane*. (A. & K. Markham Photographers)

Lancaster NX611 *Just Jane*, the
pride of the Lincolnshire Aviation
Heritage Centre. (Martin Keen)

NX611 photographed in East Kirkby's main hangar, July 2015. (Martin Keen)

Right and overleaf: Undoubtedly the best location in Europe to experience an active Lancaster, the taxiing operations at LAHC provide close access to the bomber and the glorious roar of her four Merlin 24 engines. (Martin Keen)

Right and overleaf: The *Just Jane* nose art on the port side of NX611. (Martin Keen)

Left: During her taxiing operations *Just Jane* is a glorious sight to behold. (Martin Keen)

City of Sheffield and Bomber Command crests, starboard side of NX611. (Martin Keen)

Opposite: Inside the cockpit of NX611 – a cramped space from which the single pilot would fly a mighty aircraft. To the right of the pilot's seat the bomb aimer/ front gunner's position in the nose of the Lancaster can be seen. (Martin Keen)

Above and right: LE-H and DX-F Squadron codes on NX611. For over twenty-five years NX611 had worn the aircraft letter 'C', with the wartime codes of DX- (No. 57 Squadron) and LE- (No. 630 Squadron). Following the passing of museum co-founder Fred Panton it was decided to change the aircraft code letters to 'F' (Fred) on the starboard side and 'H' (Harold Panton, co-founder) on the port side. Both codes are also historically correct, having been allocated to wartime Lancasters operating from East Kirkby. (Martin Keen)

Another view inside the cockpit of NX611.
(Martin Keen)

Above: A 'bomb's eye' view – the bomb aimer/front gunner's position inside the nose of the Lancaster. (Martin Keen)

Right: Fishpond equipment, located in the wireless operator's position, NX611. (Martin Keen)

Left: Wireless operator's position, NX611. (Martin Keen)

Post-war French ASR equipment, NX611. This equipment is likely to be removed in the future to return the Lancaster to a 1945 Bomber Command B.VII standard. (Martin Keen)

NX611, view forward from crew door, over bomb bay and towards main spar and cockpit. (Martin Keen)

View of the Lancaster's cavernous
thirty-three-foot bomb bay. (Martin Keen)

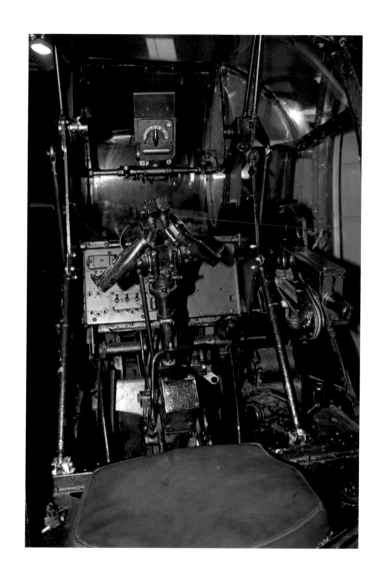

Left and right:
NX611 Fraser
Nash FN82 rear
turret (revolved
for maintenance).
(Martin Keen)

Above and next three pages: Post-winter maintenance views of NX611, with engine cowlings removed. Also, views with the cowlings refitted and fuselage and wings treated with an anti-corrosive application. (Martin Keen)

Right: Access to the rear turret over rear spar, NX611. (Martin Keen)

Above and right: Gary Bainbridge performing living history inside NX611. (Martin Keen)

Living history brings the former RAF East Kirkby and the resident Lancaster *Just Jane* to life – courtesy of authentic, dedicated and passionate groups such as Summer of '44, An Airfield Somewhere and MECo. (Martin Keen)

Surrounded by ground crew and airmen in period dress, *Just Jane* would look quite at home on a 1940s runway. (Martin Keen)

This page and opposite: History brought to life by the talented living-history re-enactors. (Martin Keen)

Right: Trying to spot enemy fighters as a gunner on a night run was not easy, and shooting them down was even harder. (Martin Keen)

Opposite and overleaf: Thanks to the dedicated members of living history groups, post-war generations are able to get a sense of what it was like to live in a turbulent time of war. It is a fitting memorial to the men and women of Bomber Command who fought for our freedom. (Martin Keen)

Left: Navigators had to keep the bomber on course under intense pressure – sometimes even enemy fire. (Martin Keen)

Left: Re-enacting a common scene from a Second World War airfield – an 8,000 lb 'cookie' blast bomb is wheeled towards the waiting Lancaster bomber by ground crew. (Martin Keen)

Right: Lancaster bomb loads on display at LAHC – left of picture is an example of the Dambusters bouncing bomb (Upkeep). Centre is an 8,000 lb 'cookie' blast bomb. Right is an example of a 12,000 lb Tallboy. (Martin Keen)

Left: A replica of a Tallboy, a 12,000 lb earthquake bomb designed by Barnes Wallis. (Martin Keen)

Right: Another of Barnes Wallis's famous yet devastating designs, the Upkeep bouncing bomb. This example is filled with concrete and was used for training purposes by No. 617 Squadron on the lead-up to Operation Chastise. (Martin Keen)

The Lincolnshire Aviation Heritage Centre is very much a family-run establishment. Fred Panton's grandchildren Andrew and Louise help co-founder Harold with the management of the museum, and it continues to go from strength to strength as a result. (A. & K. Markham Photographers)

John Phillips (far right), BCMC engineer, giving some valuable equipment an all-important health check. (Bomber Command Museum of Canada)

Above: NX611 in 1967 at Biggin Hill. (Malcolm Nason)

Above right: Author in front of FM159 prior to the spring run-up. (Gordon Wilson)

Right: FM213 at Goderich, Ontario prior to CWHM life. (John Kimberley)

Left: Greg Morrison, Lancaster Engineer and Taxi Pilot at BCMC. (Gordon Wilson)

Below: Dave Birrell, BCMC archivist and librarian, with Flt Sgt Art Sewel's donated logbook. (Gordon Wilson)

7

THE LANCASTER EXPERIENCE

There are four places where you can see a real live Lancaster during the extended summer months of the year. It is not surprising that they are in England and Canada, the two places that manufactured the Lancaster. What is surprising is that three of the places are privately run organisations trying to keep the memory of the Lancaster and Bomber Command alive. That is not to say that different levels of government have not contributed to the effort to keep these old warbirds running, of course. Once experienced, it is hard to forget the sights and sounds of four Merlins in full song – twelve in 2014 as the BBMF and CWHM Lancasters flew over the LAHC Lancaster at East Kirkby, Lincolnshire!

The Lancaster is a part of the history and heritage of Canada and the British Isles and of the freedom we have been fortunate to enjoy these past seventy years. These four aircraft are a fitting tribute to Bomber Command and the crews that served in them. The two of them in Canada are named after Victoria Cross winners. The LAHC chose a famous wartime national newspaper cartoon character, Just Jane, who was a daily pin-up girl for the *Daily Mail*.

In a letter to the Avro Company after the war, Marshal of the Royal Air Force Sir Arthur Harris, the Commander-in-Chief of Bomber Command, said of the Lancaster:

I would say this to those who placed that shining sword in our hands: Without your genius and efforts we could not have prevailed, for I believe that the Lancaster was the greatest single factor in winning the war.

BBMF

www.raf.mod.uk/bbmf
RAF BBMF Visitors Centre, Dogdyke Road, Coningsby, Lincolnshire, England LN4 4SY

The public tours started in 1986 and over 300,000 visitors have seen the Memorial Flight aircraft. The historic collection includes examples of the Supermarine Spitfire, Hawker Hurricane, Douglas Dakota and de Havilland Chipmunk.

Due to the fact that the BBMF Lancaster is administratively part of the RAF No. 1 Group, it is the most restrictive among the four museums for close access to the aircraft. Sadly, interviews and photographic opportunities are limited due to the cost of insurance for liability concerns on an active RAF station. PA474 can be seen as part of a guided hangar tour arranged by the visitor centre in cooperation with the Lincolnshire County Council.

However, the good news is that the Lancaster is highly visible during the display season. It is regularly seen at air displays, events commemorating the Second World War, and British state occasions such as the Trooping the Colour on Queen Elizabeth II's birthday. In 2014 it made 158 appearances, not including the eighteen displays and twenty-nine fly-pasts with the CWHM Lancaster during August and September.

BCMC

www.bombercommandmuseum.ca
1729 21st Avenue, Nanton, Alberta, Canada T0L 1R0

The museum is fully accessible to the approximate 25,000 visitors per year; open seven days a week during the summer and on weekends during the winter months. An eye-catching entrance to the passing highway traffic consists of two aircraft mounted on pedestals – the Canadair T33 Silver Star and the Avro CF-100 Canuck – and the black granite wall of the Canada Bomber Command Memorial. The admissions area has glass exhibit cabinets and old wartime photographs on the wall. Behind the office desk is the museum gift shop. To the left are further extensive exhibits devoted to the role and exploits of Bomber Command. The library and archives are in this area and available for research purposes. The author was given full access to the facility, which added greatly to the information in this book.

A self-guided 'walkabout' tour with provided computer tablets will take you around the Lancaster and inside the fuselage up to an observation point at the main spar. The tour stops at various points so that one can listen to the audio and watch video information. The museum also features 'QR' codes on all displays, which enable the visitor to watch video clips related to the displays. The codes link the tablet to a YouTube video on the Internet.

The museum has never sold rides for an engine run-up but has made it available to important guests and through a draw where visitors purchase tickets and a winner is drawn immediately prior to the run. The engine run-ups, both day and night, are held at various published times during the open season. My invitation was straightforward enough: Dave Birrell, a director of the Bomber Command Museum of Canada, who also wears a second hat as the librarian and archivist for the museum, invited me to be on board the museum's Lancaster for the first four-engine run-up of the 2014 season. The Friday in April was cool and dry as the aircraft was towed out of the hangar. Good weather for the Canadian prairie in spring. I stood and wondered what it would all mean to me.

I was no stranger to combat machines, but it had been forty years since I had climbed into my own Avro, a CF-100 fighter, to fly secret electronic warfare missions to protect 'our native land', as sung in the Canadian National Anthem. Another coincidence is that the museum has a CF-100 on a pedestal at the main entrance. I looked across at the black Lancaster as it sat there, silent and formidable – just me and the 'Lanc' for a few moments of contemplative respect.

It looked so big and yet it was so small. I had flown the McDonnell DC10-30 for Canadian Airlines International, and that was big, including the cockpit. The Lancaster, with a crew of seven, must have felt so small and claustrophobic to the men as they climbed aboard with their parachutes and equipment and struggled in to their confined work areas. On the other hand, it must have seemed so big a target to the Luftwaffe night fighters as they attacked from below and saw the aircraft silhouetted against the stars or searchlight beams.

It is an aircraft of contrasts – the bomb-bay doors were open and I could see the large bay, which could carry bombs weighing up to 22,000 lbs. I looked into the rear gunner's turret and wondered how anyone could get in there, let alone operate the four guns. The aircraft had what I can only describe as an arrogant and aggressive stance as it sat there on the apron with its nose in the air. I had written a book on this aircraft, and yet I understood at that moment that I did not know it all.

The daylight was fading as I returned to the warmth and light of the hangar. I now waited, with some trepidation, to return to the Lancaster in the dark and share the excitement of the engine start. Would I fail as an author, unable to capture the atmosphere on board and identify with the young men who risked their lives against appalling odds to carry out the raids of Bomber Command? I certainly have a heavy burden on my shoulders to tell their story and do justice to this magnificent aircraft, the Avro Lancaster.

Thanks to Dave and the Bomber Command Museum of Canada, I have this experience of a four-engine night start to help me in my quest. The night was planned to be coincidental with a 'Thank the Volunteers' evening, with food and libation on hand. Somehow I thought of myself as an intruder and could not really partake in all the activities provided for the hard-working volunteers. I observed the men and women who had all worked hard the previous year to not only keep the museum viable, but also to plan future growth. Perhaps in some way I was a kind of volunteer, as I would be writing about their Lancaster and promoting it and the BCMC. I enjoyed a plate of food as I wandered around looking at the various exhibits, which included a working tail turret and a cutaway Merlin engine. I marvelled at the amount of moving parts on the twelve-cylinder engine.

The time came to board the aircraft, and there was a general movement in the direction of the apron outside the hangar doors. Slightly overdressed in a fleece and parka – after all, it was April in Alberta and snow was in the forecast – I approached the front of the dark aircraft as it sat poised to come to life. After being introduced by Dave Birrell to the aircraft captain and engineer, plus a quick briefing on exiting the aircraft if a fire occurred, I was ushered to a set of steps underneath the escape hatch in the bomb aimer's compartment. The wartime crews would normally enter the aircraft door at the starboard rear of the aircraft. The engineer for this night run-up was Greg Morrison, as mentioned in chapter 6.

Once again I felt like an interloper in this alien world of the Second World War bomber crew. The war occurred before I was born. I certainly had never been near such an aircraft before, let alone been moments away from entering it. Clambering up the steep steps, I then pulled myself on to the floor of

the bomb aimer's compartment. I was guided to the steps at the rear of the compartment by a flashlight held by someone above, who I could only see from the shoes down. A few lights illuminated my progress as I passed by the pilot, perched high above me as I climbed up to main-floor level.

Squeezing past the navigator's table, I was assigned to the wireless operator's position just in front of the spar, which blocked normal progress through the fuselage. It required a certain agility to get over the space between the spar and the fuselage roof – a vertical hand-hold bar assisted the manoeuvre. It certainly would be a tight fit, especially for seven men in winter flying gear, carrying parachutes. A BCMC volunteer staff photographer, Doug Bowman of www.ArcherPhotoworks.ca, was my companion for the engine start and worked very hard in the confined space to get images of the cockpit, engine instruments and engine exhaust.

In the darkness I heard voices responding to the checklist that indicated the initiation of the start procedure. The checklists are completed by a challenge-and-response system and are heard on the spectator loudspeaker, which really adds to the atmosphere of the engine start.

PRESTART

1. PARK BRAKE	SET
2. BOOST COIL SWITCH	OFF
3. MAGNETO SWITCHES	OFF
4. MASTER FUEL COCKS	OFF
5. THROTTLES	CLOSED

Prior to the actual start, I heard some banging that echoed through the fuselage; perhaps something to do with the hydraulics or the fuel system? A few reselections of some circuit breakers – 'Try the ones along the bottom!' – and the first engine burst into life. That is, all twelve cylinders of the Rolls-Royce Merlin engine. On this particular Lancaster there is a small window on the starboard side, through which I could see the blue exhaust flames of no. 3 engine. They danced haphazardly and hypnotically like the Northern Lights. I actually enjoyed the sound of the initial rough idle, with its pops and backfires of exhaust flames before it settled down to a steady beat.

The second engine burst into life and Bowman got some good images of the two sets of engine exhausts illuminating the darkness. The noise by now had reached quite a din, with two engines at idle. The cockpit voices – pilot and engineer – were played over the loudspeakers to the crowd outside so that they could follow the engine start. When the engine next to my sitting position on the port side burst into life I thought that the propeller must surely rip through the side of the fuselage. The tip of the propeller was separated from the crew by the thickness of a sheet of aluminium. I cannot imagine what the noise inside must have been like for a six-hour mission, in spite of leather helmets with earphones that were worn.

The engines were revved up during the engine run as per the BCMC checklist written by engineer Greg Morrison. The noise is like being shut in a tin can (which it pretty much was) that is being vibrated by the deep roar of four twelve-cylinder Merlins.

WARNING:

ALL FOUR ENGINES MAY BE RUN TO 1600 RPM TOGETHER, ONLY IF THE FLIGHT ENGINEER FEELS THE TEMPERATURES WILL ALLOW IT. WHEN RUNNING ALL FOUR ENGINES TO 1600 RPM, BE SURE TO CHECK BRAKE PRESSURE BEFORE THROTTLE ADVANCEMENT. ONLY RUN AT 1600 RPM FOR A PERIOD OF NO LONGER THAN 1 MINUTE MAX.

I understand that at that time the propellers and aircraft were floodlit to great effect for the spectators; I missed that being inside. All too soon the engines were shut down to be replaced by the sound of the spectators cheering and applauding another successful four-engine start, all due to the many volunteers who made it happen. Everything had gone according to plan, which bode well for the engine starts scheduled for the next day.

I carefully exited the aircraft and marvelled at how a crew of seven could work in such close quarters over long periods of time while exposed to constant danger – a young man's game for sure. Most of the crew would have been in their twenties, which would be an advantage for the physical stress, although the mental stress would have been different as they had their full lives ahead of them – if they were lucky. I was humbled by my night-time run-up experience, and I would like to thank Dave Birrell and the BCMC volunteers for this once-in-a-lifetime experience.

LAHC

www.lincsaviation.co.uk
East Kirkby Airfield, Spilsby, Lincolnshire, England PE23 4DE

The privately run museum is well signposted on the A155, with an imposing approach featuring the original wartime entrance road and the guardhouse being replaced by a memorial to Nos 57 and 630 RAF squadrons, who flew from the wartime airfield. Approaching the admissions building, the new large hangar, built on the previous T2 hangar site, catches your attention. The museum's whole program is designed to recreate the wartime atmosphere of a Bomber Command RAF airfield. There is a memorial chapel containing the names of 848 personnel who gave their lives operating at East Kirkby. A recreated 'NAAFI' (Navy, Army and Air Force Institutes) canteen provides further atmosphere and is a full-service restaurant. The sights (memorabilia) and sounds (recorded wartime music) greet you as soon as you open the door.

The Lancaster, if it is on the hangar apron, is visible through the windows close by. Off to the right is the restored control tower, also called the watchtower, which has recreated sounds of R/T transmissions and exhibits of WAAFs manning the control desk. The original windsock is on display and has a bullet hole in it, the result of an airfield attack by a Luftwaffe Ju 88. The intended target was a group of returning Lancasters, landing after the Ladburgen raid of 4 March 1945; all landed safely, and then the airfield was raked with machine-gun and cannon fire. Four personnel were severely injured, and there was one fatality in the No. 57 Squadron briefing room.

The Lancaster experience at East Kirkby is enjoyed in many ways: a visit to the museum and displays, and – if the timing is right – a chance to witness the Lancaster taxiing, plus an interior aircraft tour, a taxi ride or even the VIP taxi ride. The weekend schedule is for three taxi rides per day, and the two-session VIP ride, held mid-week, is presently booking sixteen months ahead. The VIP ride is a full-day package starting with a morning crew briefing and two runs, morning and afternoon. Divided into two groups, you get to watch the other group on their taxi run. After a prepared lunch, the groups switch positions. A visit to the cockpit and an external walk-around completes the day. Crew members are on board to answer any questions.

There are six qualified taxi 'pilots' available and two full-time maintenance engineers on staff. The operating crew consist of a pilot, a flight engineer and a safety officer. The safety officer normally sits in the open doorway observing areas not visible to the crew in the event of public ingress. The manoeuvring area is very confined – bad for the crew, good for the public, as they can get really close to the taxiing Lancaster. On the day before the taxi runs, *Just Jane* has oil and coolant levels checked, ditto tire pressures.

On the day of the run the aircraft is towed out to the pad for a visual inspection at 09.00. By 09.15 the visitors are arriving and booking in. There is an assigned coordinator, an 'ops officer', to look after the visitor group at all times. This is followed by a visitor briefing by the crew on Bomber Command and what the aircraft will do on the taxi ride and what the 'riders' will do on board. The safety officer will assign positions on the aircraft based on specific requests ('my grandfather was a tail gunner') and general preference. A normal visitor complement fills the bomb aimer, wireless operator, navigator and tail gunner positions, plus three people standing in the mid-upper turret.

The landing strip is confirmed as suitable for taxiing (not too wet or soft) and the pilot checks that the weather is acceptable and that the fire crew is in position. Andrew Panton, general manager, financial officer and Lancaster taxi pilot, mentioned that 'the only other things that would cancel the taxi run would be strong winds and snow. The rain is not a problem except for visibility and that the ground crew get wet!' The longest straight-line taxi available is 1,936 feet, but given that this is on a thirty-acre field, there is lots of room for manoeuvring. All taxiing is done in the tail-down position.

Prior to start the aircraft battery is only used for lighting, radio and intercom, and an external trolley accumulator is used for the heavy electrical loads of the engine start. The Lancaster's four engines are numbered one to four from left to right, as seen from the cockpit facing forward. It is interesting that the left and right sides of the aircraft, facing forward, are named after the maritime designations port and starboard. All aircraft have a steady red light on the left wing tip and a steady green light on the right wing tip, once again following the tradition of the seas. A steady white light is on the tail.

The sequence of the engine start, performed by the flight engineer, is no. 3 engine followed by no. 4, no. 2 and no. 1. Once started, the engines are idled to check temperatures and pressures are in the normal range prior to taxiing. At the same time the flaps are raised, the bomb doors are closed and the trolley accumulator is disconnected from the aircraft. The pilot then gets a radio check with the fire crew to make sure of open communications. The aircraft is taxied away from the hangar towards the grass strip; a bottleneck has to be carefully negotiated between an archive build and the public enclosure. Once again, it is great for close public viewing of the Lancaster, but a challenge for the pilot.

Taxiing is done at 800–1,000 engine rpm, which is more than sufficient to sustain movement on the hard surface. The pneumatic brakes are operated by a brake lever on the control column and differentially by applying rudder pressure – no toe brakes seventy years ago for Avro! *Just Jane* is taxied at just over 50 per cent of its maximum wartime weight, with 1,364 litres of Avgas on board. While fairly easy to make shallow turns on the hard surface, it does require use of the outboard engine on the grass strip.

The taxi procedure is fairly standard, with a figure-of-eight taxi pattern followed by a run-up into wind performed at the end of the grass strip. The engines are run up to between 1,800 and 2,000 rpm, the brakes released, and the visitors are given a faster run of thirty to forty knots down the strip to give them a feel for the aircraft as it accelerates. The noise and the vibration take everyone back in history to the start of an operational sortie take-off, with crew survival unknown. Indeed, it is a sobering and emotional thought.

The Lancaster is then returned to the hangar apron for the shutdown procedure. The aircraft is guided by safety marshals as it passes close to the public enclosure. The engines are run up to 2,000 rpm in pairs to clear them out after the long idling time, first the inboard pair and then the outboard pair. The bomb doors are opened, followed by the flaps coming down. Then the four master fuel cocks are turned off simultaneously.

Just Jane is supported and maintained by the revenue generated by the taxi experience. The taxi experience started in 1995, limited to manoeuvres on the concrete area, to be followed eleven years later with the use of the grass area. Approximately 900 people annually enjoy the taxi experience. Sales and ops officer duties are performed by Fred Panton's granddaughter, Louise Bush. The LAHC is working on future plans to get *Just Jane* airborne again. Judging on the museum's past performance, this is a very attainable goal. With Louise a qualified Lancaster flight engineer, ahe and Andrew Panton form the only brother-and-sister Lancaster taxi crew in the world! Some museum, some crew, some accomplishment – Fred would indeed be proud.

Martin Keen of Silksheen Photography wrote this of his July 2007 taxi experience:

Climb up the steep red ladder and through the rear crew-access hatch on the starboard side and once inside the fuselage your eyes are drawn to the right and the steepness of the climb up to the cockpit. You next note all the obstacles in your way, including the rear spar and dreaded main spar further forward … how wartime crew, dressed in inner and outer flying suits with a Mae West life jacket and parachute harness on top, managed to operate in this claustrophobic and dark environment defies belief. It would appear the Lancaster was designed to:

A. Carry a bomb load

B. Carry equipment to facilitate delivery of the bomb load

C. Carry the crew (almost as an afterthought) to fly the aircraft to deliver the bomb load.

A taxi ride presents more than just a visual experience, it's a real assault on the senses; first you notice that distinctive 'old aircraft smell', shortly to be joined by the odour of high-octane fuel and engine oil. Strong vibrations shake the airframe as the four Merlin engines each run to 1,200 rpm, a simply glorious sound! As you taxi you notice the audience waving and hundreds of cameras pointed in your direction; the veterans and their families seem to stand out from the crowd as you edge slowly forward …

Once the run is finished you're offered the opportunity to sit in the pilot's seat. As you look out over the wings or gingerly move the rudder pedals and control column, your thoughts drift to all those that have sat here before you. The vulnerability of the crew is especially obvious; taking a moment to look around, you think of the trauma experienced by young aircrew in these aircraft, along with the sacrifice many made, and I'm not ashamed to admit that it was a very emotional experience.

CWHM

www.warplane.com
9280 Airport Road, Mount Hope, Ontario, Canada L0R 1W0

The other three museums in this book are unique (though with some similarities), but the CWHM is currently the only museum in the world where, as a museum member, you can purchase a flight certificate to have a one-hour flight in an Avro Lancaster. The flight certificates are valid for one year and, after the schedule is decided, bookings are made in April of each year. The Lancaster is not the only aircraft available for flights. Presently a total of twelve aircraft are, or will be, available for member flights. They range in size from the de Havilland Tiger Moth to the North American Harvard to the Beechcraft Expeditor to the Douglas Dakota and North American Mitchell. There is also a Consolidated Canso flying boat. Flights in these aircraft last for twenty minutes.

The flight status of each aircraft is displayed as they go through maintenance inspections or restoration to flying status. Some aircraft are available year round and others, like the Lancaster, are available during the flying season only. The flight certificate works on the principle of an upgraded membership with a portion issued as a tax receipt because the CWHM is a registered charity. The reservations may be made online or by phone.

Under the leadership of chief pilot Ray Rohrer, a group of volunteer pilots go through an extensive checkout to fly the museum's aircraft. The 'Queen of the Hangar' is the Avro Lancaster. A handful of pilots fly the Lancaster under the guidance of the Lancaster's chief pilot, Don Schofield. Schofield was an airline pilot based nearby in Toronto and started to volunteer at the museum in the late 1970s after talking with Dennis Bradley, one of the founding members. This was long before the Lancaster restoration was complete. He flew backseat in the North American Harvard, and because of his RCAF Harvard time he was able to provide some information on formation flying. He found the commute to Hamilton too long with his normal airline workload and dropped out.

Years later, when Schofield had more free time, he dropped in to see how the Lancaster restoration was going; he has been there ever since! He remembers, 'The aircraft was in a million pieces all over the hangar and my first job was making tea and sweeping the hangar floor.' A British RAF test pilot flew *VeRA* after the restoration work and, after some further work, confirmed that it was serviceable. Three pilots with previous Lancaster experience were assigned to fly the aircraft, and there were further nominees for the position. One of the nominees was a fellow airline pilot that Schofield worked with, and the topic of the Lancaster would be raised when they met. It was very quickly realised that 'there was a huge number of requests for appearances' and that the small group of pilots would not be enough to cover them.

Three airline colleagues, including Schofield, were checked out for the first full flying season of 1989. Schofield's background on the Beech Expeditor with the RCAF contributed to why he was a suitable candidate among the many who applied. Schofield has been flying, instructing and checking on the Lancaster for twenty-five years and has amassed 800 hours of Lancaster time. When the author commented that he was the 'highest-time Lancaster pilot in the world', Schofield, in his seventies, said that he 'managed to stay healthy ... it was a matter of right place, right time and I have a wife that feeds me well and a dog that takes me for a daily walk'.

It is now very difficult – nigh on impossible – to find someone who is healthy and has flown one of the two last types of other four-engine tail-dragger aircraft, the Avro York and the Handley Page Hastings. The museum must settle for two-engine Douglas (DC-3/C47) Dakota or Beech (C45) Expeditor experience. Unfortunately, Schofield's original civilian logbook was lost in the devastating hangar fire of 15 February 1993, which destroyed aircraft as well as maintenance records. The Lancaster was lucky to escape the inferno and be able to resume flying.

According to Schofield, the mandate from the licensing authority, Museums Canada, 'is for the CWHM to collect, restore, and maintain, on ground or in the air the aircraft collection. The thought being that not everyone can come to the museum to see the collection and that we should be able to take the aircraft to them.' Schofield mentioned that, in keeping with the mandate, he has flown the Lancaster over every Canadian province and nineteen of the forty-eight continental states of the USA.

The museum will consider anything that generates revenue or a donation. This includes air shows, memorial events, feature movies, photoshoots and of course the members' rides. This means that it is possible for all Canadians to see the Lancaster in the air within a reasonable distance of their home and not have to drive to Hamilton, Ontario, to see and hear the famous Merlin engines in flight. During August and September 2014, the population of the United Kingdom was able to enjoy the sights and sounds of the only two remaining airworthy Lancasters, the BBMF and the CWHM aircraft, flying in formation.

Schofield said that flying the Lancaster is a 'real blast' but does have its challenges. He mentioned that 'Second World War airplanes were designed and built under one imperative: there was a war going on, get the thing out of the door and into the hands of those who were literally taking it to war'. Perhaps quality control and longevity did not have a very high priority. The unpredictable Lancaster has something called 'diversionary characteristics'. Basically, this means that it is unstable and, unless you do something about the flight condition, it is going to get worse. Schofield explains: 'If it gets away from you, as opposed to picking itself up ... if things are getting bad, things go downhill at a modest rate and then all of a sudden it is like stepping off the edge of a cliff.' He mentioned that, as your experience grows, 'you can literally feel the aircraft and know what it is doing' and take corrective action to avoid dangerous situations. Schofield was adamant that 'you stay away from the edges of the performance envelope where you know you are going to get yourself into trouble'.

One of the major problems with the Lancaster is its lack of directional control during certain critical times of flight, such as landing and take-off. Schofield says that you can lose control very fast and that it becomes impossible to stop the aircraft leaving the runway. Training and experience are the only antidotes. This reminded the author of his own mishap after a student mishandled the rudders on a de Havilland Chipmunk and the aircraft ground-looped on to the grass before it could be stopped. The tail-dragger aircraft take a bit more attention than today's nose-wheel training aircraft when departing from or arriving on the runway. Schofield felt that 'the [Lancaster] brakes were operationally adequate, no more'.

The Lancaster was never designed for air shows. It was designed to drop bombs, which it did very effectively, and it had a short life expectancy. It was not expected to be flying seventy years later. Safety concerns in the Lancaster would never be tolerated in today's aircraft. Schofield feels that he has been lucky to fly the aircraft without any major incident; certainly his combination of military and airline flying experience, plus training and time on the Lancaster contributes to his safety record. The young Second

World War Lancaster pilots would not have the luxury of such previous experience – it was learn on the job or join the growing fatality list.

The Historic UK Lancaster Experience

In its sixty-ninth year, FM213 (KB726) returned from the land of its birth to the land of its design and flew the same skies that many of its predecessors had flown in anger and in peace. Together with PA474, it visited the old RAF Lancaster haunts and RCAF stations that once echoed with the unforgettable sound of four Merlin engines in harmony. In 2014, the BBMF and CWHM put on what was certainly the best aviation remembrance show of this decade, and perhaps longer. Some Lancaster veterans – and there are few now – said it will be the best show of the century. Two Lancasters in formation flying out of a former Bomber Command station in Lincolnshire (Coningsby) to all parts of the British Isles; how could such a thing happen? Foresight, perseverance, hard work, determination, resolve and dedication are some of the adjectives that could be applied to the private and government sources that made this happen.

During the restoration of *VeRA*, which was a Mk X maritime reconnaissance version, about two and a half tons of equipment was removed, including a fuel tank in the bomb bay. Schofield began thinking about what sort of range, speed and performance could be expected from this new version. There had never been an airplane in this configuration before. To where would the aircraft be flying? How far did the CWHM wish to go in satisfying air show requests? One of the most expensive challenges in maintenance, both in manpower and money, was the fuel-dumping system. It was removed because, as Schofield said, 'the airplane carries enough fuel for the likely distances'.

Currently, *VeRA*'s maximum take-off weight is 53,000 pounds, which, not by coincidence, is the maximum landing weight. This allows an immediate return to the airfield in the event of any problems, with no requirement to dump fuel. The airplane could, and did, operate to 66,000 lbs during the bombing campaign. The internal tanks in the CWHM Lancaster will give a nine-hour range. The Lancasters that were ferried from Victory Aircraft in Toronto flew the North Atlantic with internal fuel tanks in stages, although due to wartime circumstances they did not have the present regulations regarding holding alternate and approach fuel. Gander, Newfoundland, to Northern Ireland was certainly a possibility.

So the seeds of an overseas flight had been sown, to lay in wait for the right moment, before *VeRA* had even flown. The right moment turned out to be in 2014. The old radio racks were replaced with four seats from a crashed Beechcraft King Air, and this allowed ground crew to be carried on away trips. Initially it was cold, dark and noisy, so the unofficial policy was to limit the transit legs to less than three hours. The flights to the west coast of Canada took twelve hours out. The organisers then adjusted their schedule so that the airplane did a western circuit and they all shared the cost.

Schofield flew Regina, Saskatchewan, to Hamilton, Ontario, a journey of 2,030 nautical miles, and that was more than required to cross the North Atlantic (Gander, Newfoundland, to Belfast is 1,792 nautical miles). The idea was starting to grow with the performance and operating knowledge of the airplane that this flight was possible. Perhaps the turning point was when a delegation from CWHM visited the BBMF at RAF Coningsby to discuss setting up checklists and operating procedures for *VeRA*. Schofield was not surprised when the inevitable question arose: 'When are you guys going to bring your aircraft over?' This is when the seed turned into a plant!

In the early 1990s, the Lancaster had been flying successfully for four years; Schofield got out some maps, charts and dividers and determined that the flight was actually practical. He was already familiar with the North Atlantic because of his airline experience. He made and continued to refine a flight plan from Hamilton to Coningsby, which is approximately 3,000 nautical miles on a great-circle route. Schofield discovered that the great-circle route passed fairly close to the southern tip of Greenland and Iceland. He then planned the following route: Hamilton to Goose Bay, Labrador, to Narsarsuaq, Greenland, to Keflavik or Reykjavik, Iceland, to Coningsby. Schofield commented, 'The interesting thing about the route is that you had the ability to go ahead [an airport] or go back [an airport] if the landing airport was not available and all the legs had the ability to do that.'

The Americans took a Consolidated Liberator to Europe and damaged two engines, and with no support the trip turned into a financial disaster. The message to anyone else attempting such a flight with a vintage aircraft was that you had better have a good support plan. In spite of support from the RAF, Canadian military, Air Canada, British Airways and oil companies, it was deemed too risky by the administration at the time and the idea was dropped. The RAF approached the CWHM to come to England several times over the years, but the administration at the time demanded too much and the RAF was unable to meet the requested payment both in cash and in kind.

David Rohrer was the new incoming president and he chatted to Schofield about the flight plan that he had created to get to Coningsby. The RAF had indicated to the air show's organisers in the past that the BBMF's Lancaster would attend for free if the CWHM brought their Lancaster to England, but that they would have to pay for the Canadian one. Schofield, the only pilot able to attend, was invited to Britain for the BBMF end-of-season dinner in the autumn of 2013. He found himself away off in a corner, which, as it turned out later, was no accident. Richard Lake, managing director of Eastern Airways, talked at length with Schofield about bringing *VeRA* to England and offered to underwrite a one-month tour. Lake felt that the tour, because of its popularity, would carry itself financially. Schofield approached Rohrer with the proposal

and Rohrer said, after some thought, 'If not us, who? If not now, when?'

A delegation went to England in late 2013 to examine the complexity and practicalities of such a venture – perhaps we should say adventure! Planning, preparation and more planning was vital to the task. There were risks involved, but the CWHM was willing to accept that in order to achieve the objective of remembering and honouring our veterans – the two Lancasters flying over the fields of Lincolnshire in remembrance of all those who gave so much. The resulting business plan was to cover all costs and, if it was done right, actually show a profit, so that when *VeRA* returned to Hamilton the venture had been a financial success. With Lake's generous offer to cover any shortfall and provide financial security, plus the total support of the staff at the BBMF for the combined tour, the decision was made: the UK Lancaster Tour would take place in August and September 2014.

Al Mickeloff had worked on and off for the museum since the 1980s as a summer student, volunteer, employee and, finally, in his present position as retail sales and marketing manager. He remembered being given a job during the Lancaster restoration 'cleaning bird **** off the floor at the back at the aircraft, and other jobs you could not mess up'! His normal responsibilities include the CWHM website and newspaper, plus special events, education (20,000 children per year) and social media, which played 'a huge role in the trip'. Mickeloff remarked that 'it is a struggle to get media attention normally' in Canada. When asked about his job description he laughed and said, 'You do what you have to do sometimes to keep the doors open.'

Mickeloff concentrated on budgets – 'boring stuff' – and special projects such as the successful Corgi die-cast Lancaster model, in addition to souvenirs, the official program, the calendar, film requests, social media and website responsibilities. What turned the whole publicity scene around was auctioning the seat on the flight to England. The *Daily Mail* in England got hold of the story and it went viral. During the entire tour the whole world could track the progress of the flight by using the Flight Radar 24 website. The English media was thirsty for information and Mickeloff said that 'BBC Radio called every day for information' during the tour.

Mickeloff flew to Iceland to await the arrival of *VeRA* and liaise with the expected media coverage. Martin Keen, who contributed and arranged the images for this book, was on hand to photograph the arrival of the Lancaster in Keflavik. Richard Lake, managing director of Eastern Airways, whom Mickeloff said was 'the conduit and visionary of the UK tour', joined the aircraft for the last leg of the flight to RAF Coningsby. Mickeloff was there for the arrival and coordinated the 'show line' of approximately sixty popular media outlets, which included local and national television, newspapers and magazines.

Mickeloff said that 'right off the bat the most requested information was – are you going to fly over "Just Jane"?' He mentioned that 'we [CWHM] had a great working relationship with Andrew [Panton] and he was a great source of information and finding supplies'. All the merchandise, coming in from Canada, China and the USA, was stored at the LAHC courtesy of Andrew Panton. All four museums mentioned in this book cooperated in some way to make the tour a success and continue to do so to keep the dream alive. Mickeloff's dream came alive on 21 August 2014, when he was on board *VeRA* for a three-plane formation flight out of RAF Waddington with the restored Avro Vulcan XH558 and *Thumper*, the BBMF Lancaster.

As mentioned above, one seat on the flight to England was auctioned off on eBay to help defray costs. The winner was Matt Munson. Mickeloff mentioned that 'Munson turned into the voice of the trip in that he tweeted daily his experience and included photographs of the flight'. Two seats were auctioned for the return trip to Canada, going to Glen Manchester and Jeff Cairns. In spite of an engine problem, the tour finished in the black, which was most important to the CWHM, a privately held charity. Perhaps the old phrase of 'nothing ventured, nothing gained' was applicable to this endeavour.

Lancasters have been crossing the Atlantic on delivery flights since the first aircraft, KB700, rolled off the Victory Aircraft assembly line on 1 August 1943. Present-day navigation systems allow such accurate long-range flights that making stops within the range of the airplane is no longer required. However, that being said, Schofield was emphatic that 'all the flight planning for the UK tour was done with maximum safety in mind'.

CWHM had to spend a lot of money on new communication and navigation equipment to reach Europe. Although we like to think of North America as being an advanced aviation environment, in certain aspects we lag behind Europe. An example is VHF frequencies. North America is using 127.95, while Europe uses three-decimal frequencies like 127.953. It is this combination of the old airplane and the newest technical equipment that allows it to fly in present-day Europe. The new equipment is based on satellites, the Garmin Global Positioning system (GPS) or, as it is commonly known in the United Kingdom, satnav. The Russians have their own system called GLONASS.

Garmin combined the two systems into their Garmin GLO, which can talk to sixty-odd satellites to determine its position. The GLO has no display but will hook up electronically to your iPad, showing your position on a map of the earth. It is very small – about the size of a wallet. The scale may be adjusted to suit your requirements at any time. Schofield mentioned that 'it was extremely accurate, and after 3,840 nautical miles to our United Kingdom destination a Garmin representative commented that it would only be nine feet off the correct position'. The CWHM Lancaster had a 40 lb briefcase full of every chart, map and book that could possibly be required. Schofield operated the Garmin on approach to the UK and 'kept zooming in [the scale] as we got closer and closer and we landed in the middle of a rainstorm. We were legally flying IFR [Instrument Flight Rules] and turned final at three miles. When we went heads-up for the landing a clever young airman had turned the landing lights up to strength five so that we were able to see for the last mile.' So *VeRA* landed at RAF Coningsby out of the dark rain clouds in spectacular fashion, with the welcoming air display unfortunately grounded due to poor weather.

Despite the complexity of getting permits from the governments, both local and national, of Canada, Greenland, Iceland, the United Kingdom, the Channel Islands and Northern Ireland, everyone was on board and the process was completed by February 2014. Now it was time to put the business plan into action. However, there were challenges within the system. The Lancaster is permitted to fly in Canada under a special Certificate of Airworthiness whereby it is allowed by Transport Canada to operate under very strict guidelines despite not falling within the rules. In the United Kingdom the aviation rules and regulations are established by the European Community in Brussels, Belgium. According to Schofield, 'Old Warbirds are very much in contention over there.' Some of the member states decided to retain their own rules for historic and vintage aircraft to allow them to fly in their territory. However, regarding the UK tour, Schofield said that they made the decision that 'if it is good enough for Transport Canada it is good enough for us'.

A major hurdle was liability insurance, which was very costly and involved what is termed special drawing rights. It did not help that the civilian Lancaster does not have a type certificate. However, as with the other issues, this was solved – although it added to the expense of the tour. It is interesting to note that *VeRA* had no hull insurance because the insurance companies required three Lancaster sales to establish worth;

this being impossible, it was termed 'priceless'. It certainly is!

Flying *VeRA* to England, the altitudes used were between 5,000 and 10,000 feet and the cockpit and fuselage of the Lancaster were very cold. The aircraft was designed with rudimentary heating – must have been an Avro thing in those days, as the author froze flying the 1950s Avro CF-100. The flight was originally filed as an Instrument Flight Rules flight, but in order to stay warm the subsequent legs were filed Visual Flight Rules, weather permitting. *VeRA* does not have an automatic pilot, so all flights were flown by hand. The leg from Goose Bay, Labrador, to Keflavik, Iceland, took just over eight hours. As the airplane has two sets of controls and carried three pilots for the transatlantic stretch, they were able to switch seats and at least get up to stretch. The wartime Lancasters only had one set of flying controls. The airplane performed flawlessly and communication with the new technology was never a concern. SeeMore Productions, under the guidance of Morgan Elliott, remained on board to create a documentary for the CWHM.

An RAF navigator accompanied the crew from Iceland to Coningsby and was always on board for the flights in England in case the lead BBMF airplane went unserviceable, as that way the Canadian airplane could continue on with the scheduled events on its own. The navigator proved very helpful getting around some bad weather coming from the south-west and heading towards Coningsby. It was a race to see who would get there first. Schofield praised the cooperation of everyone involved in the arrival flight, with air traffic control picking out three suitable alternates if they were unable to land at Coningsby. The last five minutes was flown in pouring rain. The occasion was not destroyed by the diversion of the flight, and a great reception was held with veterans in attendance. The same navigator that flew down from Iceland, F/L Rich Gibbey, was on another flight – in fact, his RAF retirement flight – and he chose to do it in style with the Canadian Lancaster.

Another challenge was to have the two Lancasters flying together in formation when one was military and the other civilian. A paper plan was created and submitted and its safety was demonstrated to the RAF and CAA before public display authorisations (PDAs) were issued both individually, to the CWHM and BBMF, and collectively. It was pilot-specific and Schofield and Leon Evans had to change seats and fly the plan again to get another PDA. This involved two flights in the morning, and by 14.00 *VeRA* was airborne on the first scheduled event of the tour. Schofield mentioned that 'it was the start of fifty-eight days straight except for the days for the engine change. We lost I think just two other days for weather [not being suitable].' The three engineers under chief engineer Jim Van Dyk were really stretched and contributed an enormous effort to make the tour a success. The RAF hosted the CWHM and allowed access to the hangar and tools, etc., which was an invaluable help to the success of this possibly once-in-a-lifetime experience.

One important part of the business plan was the revenue-generating commercial side, which included a travelling shop that would follow the Lancaster around the UK. Pauline Johnstone, assistant retail manager/buyer at the CWHM, was part of the team manning the souvenir trailer. Johnstone had joined the CWHM in 1996 and had been part of the new building expansion, which included a separate gift shop. Presently the website sales are a big part of the retail business. Johnstone's previous employer was in the jewellery business, and she jokingly remarked, 'Diamonds to airplanes – a different kind of gem!'

Nine months prior to the UK tour, Mickeloff and Johnstone designed custom clothes that made up 80 per cent of the clothing brought to England for the tour. Other items for sale also included calendars, programs and crystals. The majority of the goods were sent ahead of time by sea. Clearing customs, they were put into storage in a large container at the LAHC in East Kirkby. Johnstone mentioned that 'they [LAHC] were wonderful in helping us out and we could not have done it without them'.

'The retail group was the first to leave Canada as we had to be prepared when the Lanc arrived,' recounted Johnstone. The group comprised of two staff and five long-time museum volunteers. A forty-foot low-loader trailer with fold-down sides was purchased and a driver hired to move the trailer around the various venues. The venues included air shows and fly-past locations. Johnstone estimated that, during the seven weeks, 'we put 6,000 miles on our vehicles, which was incredible. We had vehicles which followed the trailer. Sometimes it was a day show and other times we were gone for three or four days. We hit a lot of curbs [driving on the opposite side of the road] along the way!'

The group was based at The Inn at Woodhall Spa, Lincolnshire, about twenty minutes' drive from the storage container at East Kirkby. Johnstone remarked, 'The staff were really amazing and welcoming and I am happy to say that I have made some life-long friends.' Both Johnstone and Schofield were overwhelmed by the hospitality and friendliness of the people during their entire stay.

When asked if she ever went in the Lancaster, Johnstone replied, 'I must say that was a very special thing and it was a surprise. I was able to take my first ever flight in the Lanc, I had been in other aircraft but I never had been in the Lanc. There happened to be two seats available in the Lanc that was at Bournemouth the next day. That was very, very special and I will never forget that. We (David Hills and I) were actually in Duxford when we found out, so we had a three- or four-hour drive to Bournemouth and after the forty-minute flight got back in the van and drove back to Duxford but it was well worth it.' The flight was on the 24 September 2014.

Schofield commented that 'air shows in Britain are a far bigger deal than ours [in Canada]'. The locations for the air displays could be concentrated in groups and so cut down on transit time. Briefings were held at the event site or remotely, as the location of the fly-past or air show was often far from the airfield at which the Lancasters were based. Schofield gave an example of one flight where he 'flew two hours and thirty-eight minutes and did three air shows and four fly-pasts. I have never worked so hard in all my life.' This was all in close formation and these comments were from a former fighter and airline pilot. Fatigue was a constant companion but all involved were determined to make the tour a safe success.

The displays had to be commercially attractive to gain attention and cover costs. Schofield said, 'We avoid the high-traction concrete [on runways] at all costs. Landing at Coningsby we land long, and people wonder why: to avoid this type of concrete found mainly at military bases. Landing with some drift on this type of concrete we can scrub a set of [expensive] tyres.' The first shows had to show off the Lancasters in their best light so that media interest would encourage the attendance of spectators for future shows. The RAF worked on a system of pre-choreographed routines that were scripted and flown. The decision was made to, as Schofield recounted, 'tuck in behind [BBMF] and stay with them as tight as we reasonably could'. As a former military pilot who flew formation, I can assure you that this was no mean feat in a seventy-year-old airplane the size of a Lancaster with un-boosted controls. Every flight would be a workout.

It was a different show at Middleton St George, the actual home of the original V-RA and No. 419 (Moose) Squadron RCAF, from where P/O Mynarski departed on his fateful flight. The BBMF courteously stayed away and *VeRA* was the star of the show during some very nostalgic moments. The local villages and town were festooned with Canadian flags in honour of the Canadian contribution to the war effort, Bomber Command, RAF Middleton St George, No. 419 Squadron and the 'Mynarski Lancaster'. The welcome there and all over Britain was huge, beyond imagination, and Schofield said, 'It could all be summed up – the Canadians are coming.' The BBC television crew who were doing a documentary actually put down their cameras to help with the Lancaster.

David Thompson is a member of the Friends of Durham Tees Valley Airport, a group of aviation enthusiasts dedicated to promoting the airport, whose members assisted the engineers with *VeRA*s engine change. The RCAF Nos 419, 420 and 428 squadrons were stationed during the Second World War at Goosepool, Middleton St George, now known as Durham Tees Valley Airport. The following are excerpts from Thompson's blog describing the changeover of the no. 4 engine.

Saturday, 30 August

I was up at Teesside for most of this afternoon helping the Canadian engineers prepare the Merlin for its removal. There are four engineers and they worked non-stop under less than perfect working conditions and with very little technical tools and kit and had to beg or borrow quite a bit of equipment.

The spare new Merlin arrived just after 8pm and was un-loaded thanks to a loaned fork-lift truck from the airport. The plan for Sunday is to remove the damaged Merlin which has blown a supercharger seal, oil could clearly be seen in three of the cylinders once the exhaust stubs were removed, and hopefully get the new Merlin up and into place ready to plumb it in on Monday and then ground test it.

Sunday, 31 August

The engineering team numbers increased with the arrival of two Retro Track & Air (UK) Ltd engineers. The damaged No. 4 engine was removed today and on inspection by the T&A lads was found to have suffered a supercharger failure which was pretty evident when the turbine blades fell out once the carb was removed!

The replacement BBMF Merlin is a Rolls-Royce manufactured engine whilst the damaged engine is Packard built which entails a bit of swapping about of parts, non-technical description here, but I think most of the work involves altering the plumbing and harnesses?

The engineering team again put in another 8am to 8pm twelve hour day with very limited resources and thanks must go to Sycamore Aviation for use of their equipment and the Cleveland Police Air Support Unit for the use of their kettle!

Monday, 1 September

The engineers finished at 7pm tonight to go and have a pint in The Oak Tree Inn at Middleton St George which was a regular wartime haunt for the Canadians based at Goosepool. So just an eleven hour day today, just! The new Merlin has been attached to the bulkhead but a lot of the plumbing still needs to be completed before the propeller is fitted and the engine test-run.

Tuesday, 2 September

To be fair it's the five Canadian engineers who have carried the day on this one plus the two British Retro engineers who have travelled up from their base in Gloucestershire to help with fitting the new Merlin. Of the five Canadians Jim and Rick are full time engineers with the CWHM and Craig, Mike and Randy are all volunteer flight engineers on the Lanc and are classed as 'aircrew'. Nice work if you can get it!

Special mention should also be given to the members of The Friends of Durham Tees Valley Airport who have fetched and carried, swept and polished as required. The propeller was hung this morning and all of the harness work completed by mid-afternoon and then the engineers started work on refilling the engine coolant and oil before priming by hand and putting the prop boss cover on. Back to a 12 hour day today but at the end of it, not the result everyone wanted when No. 4 engine turned but sadly

failed to burn. The plan for Wednesday morning is to crack on and resolve these problems and get *VeRA* down to Coningsby as the Canadian team are desperate to make up ground and meet their commitments especially with a busy weekend coming up.

Wednesday, 3 September

The problem last night was resolved as a fuel air-lock and after bleeding and priming this morning she had a successful ground run. The Lanc then took off for a short air test of two circuits including a nice low pass before landing and pulling up alongside Hangar 1, her temporary home for the past seven days. The Canadian engineers gave up four seats on the air test to the volunteers and enthusiasts who had helped them during their stay. It was done on a prize draw, pick a number basis and yes, I didn't. *VeRA* finally left Goosepool for Coningsby at 13:25, and that was it, there she was gone and life returned to normal, sadly!

After landing from a show, the planning starts for the next one – attention is paid to loading fuel and other requirements. A crew debriefing is held and the journey log is filled out for the engineers. A question-and-answer session gets the ground crew up to speed with the condition of the aircraft and anything needing attention. A set of standard operating procedures enabled the aircrew and ground crew to operate at peak efficiency for the tight schedules to ensure the aircraft was operational for the tour.

Ray Rohrer, president of CWHM, is quoted as saying, 'At an airshow in Canada there is music and applause and cheering. When we flew shows over there, there was absolute silence and tears. And then, when we came home, we realized this airplane is just as important to Canadians [by the homecoming reception at the CWHM]. I had a tear in my eye.'

The day the CWHM Lancaster left England to return to Canada was the only time that *VeRA* led the formation. Recounting the departure,

Schofield, with a hint of emotion in his voice, said, 'When we walked out to the airplane that day there were hundreds if not thousands of people lined up at the fence and having to turn around and shake hands with those guys – there was a lot of tears. It was very emotional and I can honestly say that I have never worked with such a group of people who were so like-minded and enthusiastic and such good friends.' What a fitting tribute to the aviation enthusiasts and citizens of the United Kingdom in this day and age of predominantly negative world-news stories. Every departure from RAF Coningsby was greeted with thunderous applause when the crew exited the hangar blister and walked towards the aircraft.

The final formation group had the two Lancasters plus the BBMF's two Spitfires and two Hurricanes – a truly worthy and fitting memorial formation. It was a movie-style tour-ending scene, with 'not a dry eye in the house'. Schofield recalled, 'We took off from Coningsby, went over the Royal Air Force College at Cranwell, over RAF Waddington, up over the cathedral in the city of Lincoln, and got up to Scampton at which point the British members did a gentle bomb burst and we flew through the middle.' *VeRA* then continued on its way to Iceland, the first leg of the journey home to Hamilton, Ontario.

In its sixty-ninth year, FM213 (KB726) returned across the Atlantic Ocean to the land of its birth and flew the same skies that many of its predecessors had flown in war and in peace. Together with PA474, it visited the old Lancaster haunts and RCAF stations that once echoed with the unforgettable sound of four Merlin engines in harmony. The tour did indeed honour the veterans of Bomber Command, and left many memories for the remaining few, plus their sons, daughters and grandchildren. This book of aviation history will also help preserve the struggles of Bomber Command personnel, and the ultimate sacrifice given by some, to achieve the freedom we enjoy today.

The best of times, the worst of times and the lucky survived.

Lest we forget.

A stunning Bomber County sunset with Lancaster *Just Jane* in the foreground. How many airmen must have witnessed such a sight before taking off on a night raid against a target in occupied Europe? (Martin Keen)

Left: The Avro Lancaster, Bomber Command's 'Shining Sword'. (Martin Keen)

Above and opposite: The BBMF Lancaster, PA474, passes over NX611 during events at the Lincolnshire Aviation Heritage Centre. (Martin Keen)

This page and opposite: Views from on board the BBMF's Lancaster during a ceremonial fly-past over London. (UK Open Government Licence)

Left: A daytime static engine run for FM159. (Doug Bowman)

Right: FM159 night running at BCMC, Nanton. (Doug Bowman)

NX611 with engines running prior to taxiing at a busy museum event day.
(Martin Keen)

At BCMC during 2014 a Tallboy is hung from FM159's bomb bay, a sight not seen since the early post-war years. (Doug Bowman)

Bomber Command veterans gather in front of NX611 with re-enactors during 2014's historic Three Lanc events. (Martin Keen)

Right: Long queues form for a look, via a gantry, at NX611's cockpit. (Martin Keen)

Left: A veteran tail gunner relates his wartime experiences to an enthralled audience at one of the 2014 Three Lanc events. (Martin Keen)

This page and next two: These busy scenes at LAHC illustrate both the popularity of the Lancaster, and the unique close views of a taxi run afforded at East Kirkby. (Martin Keen)

Left: Andrew Panton, Lancaster taxi pilot, gives the signal to start engine no. 2 on NX611. (Martin Keen)

Right: Former BBMF Lancaster pilot Flt Lt Mike Chatterton (RAF, retired) performs regular taxi runs with NX611 at LAHC. Mike is one of a small number of current and former BBMF pilots who perform taxiing duties along with the museum's Andrew Panton. (Martin Keen)

Andrew Panton and Louise Bush, the first brother-and-sister Lancaster crew. Andrew taxies the Lancaster while Louise is a trained flight engineer. (A. & K. Markham Photographers)

Above: LAHC engineer Bob Mitchell gives the signal for engine start on NX611's no. 1. (Martin Keen)

Left: Martin Lawton starting no. 3 on NX611. (Martin Keen)

Right: Visitors take a look at NX611's cockpit. (Martin Keen)

Left: Sean Taylor, Lancaster safety officer, with a young taxi rider clearly enjoying his experience on board. (Martin Keen)

This page and opposite: Nocturnal Lancaster. NX611 looks and sounds tremendous at night! (Martin Keen)

Right: FM213 taxiing at Keflavik, with the Icelandic flag raised in the cockpit. (Martin Keen)

Left and opposite: The CWHM's Lancaster lands at Keflavik Airport in Iceland during her historic Atlantic crossing in August 2014. (Martin Keen)

Safely away in a heated hangar on the former military side of Keflavik Airport, FM213 takes a well-earned break. (Martin Keen)

This page: The incredible sight of two Avro Lancasters flying together in the UK during the summer of 2014. (Martin Keen)

Right and opposite page: PA474 and FM213 on the RAF Coningsby ramp prior to departure to the Channel Islands. (Keith Clifford)

Left: Lancaster PA474 and FM213 crews briefing at the BBMF facility for a busy day of air show flying. (Keith Clifford)

Above right: Running in for the Lancaster pairs display at Goodwood. (Keith Clifford)

Above left: PA474 photographed from FM213 over the English Channel heading for the Channel Islands. (Keith Clifford)

Right: Lancs at Portrush, Northern Ireland. (Bill Powderly)

Right: Members of CWHM's Lancaster crew at Middleton St George: Andy Dobson, Don Schofield and Craig Brookhouse. (Martin Keen)

Left: A suitable welcome for FM213 during her visit to the former Bomber Command RCAF airfield at Middleton St George. (Martin Keen)

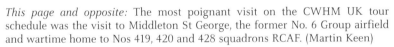

This page and opposite: The most poignant visit on the CWHM UK tour schedule was the visit to Middleton St George, the former No. 6 Group airfield and wartime home to Nos 419, 420 and 428 squadrons RCAF. (Martin Keen)

Left: CWHM's Craig Brookhouse prepares FM213's no. 4 engine for removal. This image illustrates extremely well the size of the Merlin engine's radiator. (David Thompson)

Right: Mike Charters, one of CWHM's volunteer maintenance engineers, manoeuvres with a forklift truck the replacement Merlin engine for FM213. (David Thompson)

Opposite: FM213 at Middleton St George, in a surviving wartime hangar previously occupied by Lancasters of 419, 420 and 428 Squadrons RCAF. (David Thompson)

In this photograph the Lancaster's three-blade propeller has been removed, along with the faulty no. 4 engine, a 1640hp Packard Merlin 224. (David Thompson)

FM213's chief engineer Jim Van Dyke, in a pensive mood, takes a well-earned break during the hectic hours of 31 August. (David Thompson)

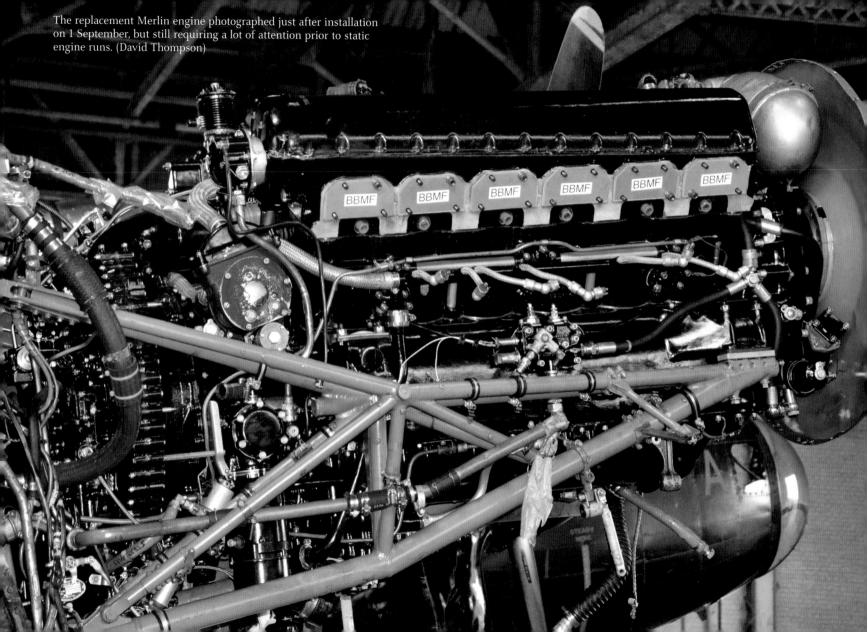

The replacement Merlin engine photographed just after installation on 1 September, but still requiring a lot of attention prior to static engine runs. (David Thompson)

A fine view of FM213 at rest in the former RAF hangar at Middleton St George. (David Thompson)

Lancaster FM213 is prepared
for ground runs on the
evening of 2 September.
(David Thompson)

Above: A sight never to be seen again – Avro Vulcan XH558/G-VLCN forms up with Lancasters FM213 and PA474. (Martin Keen)

Right: Demand for merchandise was high at the CWHM's trailer during the 2014 UK Tour. (Canadian Warplane Heritage Museum)

Above right and overleaf: Views of the historic, incredible and possibly never-to-be-repeated Three Lancs events at LAHC, summer 2014. (Martin Keen)

Above: Onlookers sporting merchandise from the historic Three Lancs events. (Martin Keen)

Right: Re-enactors give a fitting tribute to the people (and animals) of Bomber Command. (Martin Keen)

Left: Squadron Leader George 'Johnny' Johnson, the last surviving British Dambuster, with Mary Stopes-Roe, the daughter of Barnes Wallis, at the Three Lancs events. (Martin Keen)

Right: Johnny and Mary with aviation artist Neil Higgs and his exceptional artwork portraying the Three Lancs at East Kirkby. (Martin Keen)

Opposite: Familiar faces to any visitor to LAHC. Left to right: Sean Taylor, Keith Brenchley (NX611 chief engineer/flight engineer), Andrew Panton and Louise Bush. (A. & K. Markham Photographers)

Left: The CWHM were based in the BBMF hangar at RAF Coningsby during the 2014 tour. (David Thompson)

Right: FM213 on the ramp at RAF Coningsby prior to departing on the first leg of her return flight to Canada. (David Hills)

With FM213 in the lead, the BBMF escort the Canadian Lancaster away from RAF
Coningsby on their departure day, 23 September 2014. (Martin Keen)

Left: The last surviving British Dambuster, Squadron Leader George 'Johnny' Johnson, with NX611 at LAHC in July 2015. (Martin Keen)

Opposite: Remembrance – NX611 performs a poppy drop at East Kirkby. (Martin Keen)

Lest We Forget ...
(Martin Keen)

BIBLIOGRAPHY

l facts, figures and statistics must be taken as approximate; although
 were obtained from at least two reliable sources there was always a
ird reliable source which differed. These numbers would require an
tensive definition and explanation that is beyond the scope of this
ok. The approximate numbers used are sufficient to give the reader
e desired meaning.

rris, T., *Behind the Glory* (Toronto: Macmillan Canada, 1993)

show, D. L., *No Prouder Place: Canadians and the Bomber Command Experience
39–1945* (St Catherines: Vanwell Publishing, 2005)

show, D. L., *None But the Brave: The Essential Contributions of RAF Bomber
mmand to Allied Victory During the Second World War* (Kingston: Canadian
fence Academy Press, 2009)

rcusson, T. J., *Maple Leaf against the Axis: Canada's Second World War*
oronto: Stoddart, 1995)

rrell, D., *People and Planes: Stories from the Bomber Command Museum of
nada* (Nanton: The Nanton Lancaster Society, 2011)

rrell, D., *Baz: The Biography of Ian Bazalgette VC* (Nanton: The Nanton
ncaster Society, 2014)

rrell, D., *FM159: The Lucky Lancaster* (Nanton: The Nanton Lancaster Society, 2015)

shop, P., *Bomber Boys: Fighting Back 1940–1945* (UK: Harper Collins
blishers, 2008)

Christie, C. A., *Ocean Bridge: History of RAF Ferry Command* (Toronto: University
of Toronto Press, 1997)

Cotter, J., *Living Lancasters* (Stroud: Sutton Publishing, 2005)

Cotter, J., *Battle of Britain Memorial Flight: 50 Years of Flying* (Barnsley: Pen
& Sword, 2007)

Delve, K., *RAF Bomber Command 1936–1945: An Operational and Historical Record*
(UK: Pen & Sword, 2006)

Falconer, J., *Bomber Command Handbook: 1939–1945* (Stroud: Sutton
Publishing, 2003)

Forczyk, R., *Bf 110 vs Lancaster: 1942–1945* (Oxford: Osprey Publishing, 2013)

Garbett, M. & B. Goulding, *Lancaster at War* (Shepperton: Ian Allan, 1971)

Garbett, M. & B. Goulding, *Lancaster at War 2* (New York: Charles Scribner's
Sons, 1980)

Garbett, M. & B. Goulding, *Lancaster* (Enderby: Promotional Reprint Company, 1992)

Garbett, M., B. Goulding, & J. Partridge, *Story of a Lanc': NX 611* (Lincoln:
Keyworth & Fry, 1974)

Gibson, G., *Enemy Coast Ahead* (London: Michael Joseph, 1951)

Gould, J., *RAF Bomber Command and its Aircraft 1941–45* (Shepperton: Ian Allan, 2002)

Goulding, B. and R. J. A. Taylor, *Story of a Lanc': NX611* (East Kirkby:
Lincolnshire Aviation Heritage Centre, 2010)

Harris, A. T., *Despatch on War Operations: 23 February 1942 to 8 May 1945*
(London: Frank Cass & Co., 1995)

Holmes, H., *Avro Lancaster: The Definitive Record* (UK: Airlife Publishing, 1997)

Holmes, H., *Avro Lancaster* (UK: The Crowood Press, 2005)

Iveson, T., *Lancaster: The Biography* (London: Carlton Publishing Group, 2011)

Keenan, P. & A. Anderson, *The First Forty Years* (Hamilton: Canadian Warplane Heritage Museum, 2012)

Kostenuk, S. & J. Griffin, *RCAF Squadron Histories and Aircraft 1924–1968* (Toronto: Samuel Stevens/Hakkert, 1977)

March, P. R., *The Lancaster Story* (Stroud: The History Press, 2008)

McKinstry, L., *Lancaster: The Second World War's Greatest Bomber* (London: John Murray, 2009)

Moyes, P., *Bomber Squadrons of the RAF and Their Aircraft* (London: Macdonald & Co., 1964)

Page, B., *Mynarski's Lanc: The Story of Two Famous Canadian Lancaster Bombers KB726 & FM213* (Erin: Boston Mills Press, 1989)

Panton, K., *Fred Panton: Man on a Mission* (Leeds: Propagator Press, 2012)

Peden, M., *A Thousand Shall Fall* (Toronto: Stoddart, 1988)

Probert, H., *Bomber Harris: His Life and Times* (London: Greenhill Books, 2003)

Radell, R., *Lancaster: A Bombing Legend* (UK: Chancellor Press, 1997)

Redding, T., *Life and Death in Bomber Command* (Stroud: Fonthill Media, 2013)

Sweetman, B. & R. Watanabe, *Avro Lancaster: Combat Aircraft of World War II* (Random House Value Publishing, 1988)

Sweetman, J., *Bomber Crew: Taking on the Reich* (London: Abacus, 2005)

Sweetman, W., *Avro Lancaster* (New York: Zokeisha Publications, 1982)

Swift, D., *Bomber County: The Lost Airmen of World War Two* (London: Penguin Group, 2010)

The Greater Vancouver Branch of the Aircrew Association, *Critical Moments* (Vancouver: 1989)

Thompson, J. E., *Bomber Crew* (Canada: Trafford Publishing, 2005)

Wilson, G. A. A., *NORAD and the Soviet Nuclear Threat: Canada's Secret Electronic Air War* (Stroud: Amberley Publishing, 2011)

Wilson, G. A. A., *Lancaster Manual 1943* (Stroud: Amberley Publishing, 2013)

Magazines

Aeroplane (Cudham: Kelsey Publishing Group)

Airforce Magazine (LM Group)

Altitude (Winnipeg: Western Canada Aviation Museum)

Aviation News Journal Magazine (Surrey: ER Aviation and Nutrition)

CAHS Journal (Ottawa: Canadian Aviation Historical Society)

Canada's History (Winnipeg: Canada's History Society)

Canadian Aviator (Vancouver: Canadian Aviator Publishing, Nov/D 2014)

Flightlines (Hamilton: Canadian Warplane Heritage Museum)

Flypast (Stamford: Key Publishing)

Government

Various Lancaster Air Operating Manuals and Instructions; Pilot Engineer's and Technical Instructor's Notes; Maintenance Instruction Training Manuals; Handbooks published by the Air Ministry, Unite Kingdom and the RCAF, Canada, dated 1943–5.

Museum Archives & Libraries

Bomber Command Museum of Canada, Nanton, Alberta, Canada
Canadian Museum of Flight, Langley, British Columbia, Canada
Western Canada Aviation Museum, Winnipeg, Manitoba, Canada

Interviewees

Allen, A.; Bainbridge, G.; Blackman, W.; Colbeck, T.; Johnstone, P.; Mickelo A.; Morrison, G.; Panton, A.; Pearson, W.; Phillips, J.; Plenderleith, Sewel, A.; Schofield, D.; Stubley, D.